Thomas Münkel (ed.)

Artificial Intelligence in the Insurance Industry

Insider Perspectives on Opportunities, Risks, and Practical Applications of AI

2026

VERLAG
ÖSTERREICH

Thomas Münkel
has many years of experience in the insurance industry, including as Chief Administrative Officer and Chief Governance Officer at Allianz and as Chief Operating Officer at UNIQA Insurance Group. He is familiar with the insurtech sector as co-founder and CEO of Coya AG (later Luko Insurance AG) and as an investor and board member in other fintech companies. He teaches at Johannes-Kepler University in Linz on Digitalisation and Artificial Intelligence.

Bäckerstraße 1, 1010 Wien
office@verlagoesterreich.at
www.verlagoesterreich.at
Printed in Hungary

Typesetting: büro mn, 33613 Bielefeld, Germany
Print: Prime Rate Zrt., 1044 Budapest, Hungary

Bibliografische Information der Deutschen Nationalbibliothek
Die Deutsche Nationalbibliothek verzeichnet diese Publikation in der Deutschen Nationalbibliografie; detaillierte bibliografische Daten sind im Internet über https://portal.dnb.de/opac.htm abrufbar.

ISBN 978-3-7046-9852-0 (eBook)
https://doi.org/10.33196/9783704698520

ISBN 978-3-7046-9781-3 Verlag Österreich

VERLAG
ÖSTERREICH

Preface

In 2025, a group of insurance and IT experts came together to write a book on the topic of AI in the insurance industry. All of the contributing authors have been working on the topics of digitalisation, AI and insurance for many years. We felt that—although there were many studies and some scientific analyses on the subject—there were hardly any comprehensive and up-to-date practical reports. We therefore set ourselves the goal of writing an anthology that would fill this gap.

This book is primarily aimed at practitioners in the insurance industry: employees and consultants at insurers, brokers and service providers. When this book refers to insurance companies, this includes both primary insurers and reinsurers with their own licences, as well as brokers, MGAs (multiple general agents) and insurtechs. It is a book written from practical experience for practical use, not a scientific work. Accordingly, it does not claim to comprehensively cover all existing academic publications or studies on the subject.

However, it is also intended as an aid for students and for anyone who wishes to gain an overview of the current state of AI in our industry. The authors of this book are all recognised experts in their respective fields, drawing on in-depth knowledge and extensive practical experience. Nevertheless, errors may have crept in—comments and constructive criticism are very welcome.

The authors come from different areas of the insurance industry, from different countries, and have different native languages. We have therefore decided to publish both a German and an English version of this book. Some contributions were originally written in English and translated for the German edition to the best of our knowledge. In parts, AI-assisted translation tools were used, followed by careful quality control by native-speaking experts. Despite all due care, minor deviations or inaccuracies in translation cannot be entirely ruled out.

Throughout the book, the authors consistently express their personal assessments and opinions. When they refer to specific (software) products, this reflects their own experiences and preferences; no one has been paid for advertising. All authors have invested a great deal of time and care in their own (self-written) contributions.

As is always the case with an anthology of this kind, many people contributed to its creation. First and foremost, our sincere thanks go to the authors: all of them accepted our invitation and took the time to put their views on the use of AI in the insurance industry into writing, substantiating them with numerous practical examples and literature research. This work was completed within just a few months and alongside their everyday professional commitments.

A big thank you also goes to Verlag Österreich and its representative, Dr. *Marlene Steininger*. She initiated this book project by approaching me in autumn 2024 and not only convinced me of the idea, but also supported us intensively throughout the entire process with advice and practical assistance, thus playing a key role in the successful completion of this book. Special thanks also go to *Lorcán Hall*. He was able to recruit several outstanding experts as authors and drew my attention to the exciting and important topic of the use of AI for inclusive insurance—an aspect I would probably have overlooked without his valuable input. Finally, my heartfelt thanks go to my family for their support throughout this project. Thank you for everything.

Thomas Münkel

Contents

Abbreviations

A2A	Agent to Agent
AI	Artificial Intelligence
AI Act	Artificial Intelligence Act: Regulation (EU) 2024/1689 laying down harmonised rules on artificial intelligence and amending Regulations
AMC	Annual Management Charge
API	Application Programming Interface
BaFin	Bundesanstalt für Finanzdienstleistungsaufsicht (Germany's Federal Financial Supervisory Authority)
B2B	Business-to-Business
CAA	Commissariat aux Assurances (Supervisory Authority for the Insurance Sector in Luxembourg)
CEO	Chief Executive Officer
CFA	Chartered Financial Analyst
CIO	Chief Information Officer
CRM	Customer Relationship Management
CSRD	Corporate Sustainability Reporting Directive: Directive (EU) 2022/2464 amending Regulation (EU) No 537/2014, Directive 2004/109/EC, Directive 2006/43/EC and Directive 2013/34/EU, as regards corporate sustainability reporting
CSV	Comma-Separated Values
CTO	Chief Technology Officer
DORA	Digital Operational Risk Act: Regulation (EU) 2022/2554 on digital operational resilience for the financial sector
DPI	Digital Public Infrastructure
EIOPA	European Insurance and Occupational Pensions Authority
EMEA	Europe, the Middle East, and Africa
ESG	Environmental, Social, and Governance
ETL	Extract, Transform, Load
EUC	End User Computing
FAQ	Frequently Asked Question
FINMA	Eidgenössische Finanzmarktaufsicht (Supervisory Authority for the Insurance Sector in Switzerland)
FNOL	First Notice of Loss

GDPR	General Data Protection Regulation Regulation: Regulation (EU) 2016/679 on the protection of natural persons with regard to the processing of personal data and on the free movement of such data
GDV	Gesamtverband der Deutschen Versicherungswirtschaft (German Insurance Association)
GLM	General Linear Models
GPU	Graphical Processing Unit
HITL	Human-in-the-Loop
IAIS	International Association of Insurance Supervisors
IDD	Insurance Distribution Directive: Directive (EU) 2016/97 on insurance distribution (recast)
IFoA	Institute and Faculty of Actuaries
IORP	Institutions for Occupational Retirement Provision
IoT	Internet of Things
IT	Information Technology
JSON	Java Script Object Notation
KPI	Key Performance Indicator
KYC	Know Your Customer
LLM	Large Language Model
MAS	Monetary Authority of Singapore
MCP	Model Context Protocol
MGA	Managing General Agent
ML	Machine Learning
MLP	Machine Learning Parser
NAIC	National Association of Insurance Commissioners
NBB	National Bank of Belgium
NER	Named Entity Recognition
NIST	National Institute of Standards and Technology
NLP	Natural Language Processing
OCR	Optical Character Recognition
PAI	1) Principal Adverse Impact 2) Personal AI Assistants
PoC	Proof of Concept
P&C	Property and Casualty (Insurance)
RACI	Responsible, Accountable, Consulted, Informed
RAG	Red-Amber-Green
RFP	Request for Proposal
ROI	Return on Investment
SDLC	Software Development Lifecycle
SECR	Streamlined Energy and Carbon Reporting
SFDR	Sustainable Finance Disclosure Regulation: Regulation (EU) 2019/2088 on sustainability-related disclosures in the financial services sector

SME	Subject Matter Experts
Solvency II	Directive 2009/138/EC on the taking-up and pursuit of the business of insurance and reinsurance (recast)
SQL	Structured Query Language
Sub-IM	Sub-Investment Manager
TCFD	Task Force on Climate Related Financial Disclosures
TSR	Total Shareholder Return
UBI	Usage-based Insurance
UNPRI	United Nations Principles for Responsible Investment
VBA	Visual Basic for Applications

Artificial intelligence (AI) in the insurance industry—An introduction

Thomas Münkel
Insurance Manager

I. The genesis of this book

Spring 1987: As part of a management trainee programme at the Aachener & Münchener Insurance Group, I am assigned to the motor vehicle liability department of a subsidiary. My task is to evaluate major motor vehicle claims for special features, using statistical programmes for multivariate variance analysis, as we learned in our psychology studies. My trainers were amazed that a psychologist could perform such analyses on a mainframe computer, as they knew nothing about the statistics and IT courses that were part of my psychology studies.

Since then, I have been interested in the use of IT in the insurance industry, and today, almost 40 years later, with the breakthrough of artificial intelligence (AI), this topic is of double interest to me—as a psychologist and as an insurance manager. Since November 2022, with the introduction of ChatGPT 3, AI has been rapidly changing the private and professional lives of many people. *"But why write a book about AI in my industry when it will be out of date by the time it's published on?"*—this was the feedback I received from several acquaintances when I told them about this book project.

The fact that this is not the case is due, among other things, to the year 1987 mentioned at the beginning: in the 1980s, the insurance industry was still a pioneer in IT: it invested heavily in new core systems, began digitising data and used the first programs for risk analysis and product design. Today, 40 years later, it must be soberly noted that the core systems of many insurers in Europe are still stuck in the 1980s or 1990s. The use of modern hardware and software solutions often resembles a patchwork quilt. Processes that could have been

https://doi.org/10.33196/9783704698520-101

automated long ago[1] are often interrupted by additional manual entries from paper files or tedious "copy-paste" from other programmes. This drives many people in our industry to despair when they compare the possibilities of AI solutions and modern software with the reality in their companies, even though IT teams, often supported by consultants, are feverishly striving for renewal. However, such innovations almost never cover the entire process chain across all insurance lines: AI solutions are coming, but mostly slowly, incrementally and piecemeal. That is probably why this book will not be completely outdated in a few years' time. It would be nice if I were wrong in this assessment!

II. On the structure of this anthology

Although this book is a collection of contributions from various authors with different perspectives on AI, they are arranged to create a narrative arc throughout:

It begins with a general introduction to AI, covering its historical development and explaining the most important terms, by *Danilo Raponi*. This introduction is followed by a brief overview of the use of AI in various industries in order to classify the insurance industry relative to other industries.

The introduction to the specifics of the insurance industry starts with established insurers and begins with *Alexander Bockelmann's* contribution on AI in a European insurance group, followed by *Michael Zimmer's* guide to setting up an AI unit in an insurance company. The opposite pole is represented by start-ups, which can start with AI without any legacy issues. Using the example of an AI-born fintech, *Max Bachem* shows what is possible when you can start from scratch without legacy systems or heterogeneous data sets. The final practical example with a view to an entire company comes from *Igor Raičević:* he deals with the special challenges for AI at insurance brokers.

The overarching practical examples are followed by five articles on various important aspects of the insurance business, starting with the "digital underwriter". In this article, *Christoph Nabholz* and *Simon Woodward* describe "how AI is reshaping risk coverage": a key issue across all insurance lines and also an area in which digital solutions have been trialled and implemented for

1 According to *GDV (Gesamtverband der Deutschen Versicherungswirtschaft e. V.)*, Wie die Versicherer ihre Prozesse zunehmend automatisieren (11.11.2024): www.gdv.de/gdv/themen/digitalisierung/wie-die-versicherer-ihre-prozesse-zunehmend-automatisieren-183966 (accessed 21.11.2025) dark processing rates are currently around 1/3 in property and health insurance and 14 % in life insurance – a significant improvement on previous years, but still alarmingly low!

many years. The following article on "AI as a lever for inclusive insurance" highlights an often neglected aspect: AI can help to significantly simplify access to insurance cover for disadvantaged population groups or even make it possible in the first place. With "AI in the insurance process", *Michael Zimmer* takes a reality check: what is myth and what is already reality today. This is followed by articles by *Brian Walsh* on "AI use in back office and regulatory reporting" and, last but not least, the customer perspective, which *Max Bachem* examines with the exciting question of whether "customers are the drivers of AI development in the insurance industry".

The anthology concludes with an article by *Christina Lucas* that takes a "look into the crystal ball": Where is AI heading in the insurance industry? Gradual improvements or the use of AI as a lever for a fundamental transformation of the insurance industry?

Of course, there are other aspects that could be addressed on the topic of artificial intelligence in the insurance industry. For example, we do not go into detail about the various legal and governance regulations that exist on this topic. That alone could fill another book if you want to take all countries and regions into account. But we hope that this anthology provides an interesting and comprehensive overview—and if you feel that something important is missing, we will be happy to take this as a suggestion for the next edition.

III. Common basic ideas of the editor and team of authors

As an introduction to this book, below are some of the considerations that the editors and authors based their work on. These are initial hypotheses shared by all those involved in the book and represent our common view of the current (autumn 2025) status of artificial intelligence in the insurance industry.

Hypothesis 1:

The central value proposition of insurance is more relevant than ever—even in the age of artificial intelligence

The basic idea of insurance, namely providing (mostly financial) assistance in the event of a loss (insurance claim) that cannot be covered alone, remains as valid as ever: with the help of the insurer, the risk community comes to the aid of the injured party with advice (service) and action (usually money). Organising this risk community through an insurer is complex, expensive and strictly regulated in each country. This is one of the reasons why all attempts by large technology companies to gain a foothold in this industry have failed in recent decades. AI can improve many things – see the next paragraph – but it cannot (yet?) replace the core of insurance.[2] A particularly interesting aspect of this hypothesis is described in the chapter on "inclusive insurance".

Hypothesis 2:

AI has the potential to be a game changer in the insurance industry as well. However, it will not turn the insurance industry upside down in the short term.

Insurance is sensible and important – but there is still enormous room for improvement in the quality of services provided by insurers to their customers. Compared to other industries (especially in the digital age!), many of the processes and services offered by insurers seem like relics from the 1980s.[3] This is where AI can become a driver of innovation and a game changer, significantly improving service quality in a short period of time. See, for example, the concluding chapter with its "look into the crystal ball". In other parts of the value chain, however, it will most likely take years before AI is widely used.

Hypothesis 3:

The widespread use of AI is hampered in many established insurance companies by a large number of poorly integrated and hardly documented legacy systems (especially core systems).

Very few established insurers in Europe currently have an integrated portfolio management system or even a comprehensive data lake. Even if new core systems have been introduced in some insurance sectors, such as life or health insurance, there are usually large gaps in cross-sector data and processes, e.g. for an overall customer view. Cross-border IT systems are even rarer[4]. Existing systems are often poorly documented or written in completely outdated programming languages for which there are hardly any experts left today. You

2 For the general significance of insurance in today's world, see *L. Hall/P. Walsh*, Insurance and Sustainable Development: DOI:10.25546/111474.

3 Studies show, for example, a large discrepancy in the user-friendliness of digital insurance offerings vs. other industries (e.g., *EPAM*, Insurance: The Digital Paradox (2021): www.epam.com (accessed 21.11.2025) or *von Heymann*, Versicherungsbranche verliert bei digitaler Kundenzufriedenheit (22.8.2025): https://sachthemen.blog/2025/08/22/versicherungsbranche-verliert-bei-digitaler-kundenzufriedenheit/ (accessed 21.11.2025).

4 *McKinsey*, The future of AI in the insurance industry (2025): www.mckinsey.com/industries/financial-services/our-insights/the-future-of-ai-in-the-insurance-industry (accessed 21.11.2025): "a major challenge in IT transformation is undocumented legacy systems, outdated technology still in use despite no longer being supported by vendors."

can find more on this—along with possible solutions!—in the chapters with practical examples.

Hypothesis 4:

A key lever for the use of AI is access to (digital) data. Many insurers still have a lot of catching up to do in this area.

Anyone who has ever looked behind the scenes at an insurer or broker may have been surprised at how much important data, such as insurance policies, claims files and correspondence, is still stored in traditional filing cabinets. I know of very few insurers who have digitised their entire paper files (according to their own statements). Much of the data is also stored in digital data silos that are not synchronised with each other. All of this makes access to suitable data one of the biggest hurdles to the use of AI. Examples of this—again with possible solutions—can be found in the chapter on brokers, the chapter on AI in the insurance process, and the chapter on setting up an AI unit.

Hypothesis 5:

Insurance is essentially a business that involves managing risks, but AI is redefining both the meaning of risks and the way they can be insured.

Two problems are at odds with each other: first, the challenge of insuring the risks *caused by AI*, from gaps in accountability to liability for algorithms; and second, the risks arising *from the use of AI* itself, whether by insurers or their customers. This dual pressure is forcing the industry to rethink long-held assumptions about fairness, transparency and control. The article on AI in underwriting addresses this dual pressure and examines how technology is redefining the boundaries of what can (and perhaps cannot) be insured.

Hypothesis 6:

The geographical focus of this book is primarily (continental) Europe. The situation in Asia, Latin America or the Anglo-Saxon world differs in some areas.

There are major differences, particularly in the area of data protection (e.g., fundamentally different standards in the USA, Asia and Europe) and AI security (in Asia, for example, AI has more freedom in decision-making). However, the internal (IT) starting position for insurers described above is also often different in Asia than in Europe, for example, because many large insurers are simply not that old and therefore made much more consistent use of the opportunities offered by digitalisation in their start-up phase than their European competitors were able to.

Hypothesis 7:

The potential and use of AI are only just beginning; we will see rapid changes in the coming years.

We are seeing leaps in AI development almost every quarter: in the performance of large language models; in the successful use of AI in areas that until recently were considered the privilege of human intelligence; and in the simplicity of using AI tools. We are already seeing the successful use of AI in our industry under the heading of "agentic AI" or in claims settlement (see, for example, the practical chapters on "*Xaver*" or at the broker). However, given the multi-billion investments of all major tech companies and the brutal race in AI, it is very likely that further "AI revolutions" – even beyond GPT – will not take 10 years to arrive.

Hypothesis 8:

The distinctive (European) regulatory framework is both a "curse and a blessing" for insurers and customers alike.

In the European Union in particular, there are numerous laws and regulations governing the handling of data and the use of AI,[5] with the noble aim of comprehensively protecting insured persons. This has many advantages, e.g., in terms of data protection. At the same time, however, they often drive bureaucracy and slow down innovation – and hinder competition. See, among other things, the comments in the chapter entitled "A look into the crystal ball". To put it bluntly, one could say that the excessive regulations protect some insurers from truly modernising and facing competition – and customers are the ones who lose out.

Hypothesis 9:

Insurance customers will become an important driver of AI transformation.

AI applications are already a commonplace tool in many people's everyday lives. ChatGPT often replaces conventional search engines. Potential insurance customers use AI not only to compare prices, but also to compare terms and conditions, exclusions and customer reviews on a highly individual basis. This

---

5 See, for example, the European Insurance and Occupational Pensions Authority *EIOPA*, Opinion on Artificial Intelligence governance and risk management (2025): www.eiopa.europa.eu/publications/opinion-artificial-intelligence-governance-and-risk-management_en (accessed 21.11.2025).

forces insurers to respond (with AI) if they do not want to be left hopelessly behind. You can find more on this in the chapter on the customer perspective.

As mentioned, these are all hypotheses that can be discussed at length. But they should allow us to classify the positions in this anthology. To conclude this introduction, we would like to make two fundamental comments:

Firstly, in many places in this book, the use of AI in the insurance industry is viewed quite critically. This is not to downplay the remarkable progress and general openness to the use of AI in our industry. It is the authors' shared view of the current reality in practice, while fully recognising the enormous opportunities that AI offers.

Secondly, a general warning is in order here: despite all the euphoria about the potential of AI, the authors are by no means blind to the considerable risks associated with AI. We are all familiar, for example, with the article "AI 2027"[6]: The authors (recognised as proven AI experts) describe a future scenario in which artificial superintelligence could develop within this decade that would be far superior to human intelligence. To this end, AI development is outlined step by step. It ends with two possible scenarios: In the "race" scenario, the USA and China in particular compete for AI supremacy and risk everything getting out of control and ending up in a dystopia à la "The Matrix". In the "coordination" scenario, AI progress is more controlled and human-driven—but here too, there are significant (and negative) changes to everyday life. Even if this does not happen, the authors of this book are aware of the many risks as well as the great opportunities that artificial intelligence presents.

References and resources

Deloitte Belgien, Digital Insurance Maturity. Assessment of insurance digitalisation in the EMEA region (2025): www.deloitte.com/be/en/Industries/financial-services/research/digital-insurance-maturity-report (accessed 5.11.2025)

EIOPA, Opinion on Artificial Intelligence governance and risk management (2025): www.eiopa.europa.eu/publications/opinion-artificial-intelligence-governance-and-risk-management_en (accessed 21.11.2025)

EPAM, Insurance: The Digital Paradox (2021): www.epam.com (accessed 21.11.2025)

GDV (Gesamtverband der Deutschen Versicherungswirtschaft e. V.), Wie die Versicherer ihre Prozesse zunehmend automatisieren (11.11.2024): www.gdv.de/gdv/themen/digitalisierung/wie-die-versicherer-ihre-prozesse-zunehmend-automatisieren-183966 (accessed 21.11.2025)

6 *Kokotajlo/Alexander/Larsen/Lifland/Dean*, AI 2027 available under: Summary—AI 2027 (accessed 27.11.2025).

L. Hall/P. Walsh, Insurance and Sustainable Development: Partnering on Risk, Resilience, and Transformation (2025): DOI:10.25546/111474

von Heymann, Versicherungsbranche verliert bei digitaler Kundenzufriedenheit (22.8.2025): https://sachthemen.blog/2025/08/22/versicherungsbranche-verliert-bei-digitaler-kundenzufriedenheit/ (accessed 21.11.2025)

McKinsey, The future of AI in the insurance industry (2025): www.mckinsey.com/industries/financial-services/our-insights/the-future-of-ai-in-the-insurance-industry (accessed 21.11.2025)

The basics: What AI means, its history, and how AI works

Danilo Raponi
Group Head of Innovation at Generali and Managing Director of the Company's Innovation Fund

Abstract: Artificial intelligence (AI) is a concept and technology with deep historical roots and profound contemporary significance. This chapter provides an intellectual and historical overview of AI, examining what we mean by "artificial intelligence" and why defining intelligence in machines is inherently challenging. It traces the development of AI from mid-twentieth-century ambitions to today's groundbreaking achievements, explaining in accessible terms how AI systems work along the way. In a narrative that ranges from ancient myths and early automata to modern machine learning, the discussion highlights key milestones – from the coining of "artificial intelligence" in 1956 to the triumph of deep-learning algorithms in tasks like chess, Go, and conversational dialogue. The chapter analyses how perceptions of AI have evolved through cycles of optimistic hype and sobering setbacks, and how recent advances have moved AI from research labs into practical use across industries. Throughout, the treatment technological developments with broader intellectual currents about mind and computation. By gaining a deeper understanding of AI's definition, its winding history, and its underlying technical approaches (from rule-based programmes to neural networks), readers will be well-prepared for the ethical, legal, and practical questions explored in subsequent chapters.

Keywords: AI, Algorithms, Deep Learning, Definition of AI, Intelligence, KI, AI Models, Knowledge Engineering, Machine Learning, Neural Networks, Robotics, Language Models, Trial-and-Error-Iterations.

Contents

I. What is Artificial Intelligence?

For many people today, the phrase "artificial intelligence" evokes images of smart robots or science fiction come to life. In reality, AI has quietly become part of our daily routines – from the suggestions Netflix gives us, to the voice assistants such as Amazon's Alexa and Apple's Siri that respond to our queries – often without us even labeling it as AI. Still, fundamental questions remain about the nature of AI and how far it can go.

Artificial intelligence (AI) began as an audacious question before it became a technical reality. The phrase itself invites us to consider two seemingly opposite realms: the mechanical and the intelligent. What do we really mean when we talk about a machine being "intelligent"? Ever since antiquity, humans have imagined artifacts endowed with thought or life – from the bronze automaton Talos guarding the island of Crete in Greek myth to the golem of medieval legend fashioned from clay, or the man-made monster of *Mary Shelley's* Frankenstein (1818). These stories, steeped in wonder and caution, reveal an ancient dream of creating an intelligence in our own image.

Across the ages, inventors and philosophers toyed with the idea that thought might be mechanized: from Renaissance clockwork automata that mimicked the motions of living creatures to Enlightenment thinkers like *Descartes*, who wondered if animals (and perhaps even humans) could be viewed as complex machines of flesh and blood. In the late eighteenth century, audiences marveled at the Mechanical Turk, a clockwork "automaton" that could apparently play chess at a masterful level – until it was revealed that a human chess player was cleverly hidden inside. Even hoaxes like the Turk showed the breadth of popular imagination – as did new words like "robot" (introduced by Czech writer and playwright *Karel Čapek* in 1920 to denote artificial workers) – and the premium placed on the idea of a thinking machine. Still, it was only in the mid-twentieth century that this ageless dream coalesced into a scientific endeavor with the birth of AI as a field.

The modern concept of AI was crystallized by the British mathematician *Alan Turing* in 1950. *Turing* posed a question for the ages: "Can machines think?".[1] In his seminal paper, he proposed what is now known as the Turing Test – an imaginative experiment to define intelligence operationally. If a computer could converse through text in a way indistinguishable from a human, then, Turing suggested, we might be warranted to call that machine "intelligent." This bold redefinition moved the question of AI from the realm of philosophy to practical experimentation. Intelligence, Turing implied, need not be an exclusively organic property; it could potentially emerge from circuits and code.

Defining "artificial intelligence," however, has never been straightforward. Even among psychologists, there is no single definition of "intelligence" – it can variously denote abstract reasoning, learning from experience, creativity, or social skill. Small wonder, then, that AI researchers have offered varying

1 *Turing*, Computing Machinery, 433: https://doi.org/10.1093/mind/LIX.236.433.

definitions of machine intelligence, reflecting different visions of what it means for a machine to "think." Over the years, scholars have distinguished multiple paradigms for defining AI. Some definitions emphasize thinking processes (aiming to emulate the way humans think), while others emphasize behaviour (aiming to achieve results indistinguishable from human performance). Likewise, some pursue ideal rationality (machines that think or act rationally according to formal logic), whereas others prioritize human-like approaches (machines that think or act like people do, with all their heuristics and quirks).[2] Each perspective offers a lens on what matters most: the internal reasoning versus the external action, and human resemblance versus abstract perfection. One early approach framed AI as any machine behaviour that, if performed by a human, would be considered intelligent. Under this broad criterion, even a calculator performing arithmetic or a formula in Microsoft Excel might qualify. As AI pioneer *Marvin Minsky* quipped, artificial intelligence is "the science of making machines do things that would require intelligence if done by men."[3]

The ambiguity of the definition is telling: it suggests that AI is less a fixed category than a moving frontier, perpetually advancing as our machines become more capable. Indeed, a paradox often noted in the field is that the moment an AI technique becomes commonplace, we cease to call it "AI" at all – it dissolves into the fabric of ordinary technology. (As AI pioneer *John McCarthy* joked, "As soon as it works, no one calls it AI anymore.")[4] Early examples like chess-playing programmes or optical character recognition, once marvels of AI, later came to be seen as routine software tools, no longer bearing the exotic label of "artificial intelligence."

If defining intelligence itself is a philosophical challenge, adding the qualifier "artificial" raises further dilemmas. The term "artificial intelligence" was coined in 1956 by a group of visionary scientists (more on that moment in the next section), and it carried a provocative juxtaposition: joining "artificial," with its connotations of the man-made and the mechanical, to "intelligence," a trait long considered deeply human. This coupling was a deliberate rhetorical leap of faith, a statement that intelligence could be understood, engineered, and replicated. It suggested that the essences of reasoning, problem-solving, and even learning could be captured in the cold logic of a machine.

Not everyone has been comfortable with that suggestion. As soon as the idea of AI was articulated, it provoked fundamental questions: Is a machine that merely simulates intelligent behaviour truly intelligent, or only a clever imitation? In

2 *Russell/Norvig*, Artificial Intelligence, 2.
3 *Minsky* (ed), Semantic Information Processing.
4 *Meyers*, 'John McCarthy', Communications: https://cacm.acm.org/blogs/blog-cacm/138907-john-mccarthy/fulltext (accessed 15.10. 2025).

the 1980s, philosopher *John Searle* vividly illustrated this concern with his "Chinese Room" thought experiment. He imagined a person who speaks no Chinese following detailed instructions to respond to Chinese characters slipped under a door, such that to an outside observer it appears the person understands Chinese. *Searle* argued that, similarly, a computer executing a programme might convincingly simulate understanding without any real comprehension or consciousness. He distinguished "weak AI" – the use of computers to simulate thought – from "strong AI," the claim that a suitably programmed computer would actually have a mind and consciousness. In *Searle's* view, strong AI was dubious at best.[5] This philosophical debate underscores a central ambiguity in the concept of AI. Are we building tools that merely mimic intelligent behaviour, or are we on the path toward creating genuinely intelligent, perhaps even sentient, machines? Early AI research tended to sidestep the question by focusing on performance: if a programme could solve problems or answer questions in ways that would normally require human intelligence, that was achievement enough. But the tension between "intelligence as simulation" and "intelligence as real understanding" has never been fully resolved. It continues to animate discussions about advanced AI today, especially as modern systems grow more complex and human-like in their outputs. To this day, there is no consensus on whether a machine needs genuine consciousness or self-awareness to truly think, or whether convincing simulation of intelligence is sufficient for all practical purposes – a question that blurs the line between engineering and philosophy.

For practical purposes, most contemporary researchers and practitioners adopt a working definition of AI that is modest but useful: AI is the capability of a machine or programme to perform tasks that normally require human intelligence. These tasks include learning from experience, reasoning to solve problems, understanding natural language, perceiving the environment, and sometimes adapting to new situations.[6] This definition encompasses the field's breadth, from game-playing programmes and recommendation algorithms to voice assistants and autonomous vehicles. It also highlights that intelligence is not a monolith but a collection of cognitive abilities that can be addressed in piecemeal fashion. A system might excel at one intellectual task (say, identifying faces in photos) while lacking any ability in another (such as comprehending a story) – and we would still consider it an example of AI in the context of its specialized domain.

5 *Searle*, Minds, 417: https://doi.org/10.1017/S0140525X00005756.

6 *Mikalef/Gupta*, Artificial intelligence capability: https://doi.org/10.1016/j.im.2021.103434.

Another crucial distinction in thinking about AI is between "narrow AI" and "general AI." All the AI systems in existence today are examples of narrow AI: they are designed to perform specific tasks or solve specific problems. A medical diagnosis AI might be superb at recognising patterns in X-rays, and a separate language model might fluently translate sentences, but neither system possesses a broad understanding or general-purpose intelligence. General AI, on the other hand, refers to a hypothetical machine intelligence with the flexible cognitive abilities of a human across diverse domains. In other words, a general AI could learn any subject, perform any intellectual task that a person can, and perhaps even exhibit self-awareness. This remains the realm of science fiction and speculative future studies. While some researchers speculate that such an "Artificial General Intelligence" (AGI) might emerge in the coming decades, others doubt whether human-like understanding can ever be fully achieved by machines.[7] What is clear is that current AI, for all its impressive feats, is not "general" in this sense. It cannot transfer its learning from one domain to an unrelated one without significant human intervention and redesign. Most AI programmes are very far from the flexible, general intelligence humans display: an AI that plays poker cannot spontaneously learn to drive a car or cook a meal unless engineers retrain it for those tasks. In short, today's AI is brittle compared to human intelligence – it excels in narrow arenas but fails to adapt broadly. This brittleness is one of the fundamental gaps between current AI and the kind of generalized, adaptable intelligence we possess.

In sum, AI as a concept straddles a line between pragmatic engineering and profound mystery. On one side, it is a toolbox of algorithms and techniques enabling machines to mimic facets of human cognition. On the other, it is a mirror held up to human intelligence itself, forcing us to ask which aspects of our mental capacity are mechanizable and which, if any, might remain beyond the reach of silicon and code. Throughout its history, AI has been driven by a dual quest: to build useful machines here and now, and to explore the theoretical limits of mind by seeing how far mind can be replicated by artifice. To appreciate how these goals have played out, it is helpful to consider the journey AI has taken from its ambitious beginnings to the present day.

II. A brief history of Artificial Intelligence

If the concept of AI tells us what we hope to create, the history of AI reveals how close (or how far) we have come. The story of artificial intelligence is a chronicle of bold ideas, unexpected breakthroughs, and humbling reality

7 *Gignac/Szodorai*, Defining intelligence: https://doi.org/10.1016/j.intell.2024.101832.

checks. It is a history populated by visionary scientists, clever programmes, and periodic crises of confidence. Understanding this backstory provides critical context for appreciating the field's present state.

The idea of intelligent machines may be as old as imagination, but artificial intelligence as an organised field of research took shape in the mid-20th century. World War II and its aftermath provided fertile ground. The war had accelerated advances in computation – the development of electronic computers capable of performing thousands of calculations a second. These new machines immediately raised an intriguing prospect: could a sufficiently powerful computer be made to exhibit what we recognise as intelligence? In 1955, four young scientists decided to find out. *John McCarthy* (a mathematician), *Marvin Minsky* (a cognitive scientist), Nathaniel Rochester (an engineer), and *Claude Shannon* (the father of information theory) drafted a proposal for a summer workshop at Dartmouth College. In that proposal, which introduced the term "artificial intelligence," they declared their audacious hypothesis: "that every aspect of learning or any other feature of intelligence can in principle be so precisely described that a machine can be made to simulate it".[8] This 1956 Dartmouth Summer Research Project is often regarded as the formal birth of AI as a field. A few dozen pioneers gathered in rural New Hampshire to brainstorm how to make machines use language, form abstractions, solve problems, and even improve themselves. While that workshop did not immediately produce a thinking machine, it did launch a community of researchers united by a common dream. Indeed, the late 1950s and early 1960s saw a flurry of pioneering efforts that turned AI theories into working programmes. For example, in 1952 *Arthur Samuel* at *IBM* wrote a checkers-playing programme that not only followed a strategy but actually improved its play over time by learning from experience. By playing thousands of games against itself and refining its move evaluations, *Samuel's* programme steadily became a formidable checkers opponent – by 1962 it even defeated a Connecticut state champion – an early testament to the power of machine learning. Around the same time, *Allen Newell* and *Herbert Simon* developed the Logic Theorist, a software programme capable of proving mathematical theorems from the ground up. Debuting in 1956, Logic Theorist managed to prove several propositions from the Principia Mathematica, in some cases finding proofs more elegant than those published by the Principia's authors. These demonstrations, though limited to constrained domains, were enormously influential: they showed that computers could do more than arithmetic; they could engage in reasoning and improve through feedback.

8 *McCarthy/Minsky/Rochester/Shannon*, Dartmouth Proposal, 1: https://doi.org/10.1609/aimag.v27i4.1904.

The decades that followed saw alternating seasons of optimism and disillusionment – what one might call the spring and winter cycles of AI. The early years, from the late 1950s into the 1960s, were a time of heady optimism. With computers now able to churn through logical operations, some scientists believed that human-level intelligence was just around the corner. In 1965, Nobel laureate *Herbert Simon* predicted that "machines will be capable, within twenty years, of doing any work a man can do."[9] His colleague *Marvin Minsky* ventured that within a generation we would see machines with general intelligence comparable to an average human.[10] These predictions turned out to be wildly premature, but they capture the atmosphere of excitement. During this period, researchers made significant strides in programming computers to tackle tasks like proving mathematical theorems, solving algebra word problems, and playing games. The Newell–Simon team created the "General Problem Solver," aiming to devise a single programme that could solve any formal problem given the right description. Others, like *John McCarthy*, developed programming languages such as LISP specifically designed for AI problems involving symbol manipulation. There were successes: by thelate 1960s, labs had built machines that could, in limited ways, understand simple sentences, carry on rudimentary dialogues (a famous programme called ELIZA astonished people in 1966 by managing a semblance of conversation, acting as a mock psychotherapist), and even navigate small worlds (as did the wheeled robot "Shakey," an early experiment in mobile robotics that could perform tasks like planning routes and rearranging objects). Each breakthrough fueled the sense that human-like AI was not a question of "if" but "when." Even popular culture began to reflect this optimism: in the 1968 film 2001: A Space Odyssey, a computer named HAL 9000 (portrayed as capable of speech, reasoning, and even deception) personified the fascination and fears surrounding artificial intelligence in the public imagination.

Yet by the 1970s, reality set in. Many of the grand promises remained unfulfilled. It turned out that tasks which humans find effortless, like understanding the meaning of a story or recognising a face in a crowd, were fiendishly hard for machines. Early AI systems could manage neatly defined "toy" problems in small domains, but they struggled in the messy, ambiguous complexity of the real world. A U.S. government advisory panel in 1966 famously cancelled support for automatic language translation research (after millions spent) because the progress fell far short of expectations, an omen that AI's promises were running ahead of what could be delivered. In 1973, a report by the British

9 *Velik*, Quo Vadis, Intelligent Machine? 13: www.researchgate.net/publication/49595437_Quo_vadis_Intelligent_Machine.

10 *Kuipers*, Progress in AI: https://web.eecs.umich.edu/~kuipers/opinions/AI-progress.html (accessed 15.10.2025).

mathematician Sir James Lighthill delivered a harsh verdict on AI research, concluding that no substantial progress had been made in achieving artificial general intelligence.[11] Around the same time, influential critiques within the field itself further dampened optimism; a notable example was the book Perceptrons (1969) by *Marvin Minsky* and *Seymour Papert*, which demonstrated fundamental limits of one class of neural network and led many to abandon that approach as fruitless. As doubts multiplied, funding agencies grew skeptical. Detractors outside the field felt vindicated – for example, philosopher *Hubert Dreyfus* had long contended that human intelligence was largely intuitive and embodied, and thus not amenable to the purely formal techniques early AI favored.[12] His critique, once dismissed, now seemed prescient to some. Both in the United Kingdom and the United States, research grants were slashed. This period of diminished funding and waning enthusiasm came to be known as the first "AI winter." The exuberant spring of innovation was followed by a chill of stalled projects and shelved ambitions.

AI, however, is a field known for its phoenix-like resurgences. By the early 1980s, a new spring was underway. This revival centred on "expert systems" – programmes designed to replicate the decision-making of human experts in specific domains. One famous example was MYCIN, developed at Stanford, which could diagnose bacterial infections and recommend antibiotics based on a set of if-then rules crafted from interviews with physicians. Companies and governments took notice of these systems that appeared to capture human expertise in a box. A frenzy of investment followed; corporations began deploying expert systems for everything from configuring complex computer orders to credit checking and mineral prospecting. Banks used AI to decide whether to approve loans, and oil companies used it to guide drill site selection. AI buzzwords entered boardrooms. By the mid-1980s, there were dozens of startups selling "expert system shells" and custom AI solutions, and the market for specialized AI hardware (like Lisp machines) was booming. Governments also joined in: Japan launched its ambitious Fifth Generation Computer project in 1982, pouring funds into AI with the goal of leapfrogging Western computing. The United States responded with its own Strategic Computing Initiative to ensure it stayed at the cutting edge of AI and computer science efforts. It seemed AI had found a practical niche solving specialized problems, and optimism soared once again.

But the cycle of boom and bust had not been broken. Expert systems proved difficult to scale and maintain. They were brittle, often unable to handle sit-

11 *Lighthill*, Artificial Intelligence: www.chilton-computing.org.uk/inf/literature/reports/lighthill_report/p001.htm (accessed 21.11.2025).

12 *Brey*, Hubert Dreyfus: Human versus Machine.

uations that fell outside their narrowly encoded knowledge. A rule-based diagnostic programme, for example, might completely fail if a patient presented symptoms in a combination the designers hadn't anticipated. Moreover, these systems lacked any ability to learn or adapt themselves; their wisdom was entirely hand-crafted by programmers and domain experts. This knowledge engineering process was time-consuming and expensive, meaning that when conditions changed, updates were slow or nonexistent. Companies that had rushed to embrace expert systems found that maintenance costs and limitations piled up. The boom in specialized AI hardware also went bust as cheaper, general-purpose computers caught up in performance. By the late 1980s, the limitations were evident and the market for expert systems contracted, contributing to a second AI winter. Once more, enthusiasm cooled. Some proclaimed that artificial intelligence had been little more than a collection of clever party tricks that failed to deliver a truly adaptable, thinking machine.

Yet again, AI survived and adapted. The 1990s and 2000s brought gradual progress and a shift in approach that would prove decisive. Researchers increasingly turned from rule-based systems to data-driven methods. Instead of trying to articulate every rule of reasoning, why not have the machine learn patterns directly from large datasets? This idea of machine learning, which had existed since the 1950s in rudimentary forms, began to flourish as digital data and computing power grew exponentially. Statistical techniques and algorithms such as neural networks, once an obscure corner of AI research, were refined and scaled up. In 1997, a watershed moment arrived that seemed to vindicate the believers: *IBM*'s Deep Blue supercomputer defeated world chess champion *Garry Kasparov*. Chess had long been a yardstick for AI – a domain requiring foresight, strategy, and intellect. Deep Blue's victory was driven largely by brute-force computing and expert-crafted evaluation functions rather than human-like cognition, but its impact on the public imagination was enormous. For the first time, the world's chess champion had been beaten in a standard match by a machine. *Kasparov* said that at times he felt as if he faced a new kind of intelligence across the board, and his defeat made headlines around the globe. It symbolized how far AI had come since the Dartmouth conference, and it foreshadowed a future in which human champions in other domains would face similar trials.

In the first decade of the 21st century, AI quietly penetrated everyday life. Search engines like Google learned to instantly answer queries by scouring the web; spam filters learned to detect unwanted emails; speech recognition systems on phones became serviceably accurate; and recommendation algorithms began suggesting books, movies, or products tailored to our tastes. Much of this progress was fueled by machine learning algorithms finding patterns in enormous troves of data generated by the digital age. Notably, around 2012, a particular approach known as deep learning started to deliver breakthrough results. This renaissance of neural networks was catalyzed by two practical factors: an explosion of available data (thanks to the internet and ubiquitous sensors) and more powerful computers. In particular, researchers discovered that graphical processing units (GPUs) – chips originally made for fast graphics in video games – were remarkably effective at the parallel math operations needed to train deep neural networks. By leveraging GPUs and cloud computing, experiments that once took weeks could run in days or hours, enabling rapid progress. Deep learning refers to neural networks with many layers of simulated neurons, which can automatically learn hierarchical representations of data. When a deep neural network was applied to a large image dataset in 2012, it shattered previous records for recognising objects in photographs. Suddenly, AI was making headlines again for mastering tasks that had stymied earlier attempts, such as computer vision. The same deep learning methods soon achieved dramatic improvements in speech recognition and natural language processing. In 2011, *IBM* debuted its "Watson" system on the quiz show Jeopardy! and stunned the world when this AI defeated the best human contestants at a game requiring broad knowledge and nuanced understanding of clues. That same year, millions of people were introduced to AI in their pocket when *Apple* launched Siri, a smartphone voice assistant that could answer questions or perform tasks when asked in natural language. Within a few years, talking to one's phone or car navigation system felt almost routine. AI was seemingly everywhere, underpinning the rise of technology that could respond to voice commands, translate between languages flawlessly, and tailor content to our personal interests.

Another milestone of historic importance came in 2016. *Google DeepMind's AlphaGo* programme defeated Lee Sedol, one of the world's top Go players, in a five-game match. Go is an ancient board game far more complex than chess, with more possible positions than atoms in the observable universe. Prior AI attempts had struggled to play Go beyond an amateur level. AlphaGo's victory was powered by a combination of deep learning and a technique called reinforcement learning, where the programme learned optimal moves through countless games of self-play. To many, this achievement felt different from Deep Blue's chess win nearly two decades earlier. AlphaGo not only computed; it appeared to strategize and even exhibit flashes of creativity in its play. In game two of the match, AlphaGo made an unexpected move that professional players initially thought was an error – but it turned out to be brilliant, a turning point that helped secure the win. *Lee Sedol* did manage to win one out of the five games, an elusive victory that only highlighted how exceptional human intuition can be. Yet the overall result was decisive. (*Lee* would later retire from professional Go, commenting that no human could overcome the "insurmountable" skill of AI.) The AlphaGo match was a vivid demonstration of how modern AI techniques could tackle problems once thought to require uniquely human intuition.

By the late 2010s and into the 2020s, AI had undeniably transitioned from laboratory curiosity to mainstream technology. The world saw an explosion of AI applications across industries. In healthcare, algorithms began assisting in diagnosing diseases from medical images. In finance, AI systems traded stocks and detected fraud. Automakers invested heavily in autonomous driving systems. The legal profession started using AI tools for document review and research. Even in the staid insurance industry, long known for conservative practices, startups and forward-looking firms introduced AI to analyse risk and personalize policies, transforming traditional models of underwriting.[13] AI had become not just an academic endeavor but a cornerstone of innovation in the global economy.

One of the most striking developments of the 2020s has been the rise of AI systems that handle language—arguably the very domain that defines much of human intelligence. Large-scale language models, exemplified by OpenAI's GPT series, have shown an uncanny ability to generate human-like text, carry on conversations, and answer questions on an astonishing array of topics. When GPT-3 was unveiled in 2020 with 175 billion parametres (a measure of the complexity of its neural network), it stunned observers with its fluent and contextually apt responses to prompts. By 2022, AI had entered public consciousness as never before. That year, new "generative AI" systems made headlines: image-generation models such as DALL-E 2 conjured vivid artworks from text prompts, and user-friendly chatbots built on large language models could draft emails, write code, or even compose poetry on demand. For many, interacting with these systems was an uncanny experience—the line between human and machine-generated content grew blurrier. Some heralded these AI creations as the beginning of a new era, while others cautioned that they work without true understanding and can also confidently produce errors or fabrications (colloquially known as hallucinations). Nonetheless, the capabilities of AI were advancing at a pace that made even experts marvel.

Looking back from the vantage of 2026, the history of AI is a remarkable narrative of high hopes, setbacks, and ingenious rebounds. It is the story of a field that has repeatedly climbed out of its own troughs of disappointment by reinventing itself, often borrowing insights from other disciplines—whether neuroscience, statistics, or cognitive psychology. It is also a story about our relationship with our tools. Each chapter in AI's history reflects something of

13 *Galbraith*, End of Insurance, 98.

the era that produced it: the logical optimism of the 1950s and 60s, the pragmatic, expert-driven ethos of the 1980s, the data-centric globalization of the 2000s, and the deep learning connectivity of the 2010s and beyond. Through these shifts, the ultimate goal has remained in sight if not in reach: building machines that exhibit what we recognise as intelligence. That goal, at its core, is as challenging and captivating today as it was in 1956. As AI moves from solving structured games and specific tasks to engaging with the open-ended complexity of the real world, we stand witness to a new chapter – one in which artificial intelligence, for all its limitations, increasingly amplifies and mirrors the capabilities of the human mind. Recognising the transformative potential of AI, governments and industries worldwide have made AI a strategic priority. Countries are pouring resources into AI research and vying for leadership in the field, reflecting a belief that mastery of AI will confer significant economic, social, and geopolitical advantages in the decades ahead.

III. How does Artificial Intelligence work?

Having explored what AI is and how it emerged, we turn to the practical question of how AI systems operate. In simplest terms, an AI system receives information from its environment, processes that information according to some algorithmic strategy, and then outputs a result or action. Yet within that simple formulation lies a world of complexity. This section peels back the layers of AI techniques to demystify the technology – from the logic-based programmes of the early years to the learning-centric approaches that dominate today. We will also glance at the major subfields of AI – from computer vision and natural language processing to robotics – to appreciate the wide range of intelligent behaviours that researchers are striving to reproduce in machines.

Understanding how AI works in practice helps demystify the technology. Despite the almost magical impressions created by some advanced AI applications, the mechanisms under the hood are products of logic, mathematics, and engineering. In essence, AI systems are composed of algorithms – step-by-step procedures or mathematical models – that enable machines to process information and make decisions or predictions. Over the years, AI has employed a variety of approaches to achieve intelligent behaviour. Two broad paradigms have guided most AI research: the symbolic approach and the data-driven approach. While modern AI is dominated by the latter, it is useful to appreciate both, as each represents a different intuition about how to capture intelligence.

The symbolic approach, also known as "Good Old-Fashioned AI," dominated the early decades of artificial intelligence. It operates on the premise that intelligence results from manipulating abstract symbols according to logical rules.

Think of symbols as stand-ins for ideas or objects (like words in a sentence or variables in an equation) and intelligence as deriving from the correct manipulation of these symbols (like following the rules of grammar or algebra). Early AI systems were explicitly programmed with knowledge about the world in the form of rules, logic, and ontologies. For example, an expert system for medical diagnosis might contain hundreds of if-then rules provided by physicians ("IF the patient has symptom X and test result Y, THEN the likely illness is Z"). The strength of this approach is clarity: each step of the machine's reasoning can be understood by humans because it follows the rules we gave it. Some of these systems proved incredibly useful in narrow domains. However, the symbolic approach struggled with tasks that are hard to distill into clean-cut rules – which, it turns out, is most of everyday reality. Writing a rule for every scenario is impractical; there are too many exceptions, nuances, and unknowns. Symbolic AI also found it difficult to cope with uncertainty or probabilistic reasoning; classical logic is rigid, and the real world is not.

In contrast, the data-driven approach to AI, which encompasses machine learning, takes a very different path. Instead of telling the machine what to do step by step, we provide the machine with large amounts of data and let it infer patterns and rules by itself. This approach is inspired, in part, by the way humans (and animals) seem to learn from experience. We are not born with a complete rulebook for life; rather, we learn from examples, from trial and error, and from adjusting our mental models when reality surprises us. Machine learning embodies this philosophy of "learning by example." The fundamental idea is to create an algorithm that can adjust itself (its internal parameters) to improve performance on a task, given feedback or data about the right answers.

One of the earliest and most influential forms of machine learning is the artificial neural network, which has roots going back to the 1940s. Neural networks were inspired by a simplistic model of the human brain's architecture. They consist of layers of interconnected "nodes" or "neurons" that transmit signals to each other. Each connection has a weight that can be tuned. In the beginning, the network is like a novice, its connection weights essentially random. Then the network is trained on data – for instance, a collection of images along with labels indicating what each image contains. The training process adjusts the weights through many iterations, gradually improving the network's accuracy. (This training process typically relies on an algorithm called backpropagation – developed in the 1980s – which efficiently computes how each connection weight contributes to the error and nudges it in the direction that reduces mistakes.) By the end of training, the neural network has formed an internal model that can, say, recognise a cat in a photo even if it has never seen that exact photo before. Importantly, it does this without anyone ever explicitly programming a rule like "IF you see pointed ears, whiskers, and a tail, THEN it's probably a cat." Instead, the network autonomously develops its own criteria for cat recognition by statistically weighing countless features in the images. The result is a form of learned expertise that can appear eerily perceptive. Modern image recognition AIs can outperform humans at certain tasks, such as distinguishing subtle differences in medical scans, precisely because they have learned from vast datasets of images.[14]

The current state-of-the-art in AI heavily favors these learning-based methods, especially deep learning, which is essentially neural networks on a grand scale. "Deep" networks are so called because they have many layers of neurons – sometimes dozens or even hundreds – allowing them to learn complex, multi-level representations of data. For instance, in a deep neural network trained to recognise speech, the first layer or two might learn to detect basic sounds (phonemes), the next layers might recognise combinations of sounds as syllables or words, and higher layers might capture the structure of sentences. Similarly, for image analysis, lower layers pick out edges and textures, while higher layers identify shapes or specific objects. This hierarchical learning is powerful because it lets the machine build abstract concepts from raw inputs. A remarkable aspect of deep learning is that these networks often find ways to solve problems that their human creators don't explicitly understand – the "knowledge" is distributed across thousands or millions of small weight adjustments rather than in tidy rules. This can make them something of a "black box." We know they work, and we can measure their performance precisely, but interpreting exactly how a complex network makes a given decision is not always straightforward.

Besides neural networks, other important techniques remain part of the AI arsenal. Decision trees, for example, learn by splitting data into branches based on features, somewhat like a flowchart that ends in decisions or predictions. Support vector machines, another method, find optimal boundaries between different categories of data in a multidimensional space. Some algorithms even mimic evolution – so-called genetic algorithms "breed" and mutate solutions to gradually improve them from generation to generation. There are also clustering algorithms that can discover natural groupings in unlabeled data (for instance, to segment customers by purchasing behaviour or to identify communities in a social network). Each of these techniques has contributed to AI's toolkit. In recent years, however, neural network-based approaches have eclipsed most others in terms of headline-grabbing results and real-world deployments.

To illustrate concretely how an AI system works, consider something like a voice-activated virtual assistant on a smartphone. When you ask a question

14 *LeCun/Bengio/Hinton*, Deep Learning 436: https://doi.org/10.1038/nature14539.

aloud ("What's the weather tomorrow?"), the audio waveform of your voice is first processed by a speech-to-text AI, often a deep neural network trained on thousands of hours of speech. That network converts the sounds into text by probabilistically determining which sequences of letters or words best match the input audio. The recognised text ("What's the weather tomorrow?") is then fed into a natural language understanding system. This might involve yet another AI model that parses the grammar and extracts meaning – in this case, identifying that the user is asking for a weather forecast for tomorrow. The assistant then queries a database or weather API for the information. Once it has the answer (say, "It will be 75 degrees and sunny"), it uses a text-to-speech AI model to synthesize a human-like voice to speak the answer back to you. Each of those steps (speech recognition, language understanding, and speech synthesis) relies on AI algorithms that have learned from data. The designers of the system did not programme specific responses for every possible weather query; instead, they built models that can handle a wide variety of inputs by generalizing from examples.

While machine learning has proven astonishingly effective, it comes with its own set of challenges and considerations. First, these systems are only as good as the data they are trained on. If the data contains biases or errors, the AI will likely reflect them. For instance, an AI trained on historical hiring data might inadvertently learn to favor male candidates if, in the past, those candidates were hired more frequently – not because gender is relevant to ability, but because it was correlated with past decisions. Ensuring fairness and eliminating bias in AI models is thus a crucial and ongoing area of work. Second, machine learning models can fail in unpredictable ways when they encounter situations outside the distribution of their training data. A self-driving car's vision system might be nearly perfect under normal conditions but make a bizarre mistake when confronted with an unusual scenario or visual illusion it was never trained on. Unlike a human driver, the AI lacks common sense and real understanding; it cannot reason about a completely novel situation except by analogy to what it already knows. In fact, deep learning models can sometimes be too sensitive to the specific statistical patterns in their training data: researchers have found that adding an almost imperceptible layer of noise to an image can cause a state-of-the-art classifier to confidently mistake a turtle for a rifle or a stop sign for a speed limit sign. Such bizarre errors, termed adversarial examples, underscore how alien an AI's way of "seeing" can be compared to human perception.

Another important aspect of how AI works is the concept of reinforcement learning, which differs from the typical supervised learning scenario of training on labeled examples. In reinforcement learning, an AI agent learns by interacting with an environment and receiving feedback in the form of rewards or penalties. This is akin to training a pet with treats and scoldings, except the "pet" here might be a piece of software learning to play a video game. The agent tries actions at random initially, and over time, it figures out which actions lead to higher cumulative rewards. This technique proved critical in the success of game-playing AIs like AlphaGo and is also used in robotics and operations research for optimizing sequences of decisions.

In practical deployment, AI systems often combine multiple techniques and are embedded in broader software architectures that handle data input and output, user interfaces, safety checks, and more. For example, an autonomous drone uses AI-based computer vision to interpret its surroundings and reinforcement learning to make flight decisions, but it also relies on traditional control theory to maintain stability and on conventional software engineering for fail-safes and communication.

To the outside observer, the performance of a well-tuned AI can seem almost miraculous. But seen from the inside, it is a product of many trial-and-error iterations, enormous amounts of data, and carefully designed algorithms that leverage statistical patterns. There is no single "brain" or magic spark inside; rather, intelligence emerges from the coordinated action of many simple computations. In a neural network, for example, each "neuron" is essentially computing a weighted sum of its inputs and passing it through a simple non-linear function. That alone is not intelligent; it is the accumulation of millions of such operations, arranged in just the right way and informed by experience, that gives rise to what we perceive as an intelligent action or decision.

It is also worth noting that AI does not work in isolation from human contributors. The current AI boom has been propelled not only by algorithms, but by the availability of large datasets (often curated or generated by humans) and by immense computing infrastructure. The phrase "artificial intelligence" might evoke a self-sufficient machine mind, but in reality, today's AI often relies on an ecosystem that includes human data annotators, domain experts who shape the objectives, and engineers who tweak and maintain the systems. AI emerges from this socio-technical network; the "artificial" intelligence is in many respects a distillation of collective human effort and knowledge, automated and accelerated by computational power.

As AI systems become more embedded in society, understanding how they work is no longer just a technical question but also a matter of transparency and trust. The opaqueness of complex models (the "black box" issue) has led to a push for explainable AI, seeking techniques to make AI decision-making more interpretable to humans. For example, an image recognition network can be probed to visualize which pixels or features it focused on when labeling a picture, revealing whether it "looked at" the relevant object or was distracted by background patterns. Similarly, complex models can sometimes be approximated by simpler surrogate models (like decision trees) that give humans a rough sense of the logic. These efforts at interpretability aim to turn the black box into a glass box, so to speak, enabling users to trust (and if needed, challenge) AI-driven outcomes.

In reflecting on how AI works, we come full circle to the observation that every advance in AI forces us to confront new questions about ourselves. We build machines to perform tasks that require intelligence, and in doing so, we tease apart the subcomponents of intelligence itself. We learn, for instance, that much of image recognition can happen without "understanding" – a computer can recognise a face without knowing whose face it is or what a face signifies in a cultural sense. We learn that logic alone is not enough; the messy, intuitive pattern-matching that our brains do turns out to be immensely powerful, and we have had to invent statistical learning to mimic that ability. Each method in AI, from rule-based systems to deep neural networks, captures something of what we think intelligence entails, yet each also reveals its own blind spots. In the gaps of what our programmes cannot do, we often discover the subtlety of our own cognitive skills.

Artificial intelligence is not a static thing a machine has or does not have. It is an evolving collection of methods that extends human ingenuity. In the quest to build AI, we have repeatedly been humbled by the complexity of our own intelligence. But we have also been ingenious in finding pathways to make machines exhibit slivers of that intelligence. As we proceed, the line between human and machine capabilities shifts. Popular culture captures this ambivalence: in film and fiction, AI is portrayed variously as a friendly servant (as in R2-D2 from Star Wars) or an existential threat (as in the rogue Skynet in The Terminator). These dramatic imaginings underscore both our deepest hopes and fears about what real-world AI might become. If there is a lesson from the history and workings of AI, it is that intelligence – natural or artificial – thrives on learning, adaptation, and the interplay of ideas over time. One thing is certain: AI will continue to evolve, and with it, our questions will evolve as well.

References and resources

Brey, Hubert Dreyfus. Human versus Machine, in Achterhuis (ed.), American Philosophy of Technology: The Empirical Turn (2010) 37–63

Capek, R. U. R. (Rossum's Universal Robots) (1920)

Galbraith, The End of Insurance As We Know It (2019)

Gignac/Szodorai, Defining intelligence: Bridging the gap between human and artificial perspectives, Intelligence, Vol 104 (May-June 2024): doi.org/10.1016/j.intell.2024.101832

Kuipers, Progress in AI: https://web.eecs.umich.edu/~kuipers/opinions/AI-progress.html (accessed 15.10.2025)

Kurzweil, The Singularity Is Near. When Humans Transcend Biology (2005)

LeCun/Bengio/Hinton, Deep learning. Nature 521, 436–444 (2015): doi.org/10.1038/nature14539

Lighthill, Artificial Intelligence: A General Survey, Artificial Intelligence: A paper symposium (1973): www.chilton-computing.org.uk/inf/literature/reports/lighthill_report/p001.htm (accessed 21.11.2025)

McCarthy/Minsky/Rochester/Shannon, (2006). A Proposal for the Dartmouth Summer Research Project on Artificial Intelligence, August 31, 1955. AI Magazine, 27(4), 12: doi.org/10.1609/aimag.v27i4.1904

Meyer, B., 'John McCarthy', Communications of the ACM (28 October 2011): https://cacm.acm.org/blogs/blog-cacm/138907-john-mccarthy/fulltext (accessed 15.10.2025)

Mikalef/Gupta, Artificial intelligence capability: Conceptualization, measurement calibration, and empirical study on its impact on organizational creativity and firm performance, Information & Management, Vol 58, 3 (April 2021): doi.org/10.1016/j.im.2021.103434

Minsky (Hrsg), Semantic Information Processing (1968)

Minsky/Papert, Perceptrons. An Introduction to Computational Geometry (1969)

Russell/Norvig, Artificial Intelligence: A Modern Approach (2010)

Searle, J. R., Minds, brains, and programs. Behavioral and Brain Sciences (1980), 3(3), 417–424: doi.org/10.1017/S0140525X00005756

Turing, Computing Machinery and Intelligence (1950), Mind, 59, 433–460: doi.org/10.1093/mind/LIX.236.433

Velik, "Quo Vadis, Intelligent Machine?" BRAIN. Broad Research in Artificial Intelligence and Neuroscience, 1 (4): 13–22 (2010): www.researchgate.net/publication/49595437_Quo_vadis_Intelligent_Machine

Use of AI in various industries

Thomas Münkel
Insurance Manager

Abstract: This brief overview compares the use of AI in insurance companies with other financial service providers and other industries in general. The result is a largely consistent picture, according to which the use of AI in the insurance industry lags significantly behind other industries.

Keywords: Artificial intelligence, AI, market comparison, financial services

Contents

I. Introduction

The use of AI in an industry comparison will only be briefly touched upon here. There are many studies[1] that examine a wide variety of industries, regions, subject areas and evaluation criteria for the use of artificial intelligence. They are often updated several times a year. Therefore, the following pages only provide a few examples of more recent studies that shed light on this topic and provide starting points for those who want to delve deeper into an industry comparison.

1 E.g., *ACORD*, Insurance Digital Maturity Study (2025): www.acord.org/marketplace-pages/product-detail/acord-insurance-digital-maturity-study-(2025-edition) (accessed 27.1.2026); *Deloitte Belgien*, Digital Insurance Maturity. Assessment of insurance digitalisation in the EMEA region (2025): www.deloitte.com/be/en/Industries/financial-services/research/digital-insurance-maturity-report (accessed 5.11.2025) and *Evident*, The Evident AI Insurance Index. Benchmarking the AI maturity of the largest insurance companies in North America and Europe (2025): https://evidentinsights.com/insurance-ai-index/ (accessed 16.11.2025).

https://doi.org/10.33196/9783704698520-103

II. AI use by financial service providers

In addition to insurers, the financial sector mainly comprises banks and other financial service providers (e.g., leasing providers, building societies, credit card companies, asset managers, payment service providers, etc.). Various studies show that there are striking differences here. For example, a survey of approximately 1,400 IT and data managers revealed significant differences between insurers and other industries. In this study, insurers largely considered themselves to be in the early stages of AI implementation, while other industries considered themselves to be more advanced. This was also explained by the outdated core IT systems of insurers and the extensive regulation of the industry.[2] Compared to other financial service providers, insurers placed particular emphasis on comprehensive data and model governance compared to banks, for example (56 % vs. 39 %). Given that banks are also heavily regulated, the difference is striking. Another surprising observation is that insurers use AI less than other industries to evaluate unstructured data.

Similar explanations for these differences were found in a study conducted at the *University of Limerick,*[3] in which insurance managers were asked what they considered to be the biggest obstacles to the use of generative AI. The main factors cited were strong regulation, a lack of trust in AI and a risk-averse mindset. However, the picture is not quite so clear-cut: for example, in a Germany-wide AI market study[4], *PwC* sees insurers ahead of banks in the use of AI in Germany. In this study, 85 % of insurers stated that they allow the use of GenAI, while only 60 % of banks did so.

III. AI comparison between insurers:

Of course, not all insurers can be lumped together: there are huge differences in the scope and quality of AI use among insurers. A particularly systematic and detailed analysis comes from *Deloitte Belgium,*[5] which in 2025 commissioned

2 *Iron Mountain:* AI maturity in the insurance industry (Juli 2025): https://resources.ironmountain.com/whitepapers/a/ai-maturity-in-the-insurance-industry (accessed 16.11.2025).

3 *Owen/Mullins/Sheehan*, Generative AI Adoption and Barriers: The Case of the Insurance Industry (2025): http://dx.doi.org/10.2139/ssrn.5227619.

4 *PwC*, Einblicke zur Künstlichen Intelligenz im deutschen Finanzsektor (2025): www.pwc.de/de/finanzdienstleistungen/einblicke-zur-kuenstlichen-intelligenz-im-finanzsektor.html (accessed 16.11.2025).

5 *Deloitte Belgien*, Digital Insurance Maturity. Assessment of insurance digitalisation in the EMEA region (2025): www.deloitte.com/be/en/Industries/financial-services/research/digital-insurance-maturity-report (accessed 5.11.2025).

experts to examine the maturity of digitalisation (including AI) among insurers in the EMEA region based on functionality and user experience using clear criteria. Unsurprisingly, there were massive differences between digital laggards and champions in all EMEA countries. Here, too, the conclusion already mentioned several times applies: "There is a need for significant investment in insurers' back-end systems to overcome current limitations and achieve true service capabilities"[6].

The *Evident* AI – Insurance Index[7] (which claims to be the "global standard for AI maturity") reveals enormous differences among the 30 largest insurers based in the US and Europe in its latest ranking from June 2025. The study not only examined AI innovations, but also assessed talent, leadership and transparency. The latest *ACORD* Insurance Digital Maturity Study,[8] which examines the digital maturity of over 200 of the largest insurers worldwide, comes to similar conclusions.

IV. AI maturity in different industries

Accenture conducted an industry comparison examining AI maturity based on various criteria for different industries.[9] In each case, the insurance industry was placed in the bottom third, with (relative) progress, but still more laggards than pioneers in a cross-industry comparison. Now, one can argue about the exact positioning. However, experts will probably agree that the insurance industry is approaching the topic of AI relatively slowly. This is all the more surprising when you consider that there is hardly any other industry whose core business relies so heavily on data, language and (risk) probabilities – ideal for the comprehensive use of AI, right? One possible reason that is often cited is that insurance managers tend to be risk-averse and are therefore more cautious than others when it comes to adopting new technologies. Perhaps. More relevant, however, seems to be the massive regulation of insurance companies, which is more pronounced in Europe than in almost any other industry.[10]

---

6 *Deloitte Belgien*, Digital Insurance Maturity Report, 29: www.deloitte.com/be/en/Industries/financial-services/research/digital-insurance-maturity-report.html.

7 *Evident*, The Evident AI Insurance Index. Benchmarking the AI maturity of the largest insurance companies in North America and Europe (2025): https://evidentinsights.com/insurance-ai-index/ (accessed 16.11.2025).

8 *ACORD*, Insurance Digital Maturity Study (2025): www.acord.org/marketplace-pages/product-detail/acord-insurance-digital-maturity-study-(2025-edition) (accessed 27.1.2026).

9 *Accenture*, The art of AI maturity – Advancing from practice to performance (2022), 34: www.accenture.com/content/dam/system-files/acom/custom-code/ai-maturity/Accenture-Art-of-AI-Maturity-Report-Global-Revised.pdf (accessed 16.11.2025).

10 See also *Lucas*, Where AI meets insurance (in this volume) 181 ff.

Garner,[11] based on the Digital Acceleration Index by *Boston Consulting Group*, concludes that although insurance companies have accelerated digitalisation and the use of AI since the coronavirus pandemic, they still lag behind almost all other industries. This is unlikely to have changed much today, as all industries are investing heavily in the use of AI. The situation looks somewhat better according to the latest study on the AI Readiness Index by *HG Insights*:[12] There, the insurance industry ranks in the top half of all industries surveyed.

Oxford Economics and *ServiceNow* conducted a structured survey of nearly 4,500 managers worldwide in various industries in 2025 on the use of AI in their companies.[13] They came to the surprising conclusion that the AI maturity index they surveyed in 2025 across eleven industries and 16 countries had fallen by 9 percentage points compared to the previous year. They attribute this to the fact that the speed of AI innovation is overwhelming companies' ability to quickly implement AI on a larger scale. They identify a gap between bold AI visions at the top level and the appropriate guidelines for company-wide implementation of AI innovations. And when comparing industries, a familiar picture emerges: the insurance industry ranks last in the "pacesetters" ranking, and in a regional comparison, Germany lands in the bottom third.

These study data support the theses put forward in the introductory chapter, according to which the insurance industry is currently still lagging behind in exploiting the potential of artificial intelligence. The following articles in this book deal with what is already possible today and works in practice, and how to proceed with a high probability of success.

References and resources

Accenture, The art of AI maturity—Advancing from practice to performance (2022). Available at www.accenture.com/content/dam/system-files/acom/custom-code/ai-maturity/Accenture-Art-of-AI-Maturity-Report-Global-Revised.pdf (accessed 16.11.2025)

11 *Garner*, How Digitally Mature Are Insurance Companies in 2023? www.cortical.io/blog/how-digitally-mature-are-insurance-companies-in-2023 (accessed 16.11.2025) "(...) insurance still lags behind almost all industries, including healthcare, finance, and consumer goods".

12 *HG Insights*, GenAI Readiness Report: The Most AI-Mature Companies in 2025 (2025): https://explore.hginsights.com/genai-readiness-report-2025 (accessed 16.11.2025).

13 *ServiceNow*, Enterprise AI Maturity Index 2025 (2025): www.servicenow.com/content/dam/servicenow-assets/public/en-us/doc-type/resource-center/white-paper/wp-enterprise-ai-maturity-index-2025.pdf (accessed 16.11.2025).

ACORD, Insurance Digital Maturity Study (2025). Available at www.acord.org/marketplace-pages/product-detail/acord-insurance-digital-maturity-study-(2025-edition) (accessed 27.1.2026)

Garner, How Digitally Mature Are Insurance Companies in 2023? Available at www.cortical.io/blog/how-digitally-mature-are-insurance-companies-in-2023 (accessed 16.11.2025)

Deloitte Belgium, Digital Insurance Maturity Report 2025, August 2025, available at: www.deloitte.com/be/en/Industries/financial-services/research/digital-insurance-maturity-report.html (accessed 16.11.2025)

Evident: The Evident AI Insurance Index, available at https://evidentinsights.com/insurance-ai-index/ (accessed 16.11.2025)

HG Insights, GenAI Readiness Report (2025). Available at GenAI Readiness Report: The Most AI-Mature Companies in 2025 (accessed 16.11.2025)

Iron Mountain: AI maturity in the insurance industry, July 2025. https://resources.ironmountain.com/whitepapers/a/ai-maturity-in-the-insurance-industry (accessed 16.11.2025)

Owen/Mullins/Sheehan, Generative AI Adoption and Barriers: The Case of the Insurance Industry (2025): http://dx.doi.org/10.2139/ssrn.5227619

PwC, Insights into artificial intelligence in the German financial sector (2025). Available at Insights into artificial intelligence in the financial sector 2025 – PwC (accessed 16.11.2025)

ServiceNow: Enterprise AI Maturity Index 2025 (2025). Available at Enterprise AI Maturity Index2025 (accessed 16.11.2025)

AI in a European Insurance Group

Alexander Bockelmann*
Group CTO, Baloise Group

Abstract: This chapter shows how AI and machine learning approaches are used strategically in insurance companies from the perspective of a Chief Technology Officer (CTO). The author highlights the strategic importance of AI in insurance using the example of the Baloise Group. He presents specific use cases and describes how companies such as Baloise are successfully implementing AI – from embedded AI to high-code solutions. The focus is not only on technological aspects, but also on cultural, ethical and organisational challenges.

Keywords: Artificial intelligence, AI, Baloise, Helvetia, CTO, fraud detection, claims settlement, IT, cloud computing, embedded GenAI, self-service GenAI, low-code enablement, high-code enablement, LLM, large language model, machine learning, risk assessment, AI regulation, high-risk AI systems, GDPR, IDD, DORA, governance, underwriting, EU AI Act, process automation, change management, digitalisation, foundation models, Baloise FX

Contents

* This contribution was written in German by the author. The present version is a translation into English. The contribution appears in its original form in the German edition of this book: *Münkel* (Hrsg), KI in der Versicherungsbranche (2026) https://doi.org/10.33196/9783704698513.

I. AI in the insurance world

Artificial intelligence (AI) is fundamentally changing the insurance industry, albeit more slowly than some had expected: the gap between expectations of AI and its actual applications is growing. AI is already becoming an increasingly important component of standard solutions and in-house developments, helping to continuously optimise business capabilities and processes. Applications range from optimising internal processes to developing new business models. The example of the *Baloise Group* clearly shows how innovation, data expertise and technological strategies interact to implement efficient innovation for customers and partners as well as employees and shareholders.

A. *Baloise*—Swiss innovation and service for Europe

The *Baloise Group*[1] is a major Swiss insurance group headquartered in Basel. It offers a wide range of insurance solutions in the non-life and life sectors, as well as asset management and banking services. With around 8,000 employees, *Baloise* operates in Switzerland, Belgium, Germany and Luxembourg. In 2024, the *Baloise Group* had around 6 million customers and a business volume of CHF 8.6 billion.[2] *Baloise* is known for its innovative financial and service solutions, was named one of Switzerland's most innovative insurers in 2023[3] and

1 www.baloise.com.
2 www.baloise.com/dam/jcr:449f7aa0-a73c-4f26-a539-c1f19bd20714/geschaeftsbericht-bg-2024.pdf.
3 *Baloise*, www.baloise.com/de/home/news-stories/news/medienmitteilungen/2023/baloise-zu-den-innovativsten-schweizer-versicherern-2023-gekuert.html (accessed 23.7.2025).

won the "Top Service Germany" competition in 2024 for exemplary customer focus and service quality.[4] In April 2025, the insurance groups *Baloise* and *Helvetia* proposed a merger of equals, which was approved by shareholders in May 2025 and is currently awaiting approval from the relevant authorities. As of October 2025, approvals had been obtained from the EU and the Swiss Competition Commission. This means that the work is well on track for a closing in December 2025.

B. AI as a strategic imperative for insurance CTOs

The history of information technology (IT) is characterised by regular disruptive innovations that fundamentally change working methods, employee skills, IT development and IT applications.

Classic examples of this are the introduction of the mainframe (e.g., OS/360 *IBM*, 1960s)[5], the personal computer (e.g., *IBM* PC Model 5150)[6], the Internet (1990s), and cloud computing (e.g., AWS Start 2006).[7] These and other IT trends and developments have since influenced IT in companies, enabled new business processes and capabilities, and fundamentally changed the architecture of corporate IT.

Not every IT trend becomes such a disruptive event and strategic success factor and/or makes sense for every company in terms of content. Ultimately, IT is a means to an end, and that end is the efficient, high-performance, secure and innovative support of a company's goals. A CTO should therefore analyse IT trends, question them and evaluate their potential benefits for their business context.

From today's perspective, AI appears to be a disruptive IT event, the impact of which, in my opinion, can only be properly assessed in retrospect. Today's AI technology, and especially the genAI technology available since 2022, such as ChatGPT,[8], is still young and rapidly evolving for broad and scaled use in regulated industries such as insurance, banking and healthcare. Between 2022 and 2024, numerous so-called large language models (LLMs) with ever-in-

4 *Baloise,* www.baloise.de/de/ueber-uns/auszeichnungen.html (accessed 23.7.2025).
5 *Wikipedia,* https://de.wikipedia.org/wiki/OS/360 (accessed 23.5.2025).
6 Tynan, IT-Meilensteine: 12 Technologien, die die Welt verändert haben (7.10.2010): www.cio.de/article/3664567/12-technologien-die-die-welt-veraendert-haben.html (accessed 21.11.2025).
7 Baigorri, The Cloud Wars: A Battle for Dominance (2.10.2024): www.cloudinstitute.io/aws/the-cloud-wars-a-battle-for-dominance/ (accessed 21.11.2025).
8 *Wikipedia,* https://en.wikipedia.org/wiki/ChatGPT (accessed 8.8.2025).

creasing scaling of training data and capabilities have emerged, bringing about an upswing in AI adoption in businesses.

These LLMs and their growing generative and multimodal capabilities are now opening up new opportunities for optimisation and innovation that were previously not possible, or at least not as efficiently, with traditional methods of data analysis and processing.

This will have a significant impact on the IT landscape, its processes, the necessary skills in the IT workforce, and the required external partner and innovation network in the medium term, making it a strategic issue for CTOs. AI and LLM-based IT applications have thus long since become more than just a testing ground for innovation departments. In many companies, the use of AI and, in particular, LLM-based solutions has consequently shifted from an experimental approach with many small experiments and pilots to a few, but larger-scale use cases. This has led to a trend towards a strategic imperative to increase efficiency within the company in the future, enable process innovation and increase customer interaction and loyalty. AI can also lead to new products and services, thereby expanding business models.

For insurance CTOs, the underlying technology is nothing new. Most financial institutions have been working with simple and complex mathematical models, machine learning approaches and comparable methods for years and decades, e.g., in the context of premium calculation for a defined risk (pricing), in actuarial models, in risk assessments, in fraud detection or in the field of process automation, such as information extraction from documents or conversation recognition in customer service.

Despite all the AI and LLM euphoria, it should be noted that, from a practical and IT perspective and regardless of regulatory, ethical, data protection or security requirements, the necessary IT solutions for the application of AI for scaled use cases are often not yet available in a standardised form.

Due to the rapid pace of technological development, today's AI infrastructure is likely to be tomorrow's AI legacy. AI investments are therefore always subject to a cost/benefit analysis in order to leverage the potential of the technology and the opportunity for, thereby enabling the further development of the organisation, employees and business capabilities in line with the business context.

II. AI as a lever for innovation and efficiency

Artificial intelligence is currently changing the insurance industry slowly, but at an increasing pace and scope. While classic machine learning models have been in use for years, modern AI approaches are opening up new possibilities, from the automation of repetitive tasks to the development of personalised communication and services. This chapter highlights both the practical challenges and opportunities arising from AI integration and uses concrete examples to show how insurers such as *Baloise* are exploiting this potential.

A. Challenges for the use of AI in practice

Insurance companies have been successfully using mathematical models and rule-based algorithms for various purposes within their organisations for many years. These approaches have been and continue to be used to analyse data, forecast trends, calculate financial and actuarial figures, and optimise processes and innovation within the company.

A desirable and important feature of these models is the traceability of their results in specific individual cases and in general.[9] This can best be illustrated using a classic rule tree. Is condition A fulfilled? If yes, then do B; if no, then do C, etc. Experts can develop these types of models based on empirical values, read and understand them, and generate a predictable output with the same input. Modern machine learning methods and AI applications now create new challenges for practical application, which are discussed in more detail in other sections of this book and will only be briefly outlined here.

1. Regulatory requirements

In addition to technical and organisational aspects, regulatory requirements also pose a key challenge for the use of AI in insurance companies. Both the EU and Switzerland have various legal frameworks in place, particularly with regard to transparency, governance and data protection in AI applications.

In the EU, the Regulation laying down harmonised rules for artificial intelligence (AI Regulation)[10] defines a risk-based regulatory framework that sets

9 *Fraunhofer-Gesellschaft,* Maschinelles Lernen: Kompetenzen, Forschung, Anwendung, 30ff (2018): www.bigdata-ai.fraunhofer.de/de/publikationen/ml-studie.html (accessed 21.11.2025).

10 Regulation (EU) 2024/1689 of the European Parliament and of the Council of 13 June 2024 laying down harmonised rules on artificial intelligence, available at http://data.europa.eu/eli/reg/2024/1689/oj.

out extensive requirements, particularly for so-called high-risk AI systems. This includes documentation requirements, human oversight, and the traceability of decisions.[11] In addition, the provisions of the General Data Protection Regulation (GDPR)[12] must be observed, which is particularly relevant to the processing of personal and sensitive data by AI systems and also covers aspects of the IDD (Insurance Distribution Directive[13]) and DORA (Digital Operational Resilience Act).[14]

Insurance companies that have long used statistical models in actuarial practice are faced with a crucial question: Are these traditional models classified as "artificial intelligence" within the meaning of the AI Regulation or not? The answer to this question has far-reaching implications for transparency, governance and compliance requirements.[15]

Models that do not have features such as autonomy, adaptability or self-learning capabilities are unlikely to fall under the definition of AI systems within the meaning of the AI Regulation. This applies in particular to classic, deterministic models without dynamic learning components. Recital 12 of the AI Regulation clarifies that traditional software systems that merely follow predefined rules (e.g. "if-then" rules) or simple statistical approaches do not fall under the definition. It emphasises that the ability to learn from data and develop models is a key feature. This implicitly excludes systems that lack autonomy and adaptability from the regulatory scope of the AI Regulation.

The situation is different for pricing and underwriting solutions that contain AI components or exhibit such characteristics (self-learning, autonomy, adaptability). These systems are generally classified as "high-risk AI" and are therefore subject to the comprehensive requirements of the AI Regulation. These range from requirements for data quality and fairness, technical documentation, transparency and explainability, to human control and regulatory registration.

11 See, for example, *Feiler/Forgó*, AI Regulation (2024).

12 Regulation (EU) 2016/679 of the European Parliament and of the Council of 27 April 2016 on the protection of natural persons with regard to the processing of personal data http://data.europa.eu/eli/reg/2016/679/oj.

13 Directive (EU) 2016/97 of the European Parliament and of the Council of 20 January 2016 on insurance distribution, available at http://data.europa.eu/eli/dir/2016/97/oj (accessed 3.10.2025).

14 Regulation (EU) 2022/2554 of the European Parliament and of the Council of 14 December 2022 on digital operational resilience in the financial sector http://data.europa.eu/eli/reg/2022/2554/oj.

15 *Actuarial Association of Europe (AAE)*, Navigating Europe's AI Act: Insights for actuaries and the insurance sector (2025): https://actuary.eu/wp-content/uploads/2025/03/AAE-Discussion-Paper-Navigating-Europes-AI-Act.pdf (accessed 21.11. 2025).

National supervisory authorities such as BaFin (Germany), NBB (Belgium), CAA (Luxembourg) and FINMA (Switzerland) are guided by the AI Regulation, but set their own priorities. BaFin requires clear governance, transparent model responsibility and active model risk management when dealing with algorithms. The NBB and CAA also emphasise the importance of explainability and data protection, drawing heavily on the principles of EIOPA.

FINMA pursues a principles-based approach and integrates AI-relevant requirements into existing regulations, for example in the areas of outsourcing, IT governance and operational risks. While the EU is following a rule-based approach with the AI Regulation, Switzerland is opting for a more flexible but no less demanding implementation using largely existing regulatory instruments. For insurance companies, this means that AI projects must be set up and documented in a manner that is not only technologically sound but also regulatory compliant. The challenge lies in harmonising the speed of innovation with regulatory compliance. This is particularly true for cross-border applications in pan-European (insurance) companies. Here, an AI use case may be subject to different regulatory requirements.

At *Baloise*, this technological and regulatory development has led to a number of new internal governance activities. Internal AI regulations have been defined, which are developed and controlled by a new AI Governance Board and integrate regulatory and internal requirements into the system of directives. An inventory of all existing AI applications is being compiled and an approval process for all new AI applications is being introduced. Based on their characteristics and data access, a risk assessment and classification is carried out, resulting in requirements for each risk level. These are defined in a corresponding risk management standard, and internal governance compliance with the necessary controls and documentation requirements is incorporated into the risk management processes.

Regulatory requirements in the sense of minimum regulation are helpful for a transparent, risk-based and ethical approach to AI. As the technology develops and experience in dealing with AI and regulatory requirements grows, there will be learning effects and adjustments. Internal processes and procedures should anticipate this and allow for a certain degree of flexibility.

2. Traceability, transparency and explainability of models

Transparency is often the easiest framework condition to fulfil in practice. The development, responsibility and use of AI-based models can be transparently and comprehensively documented with appropriate processes and tools. According to the EU General Data Protection Regulation, a model is considered explainable in the context of an individual decision if the key influencing factors can be identified.[16] The complete traceability of complex neural networks or LLM models is not possible in practice, and increasing the traceability and explainability of AI is one of the ongoing and future research topics in AI research·

3. Efficiency and costs of AI calculations and data transformations

Until recently, AI was still considered a driver for cloud adoption. In order to use AI and LLMs successfully, data had to be available in the cloud for the AI or LLM. Public cloud infrastructure and/or AI and data services were prerequisites for the realisation of use cases. Meanwhile, security and data protection requirements, increasing cost pressure and realisable efficiency potentials in the private cloud environment are driving some companies to repatriate parts or complete AI or data solutions and migrate from the public cloud to a private cloud or a local data centre[17].

4. Data literacy and data culture in companies

For many practical applications in companies, the availability of high-quality and comprehensive training material and/or contextual data is crucial. Today, this is often still a limiting factor because the fundamental investments in a data culture and in data transparency and quality have not been made. Historically grown data silos make holistic data access difficult, and insufficient or incorrect data can lead to poor quality AI results.

5. Change management and acceptance of new processes

Maximising the benefits of AI use cases requires a fundamental rethinking of processes and procedures, which are often built around system limitations and media breaks and have only been partially optimised. In contrast to classic process automation, AI-based optimisation approaches enable flexible, new solutions that often challenge the status quo. It is no longer just a matter of partial optimisation, but of rethinking alternatives, often with limited or no integration of employees in the process. Alternatively, process and decision optimisations are implemented as assistance solutions so that employees are

16 *Fraunhofer-Gesellschaft,* Maschinelles Lernen: Kompetenzen, Forschung, Anwendung, 30ff (2018): www.bigdata-ai.fraunhofer.de/de/publikationen/ml-studie.html (accessed 21.11.2025).

17 *Gross,* CIOs überdenken Public Cloud angesichts ihrer KI-Strategie (22.7.2025): www.cio.de/article/4024939/cios-uberdenken-public-cloud-angesichts-ihrer-ki-strategie.html (accessed 21.11.2025).

always involved in the process. These new approaches must be conceived and ultimately accepted.

To achieve this, a new type of leadership, communication and transparency is necessary. Ideally, managers should not only allow the changes, but actively promote them. Managers are multipliers for their teams. Well-trained and communicatively supported managers understand the strategic importance of AI and can anchor the topic constructively and positively in their teams. This requires technical and communicative training for managers on the topic of AI, parallel to the development of AI skills among employees. Transparent communication about the goals, benefits and effects of AI projects on processes and responsibilities is an important process for achieving transparency, trust and support for implementation within teams. Co-creative approaches are also a good first step, as they allow teams to learn how to actively work with AI and experience the advantages of AI-based support for recurring activities.

Momentum and positive results motivate AI-based transformation. Measuring and transparently communicating project KPIs (key performance indicators) thus support the acceptance of AI. And especially in AI projects, it is important that employees see and understand that the technology is being used responsibly. The introduction of AI should follow clear guidelines and be in line with the culture and values of the company.

Like any transformation, the AI transformation of processes and decision-making paths requires comprehensive change management support for successful implementation. As is so often the case, the successful introduction of AI solutions is only a minor technical challenge. Often, work on the model accounts for 10 % of the effort, work on the technology accounts for 20 % of the effort, and 70 % is work in the change management area with its various topics of leadership, communication, training, integration and regulation.

6. Size matters

AI-based optimisations often require relevant volumes to achieve a factual business case. When introducing and training a voice robot in *Baloise*'s customer service department in Switzerland, very good results were only achieved after at least 10,000 calls had been processed. Prior to this, the recognition rate of the numerous dialects spoken in Switzerland and the recognition rate of the caller's intention were not yet sufficient.

7. AI is no longer a pilot project—measurable results are expected

Although AI technologies continue to develop rapidly, conducting pure "proof of concepts" is no longer acceptable today. In practice, concrete success KPIs are expected from AI investments. Investments and use cases therefore often focus on increasing efficiency, profitable growth through pricing and underwriting optimisation, and the development of new premium services to increase revenue profitably. Despite these challenges, AI offers enormous opportunities for the insurance industry.

B. Opportunities for the practical use of AI

A fundamental task for CIOs/CTOs is the continuous IT-based optimisation of their respective business models and processes. Since the dot-com bubble at the latest, this has increasingly involved the digitalisation and automation of business models, customer interaction and internal processes.

Automation was mostly rule-based and static and, given a certain degree of variability and further development in the business environment, requires constant updating and maintenance. In future, learning and adaptive AI-based processes and automation could offer new, more flexible and self-optimising opportunities that traditional IT solutions have not been able to provide to date.

Another area of automation and optimisation lies in data-driven analysis and decision-making. In many cases, AI-based solutions are superior to traditional machine learning approaches or alternative technologies. In practice, however, both technologies are often complementary. For rule-based and/or narrow applications, traditional machine learning approaches are often still more efficient.

Table 1: Comparison of machine learning and AI applications

Dimension	Traditional machine learning	AI/LLM-based Solutions
Area of application	Specific, rule-based	Flexible, context-related
Depth of automation	Task-related	Cross-task and/or cross-workflow
Customer interaction	Script-based	Adaptive, multimodal
Adaptability/learning ability	Periodic	Continuous, dynamic
Pace of innovation	Medium	High, iterative

Typical AI use cases in the insurance industry are described in detail elsewhere in this book. At *Baloise*, we often see use cases in the following areas.

1. Automation of routine tasks

AI automates repetitive tasks such as data entry, document verification and simple customer enquiries, giving employees more time for more complex activities. One example is the "Balscan" app, which can be used to efficiently capture sales leads by photographing old contracts and automatically extracting data and generating leads.

2. Improved risk assessment, fraud detection and claims settlement

AI models can recognise patterns in large data sets to assess risks more accurately and thus enable more differentiated premium calculations. Similarly, analogue pattern recognition can identify fraudulent activities at an early stage, e.g. in the context of fraud detection and AI-based optimisation of detection rules for fraudulent claims. AI-supported fraud management is being used successfully in several *Baloise* business units and is being continuously developed.

Another example is AI-optimised claims settlement. AI optimises the claims settlement process thanks to automatic data completion, more precise claims assessment and automated communication processes, resulting in significant efficiency gains and increased profitability.

3. Personalisation of products and services

AI enables the rapid and efficient personalisation of customer communications and interactions. At *Baloise*, it is also used to personalise products and services. By analysing customer data, AI can develop tailor-made offers and make customer interactions even more personal (e.g., event-based marketing). Personalised customer communication through AI or traditional approaches is now an industry standard and a customer expectation. Deviations from this can affect competitiveness.

4. New business models

On the IT side, AI enables the development of completely new products and services based on predictive analytics and personalised recommendations. Various examples of vertical or horizontal expansion can already be seen on the market.

So far, there do not seem to be any truly transformative innovations in the insurance industry in terms of business models. In my opinion, the core business of insurance, i. e. covering existential risks (such as illness or death) and significant possessions (cars, houses, valuables), is fundamentally not very variable. AI can and will transform the information, policy issuance and claims processing processes over time. However, the basic model of insurance in the sense of covering existential risks on the basis of risk equalisation across a community will not change in the foreseeable future. I therefore consider the basic solidarity and insurance model based on contribution to be stable. The operationalisation of the business model, customer interaction, risk assessment and internal and external customer/partner processes will continue to evolve with significant technological innovations, including with and through AI.

C. Four new AI-based value drivers in case processing

The transformative nature of AI-based innovation is evident in insurers' case processing. New AI-based value drivers make the use of data and AI, e.g. in case processing in insurance, more valuable than traditional technologies. These value drivers are largely specific to AI-based optimisations and thus additive to traditional optimisation techniques and potentials.

1. Useful data extraction

The manual capture and processing of physical documents is time-consuming and prone to errors. AI recognises and processes information in various types of documents and enables content and data extraction and, on this basis, automated case closure processing if necessary. Example: SmartFix at *Baloise* recognises, indexes and triages documents and customer letters. For customers, this speeds up the processing time for their requests.

2. Triage and process control

Efficient classification and assignment of cases is crucial. AI systems can identify risks and detect fraud at an early stage, which can lead to significant cost savings. Examples such as *Baloise's* "leakage detection" show how AI contributes to the optimisation of claims settlement processes. Similarly, voicebots in customer service can identify customers in a customer-friendly manner and in natural language, understand their concerns and either direct them to self-service or to the relevant customer advisor.

3. Information gathering

The daily gathering of information in case processing is often tedious. AI-based assistants (e.g., *Baloise* GPT2.0, our internal LLM chat) can bring together relevant information from various internal and/or external sources, which increases efficiency and enables informed decisions.

4. Text generation and text assistant

AI models can automatically compose texts in various formats, which significantly speeds up the creation of quotations, reports or other customer-relevant documents. This reduces the workload for employees and ensures consistent communication. In international environments, the growing multimodal translation capabilities also add value.

III. AI implementation strategies: embedded, self-service, low-code and high-code

The scaled introduction of AI in an insurance company requires more than just technology. It is a major change management task with requirements for AI governance (e.g., EU AI Act), AI awareness and employee training, skill management in IT and specialist areas, and other aspects.

From an implementation perspective, *Baloise* relies on four complementary strategies to integrate AI into its business model in an effective, efficient and scalable manner. The aim is to realise efficiency potential and tap into new forms of value creation. AI is not viewed as an isolated technology, but as a strategic tool for the further development of processes, services, and business models. The strategy is based on four complementary implementation paths that address different levels of maturity, target groups and areas of application.

A. Embedded GenAI/AI—Use of integrated intelligence

AI functionalities in standard software provide an easy entry point into AI usage. These embedded AI approaches enable the rapid and low-risk introduction of AI without the need for extensive technical adjustments. In practice, this can be seen, for example, in the use of AI capabilities within a standard CRM solution for automated conversation summarisation or in our desktop publishing solution, where AI-generated social media content is created. AI is also used in input management, for example through automatic and integrated document recognition and triage. These applications show how existing systems can be enhanced with AI functionalities to increase operational efficiency.

With the growing integration of AI into standard software, this is an efficient and low-risk way to bring AI support to specific processes and domains. Use is often intuitive for users and requires little dedicated training. Data access and context are provided and predefined in the standard solution.

The challenge with this approach is the potential for sub-optimisation at the level of individual processes. By definition, cross-system and workflow-based opportunities cannot be addressed unless the standard software is used as such a workflow tool. "Agentic AI" approaches, in which multiple AI agents are orchestrated and controlled by a comprehensive AI along a task or process, could break down these barriers in the future. This requires the ability to access the individual AI-supported capabilities in the various standard software products. It remains to be seen how standard software manufacturers will position themselves here and which integration standards will prevail.

Another challenge may be that the use of embedded AI applications can be opaque to the user, making risks and compliance requirements for the use of AI solutions more difficult to control and ultimately more difficult to implement.

In addition to embedded AI, another implementation strategy for AI at *Baloise* is the use of self-service solutions.

B. Self-service GenAI—democratising the use of AI

A forward-looking component of *Baloise's* AI strategy is empowering employees to use generative AI independently. Intuitive interfaces and targeted prompt engineering enable employees to create content and develop use cases without in-depth IT or programming knowledge.

In practice, this can be seen in predefined smaller use cases, such as the "Job Assistant", which automatically creates job advertisements from new role descriptions, or in the "HR and Real Estate Toolbox", which provides templates and tools for specific departments, supporting employees in recurring tasks and reducing their workload by reusing defined prompts for specific tasks. This approach promotes a company-wide culture of innovation, as explained in the next section, and strengthens the digital sovereignty of the departments.

The approach is limited by the integrated internal data available to all employees, which generic generative AI services or the user has access to. Likewise, we do not currently have any "agentic AI" capabilities available in self-service, which limits the potential complexity of self-service use cases.

The resulting development of general AI and prompting capabilities among the workforce is seen as an essential part of the skill profile of employees and as an investment in the company's future, and is supported by numerous learning opportunities.

If generic self-service AI offerings are not sufficient for the respective business purpose, they can be enhanced with low-code methods. These usually require little or no programming skills and can be used by a broad range of employees.

C. Low-code enablement—AI through citizen development

The third AI implementation strategy, low-code enablement, is becoming increasingly popular. This approach empowers specialist departments to develop AI-supported applications independently using low-code or no-code platforms.

This form of citizen development allows specific micro-cases to be implemented efficiently, for example to automate sub-processes or create interactive dashboards. To this end, *Baloise* uses standardised solutions and applications from hyperscalers, among other things, which are made available throughout the group.

This strategy is aimed in particular at business users with technical affinity who want to create productive solutions without in-depth programming knowledge and who do not want to be limited by the sometimes lengthy prioritisation and requirements processes.

Low-code applications complement the self-service approach with a structured development environment offering a higher degree of customisation for the respective use case. The challenges lie in ensuring governance, quality and scalability. It is also helpful to distinguish clearly between IT-supported and IT-implemented use cases. At *Baloise*, the low-code model scales from simple, local prompt-based agents to IT-supported low-code solutions, in which, for example, internal data access is implemented by IT as the basis for decentralised low-code use cases. Overall, this approach opens up new innovation potential, as it directly integrates the creativity and process knowledge of the specialist departments into solution development and allows decentralised implementations within defined solution patterns and complexities.

If these solution patterns and complexity limits are exceeded, one enters the realm of high-code applications. These are usually developed by IT experts based on business requirements and then made available to users as self-service.

D. High-code applications—tailor-made solutions

For more complex requirements, *Baloise* develops its own AI applications or integrates foundation models such as GPT or Gemini into existing systems and processes. These high-code approaches require technological depth, but also offer maximum flexibility and customisation options for specific use cases. One example is the automated analysis of documents to increase efficiency in contract review. Such solutions are particularly useful where standard software reaches its limits or where specific requirements exist and/or external or dynamic data is used. In these more complex AI use cases, IT implements and operates the AI solution for the specialist department in the same way as classic applications.

The challenge with this approach is ensuring the necessary AI infrastructure for setup, operation, governance, security, reporting, and the fulfilment of other internal and regulatory requirements for AI solutions. This approach also requires the development of internal skills and capacities and, as a rule, a network of strategic external partners to support the various aspects of the solution.

E. Opportunities, challenges and prospects

With its four-stage approach, *Baloise* is pursuing a differentiated and practical AI implementation strategy. The combination of embedded solutions, self-service offerings, low-code approaches and individual high-code applications enables the widespread use of AI across different business areas, processes and use cases. Particularly noteworthy is the strategic balance between centralised control and provision of AI infrastructures and decentralised innovation capabilities, which enables and realises broad potential for innovation.

At the same time, this approach also presents challenges. The parallel use of different technologies requires a consistent governance model that ensures transparency, data protection and model responsibility. Quality assurance in the self-service and low-code area is also not trivial. Without appropriate employee training and formal approval processes, there is a risk of inconsistent results and a lack of transparency regarding new AI use cases. In addition, the integration of external foundation models can raise questions of data sovereignty, licensing, monitoring, security and internal billing. Individual developments, on the other hand, are maintenance-intensive and tie up resources in the long term.

This gives rise to clear areas for action in the future. Establishing a central AI governance framework and process helps to channel AI use across the company in a process-oriented manner, make it transparent and apply appropriate controls depending on the use case. The establishment of a centralised, scalable and expandable AI infrastructure standardises AI solution approaches for low-code and high-code use cases and facilitates the implementation of necessary data protection, security and monitoring processes. At the same time, data competence within the organisation should be further strengthened in order to enable self-service and low-code models in a targeted manner and to expand them where appropriate. The integration of explainable AI methods can and should increase the traceability of AI value contributions, particularly in regulated areas such as underwriting or claims management. Last but not least, stronger networking with external innovation ecosystems, for example through cooperation with start-ups, research institutions or strategic partners, offers the opportunity to secure early access to new developments, technologies and talent.

F. Practical example: *Baloise* FX: AI-optimised pension planning

Baloise is increasingly using AI-based solutions. Due to the relatively young technology, most AI use cases are so-called "embedded AI" solutions, in which standard software is enriched with AI components. This includes, for example, text recognition for incoming documents, voice robots in customer service, and FAQ bots for customers and employees.

In addition to these, employees are also increasingly using AI in self-service. Either via solutions such as *Microsoft's Copilot* or in the form of predefined use case prompts/agents, e.g., for translations, document queries or comparisons, data and document compilations, etc. These recurring use cases have been stored as a low-code solution with a standard prompt that employees can predefine and use. These AI-based individual solutions are made available in a prompt library or as an AI agent.

An example of a high-code implementation is the *Baloise* FX Assistant for financial and pension advice.

With its own bank, asset manager and insurance company, *Baloise* is uniquely positioned in Switzerland to offer customer-friendly, innovative and holistic financial planning and pension advice.

Pension advice is a complex subject area that requires consultants to have the appropriate expertise and training in order to provide comprehensive advice, and it is time-consuming to prepare and implement. In this environment, customers' starting points, goals and wishes are much more heterogeneous and personalised than when taking out motor vehicle insurance.

Baloise FX is a genAI-based assistant for financial and pension planners that critically examines and optimises existing financial plans based on customer information provided by the pension advisor and develops detailed alternative proposals and arguments for these. It is based on a digital database of around 70,000 pension and financial plans that have already been carried out over the years.

Combined with the financial expertise of the pension advisor, this optimises pension advice on a data-driven basis and makes it more scalable for the pension advisor. The AI takes over the personalised development of options based on customer and advisor input and creates personalised documents for the planned consultation.

The added value for the customer lies in receiving optimised and transparent pension planning, which is based not only on the advisor's financial expertise, but also on experience gained from over 70,000 advisory processes. This allows for transparent comparability between customers with similar life situations and planning goals. New alternatives from customer interactions can also be integrated directly and quickly into the analysis and recommendation.

This approach was implemented as a high-code solution with the integration of digital data from historical consultations and the use of a genAI language model for data analysis, argumentation development and option presentation. The genAI model also controls the creation of personalised consultation documents. From the perspective of pension advisors, the solution is now a self-service tool that forms part of their preparation for consultations.

References and resources

Actuarial Association of Europe (AAE), Navigating Europe's AI Act: Insights for actuaries and the insurance sector (2025): https://actuary.eu/wp-content/uploads/2025/03/AAE-Discussion-Paper-Navigating-Europes-AI-Act.pdf (accessed 21.11.2025)

Baigorri, The Cloud Wars: A Battle for Dominance (2.10.2024): www.cloudinstitute.io/aws/the-cloud-wars-a-battle-for-dominance/ (accessed 21.11.2025)

Feiler/Forgó, KI-VO (2024)

Fraunhofer-Gesellschaft, Maschinelles Lernen: Kompetenzen, Forschung, Anwendung, 30 ff (2018): www.bigdata-ai.fraunhofer.de/de/publikationen/ml-studie.html (accessed 21.11.2025)

Gross, CIOs überdenken Public Cloud angesichts ihrer KI-Strategie (22.7.2025): www.cio.de/article/4024939/cios-uberdenken-public-cloud-angesichts-ihrer-ki-strategie.html (accessed 21.11.2025)

Tynan, IT-Meilensteine: 12 Technologien, die die Welt verändert haben (7.10.2010): www.cio.de/article/3664567/12-technologien-die-die-welt-veraendert-haben.html (accessed 21.11.2025)

AI in the insurance industry—How to set up an AI unit?

Michael Zimmer
Chief Data and AI Officer, W&W Group

Abstract: This chapter outlines the essential steps and success factors for establishing an AI unit within insurance companies. It explains how organization, governance, responsibilities, and technology interact to create a sustainable structure for leveraging Artificial Intelligence. In addition to organizational anchoring and clear role definitions, the chapter addresses requirements for platforms and integration patterns. Practical examples illustrate how ideation and development processes can be designed to involve business units and deliver initial value cases quickly. Furthermore, regulatory aspects such as the EU AI Act and the importance of interdisciplinary teams and management buy-in are highlighted. The chapter serves as a guide for insurers aiming to implement AI strategically and sustainably.

Keywords: Artificial Intelligence, AI Unit, Governance, Organizational Structure, Platform Management, Ideation, Development Process, Insurance Industry, EU AI Act, Hub-and-Spoke, Interdisciplinarity

Contents

https://doi.org/10.33196/978370498520-105

I. Introduction

The topic of artificial intelligence (AI) is very important for insurers. But what does the introduction of an AI unit mean for a company? If an insurance company wants to establish the topic of AI and set up an AI unit at the same time, a number of questions need to be answered. What is the best form of organization? What tasks does the unit have? How will it be integrated into existing business and technical processes and, ultimately, quite trivially, how will it be financed? For software providers and consulting firms, the rapid introduction of POCs, ideally with an external partner, is often the best way to achieve the desired results. But is this really the way to identify cases, approach the topic strategically, promote talent and create Value in the first place? This chapter is intended to show in a practical way how a company can set up an AI unit in a targeted manner in order to approach the topic of AI pragmatically and enable the stakeholders (customers, employees and the company itself) to benefit from AI. This is necessary insofar as current studies show that 95 of the GenAI projects implemented do not generate any value.[1] The chapter addresses a holistic view for larger corporate structures, but can also be adapted to medium-sized insurance companies. Not all functions and steps are required here, but a conscious selection of the relevant building blocks. The challenges, measures and solutions presented are based on the author's experience in setting up various AI units in the German and international insurance environment.

Since the introduction of ChatGPT by OpenAI on 30 November 2022, the topic of AI has arrived within the population in general and in German companies in particular. The possibilities of generative AI in particular, coupled with falling costs[2], have led to more and more companies addressing the topic of AI. In the perfect marketing world of providers, there is a simplicity to the development of AI solutions that has led to great expectations on the part of management[3]. At the same time, however, there is now also disillusionment, as value is only realized to a limited extent, implementations are

1 *Challapally/Pease/Raskar/Chari*, State of AI in Business 2025, 3, The GenAI Divide. Project NANDA at MIT (2025): www.artificialintelligence-news.com/wp-content/uploads/2025/08/ai_report_2025.pdf (accessed 10.5.2025).

2 Cf. *Microsoft*, Azure Open AI Dienste – Preise: https://azure.microsoft.com/de-de/pricing/details/cognitive-services/openai-service/ (accessed 21.11.2025).

3 See *McKinsey*, The state of AI in 2025: Agents, innovation, and transformation (2025): www.mckinsey.com/capabilities/quantumblack/our-insights/the-state-of-ai (accessed 19.5.2025): Cost reductions in operations and sales of around 55 % were already predicted here in 2023 and economic potential of up to EUR 4.4 billion was forecast.

more complex than planned and organizations seem overwhelmed by the introduction of AI.[4]

It is therefore not surprising that a large number of national and international insurance companies are trying to drive the topic of AI and set up the associated AI units. The topic of "in-house AI" is often new to decision-makers in the insurance industry and resembles a closed book with seven seals, normative statements by many self-proclaimed experts, exaggerated expectations on the part of manufacturers and the implementing consulting firms.

In general, the following question patterns can be derived here, which are frequently asked by decision-makers:

- How do I start using AI successfully?
- What can be achieved with AI?
- How do I organize the topic of AI in a corresponding unit?
- What employee skills are required?
- Who is responsible for AI?
- Are there established technologies that I should use?
- What (legal) frameworks and regulatory requirements need to be observed?
- What is the separation of tasks between business and specialized AI areas?
- How do I keep the self-developed AI solutions fit for the future?

In general, the successful introduction of AI does not have to be complicated. However, it is necessary to take a well thought-out, interdisciplinary approach with a clear plan. Interdisciplinarity is crucial here in order to create a common AI platform with clear responsibilities and control structures between business, AI and IT. Based on data and AI governance frameworks that have been established for years[5], the following four core areas can be derived for setting up an AI unit. These are:

- The organization in the sense of process and organizational structures,
- Governance with the associated KPIs for control
- the definition of the tasks of an AI unit and
- the identification of the relevant technologies as a kind of a technical toolbox.

Fig. 1 shows these core areas graphically. They are described and categorized in this chapter. In order to create a better understanding, the text uses fictitious and focused examples.

4 *Zwingmann*, The Augmented Advantage (2025): https://blog.tobiaszwingmann.com/ (accessed 21.11.2025) and *Challapally/Pease/Raskar/Chari*, State of AI in Business 2025, 1 ff: www.artificialintelligence-news.com/wp-content/uploads/2025/08/ai_report_2025.pdf (accessed 10.5.2025).

5 Cf. on this *Hanke/Zimmer*, Self-Service und Governance im Data-Science-Umfeld: der emanzipierte Anwender in: Haneke/Trahasch/Zimmer/Felden (Hrsg), Data Science—Grundlagen, Architekturen und Anwendungen[2] (2021) 161–176.

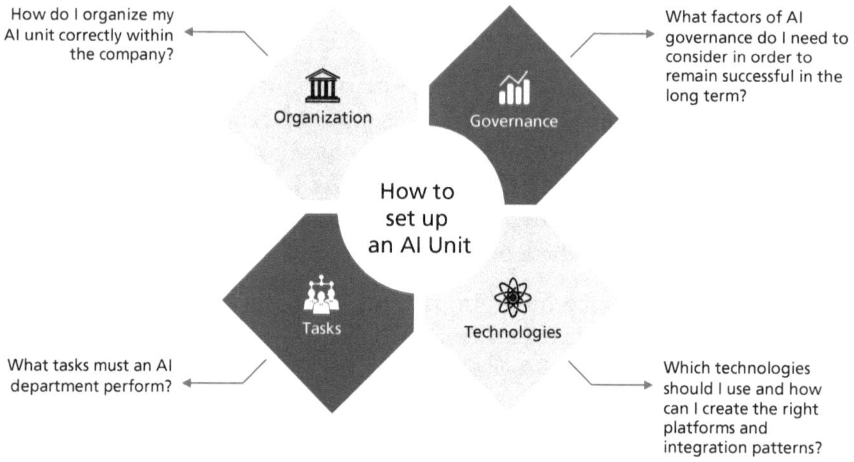

Fig. 1: Relevant topics in the development of an AI unit[6]

II. Tasks of an AI unit

When introducing AI, it is essential for managers to address a number of fundamental issues. These are trivial things such as management buy-in, moderation within the different interests of a company or clarification of relevant skill profiles and their procurement. The following core tasks of an AI unit can be derived from the author's experience:

- Home base
- Obtaining management buy-in
- Devil's advocate for AI
- AI platform management
- Ideation, development, operation and further development of AI applications and services
- "Compliance function" for AI in terms of first and second line.

A. Home base for data scientists

The first task of the AI department is about the people themselves. In recent years, AI developers, known as data scientists, have mostly been deployed in a distributed and decentralized manner. A common community with prede-

6 The figures in this contribution also appear in the chapter authored by the same author in Haneke/Zimmer/Trahasch (Hrsg), Artificial Intelligence for Business Analytics (2026), dpunkt.verlag. Reproduced with kind permission.

fined standards, a mindset and a forum for dialogue was rare here. However, experience shows that it is helpful to establish the AI sector in such a way that like-minded data scientists have a home base. This promotes exchange, creates a community and ultimately controls development centrally with standards and guidelines. This is extremely important, as data scientists who are left on their own, often shortly left the company after only a few years. The topic of AI platform standards and regulation must also be disseminated. Here, exchange in the home base can be used to share common standards and guidelines. In the end, the core task is about people, the talent, their conviction and the creation of a good working atmosphere.

B. Get management buy-in

As is usually the case when introducing new technologies, the support of top management is also of great importance when introducing AI. For this reason, it is a critical success factor to obtain a clear commitment and management buy-in at C-level right from the start.[7] Especially when it comes to allocating budgets, building platforms, changing the organization and integrating AI into the company. The development of a clearly defined roadmap is of great importance here to share a vision and get the management buy-in.

This enables the expectations of the C-level to be recorded, discussed and managed. The focus here should be on defining the main tasks for the first two to three years to clarify what can be implemented by the AI unit by then and what investments are necessary. In this way, it is possible to avoid fueling overly high expectations of AI with quick—directly monetarily measurable—value without making the fundamental investments in advance. Experience shows that such a problem is usually only solved once an initial benefit has been demonstrated. This chicken-and-egg problem should be resolved in advance to avoid running into monetary challenges and false expectations.

On the positive side, it should be noted that this dilemma can be solved without a large investment of millions, even if this would of course be desirable for every AI manager.[8] In most cases, however, an AI manager is faced with tight budgets and high and sometimes unrealistic expectations from external consultants and software developers.

It is therefore crucial to develop a clear roadmap and defined metrics to measure success and ultimately prove the predicted benefits. Realistic initial budgets

7 See *Bischof*, POC erfolgreich, doch was nun? (2025): www.it-finanzmagazin.de/ki-transformation-poc-218497/ (accessed 10.5.2025).

8 Cf. Vgl. *Zimmer/Diemann,* Von einer Bi-Landschaft zum Data &Analytics Ökosystem in: Haneke/Trahasch/Zimmer/Felden (Hrsg), Data Science[2] 143–160.

must also be defined. However, these often amortize in year two and can show a positive ROI (return on investment). In general, the motto is: "Think big, start small!" Table 1 shows examples of tasks involved in setting up an AI organization for the first year.

Table 1: Exemplary tasks in the first year[9]

Topic	Task	Objectives	Tasks
Strategy	Creation of a (data) and AI strategy	Specification of initial standards and a direction of travel	Create strategy
Create foundations	Building an AI platform	Creation of an AI platform	Building the platform
			Ensure cost-efficient implementation
Ensure compliance with the EU AI Act	Ensure regulatory compliance	Fulfilling the requirements of the EU AI ACT and other regulations or laws	Implementation of an EU AI Act framework, creation of an AI operating agreement, implementation of audit requirements
Creating value with AI	Descriptive AI cases	Provide initial cases for integration	Implementation of cases
	Knowledge bot as a standard service	Development of knowledge bots as a standard application	Patterns for scalable knowledge bots
	Expansion of document-based services	Provision of own AI services	Digitalization of the entire inbox
			Improved classification in input management
Data	Development of data to support AI cases	Ensuring the supply of data from operational and planning systems	Create value case & roadmap for incremental development

C. Devil's advocate for new solutions—educate and create awareness

"When setting up an AI unit, it is important to raise awareness and manage expectations effectively right from the start. This concerns both the possibilities and limitations of AI as well as the feasibility of initial ideas from the specialist area. In addition, the duration of the development of basic structures and the unit should be made transparent.

9 *Zimmer*, Aufbau einer KI Organisation, in Haneke/Zimmer/Trahasch (Hrsg), Künstliche Intelligenz für Business Analytics 128, Tab. 9.1.

Clear communication is crucial in order to avoid frustration and rejection among the workforce. By presenting a clear roadmap and implementing the first smaller use cases, the company can take the workforce along on the AI journey and establish itself as a center of excellence through initial successes with the specialist departments."

But what does this mean in concrete terms? The following example will illustrate this.

> As a manager in the field of artificial intelligence, it is extremely important both to explain the potential of AI in company processes and to openly address its limitations. Especially in times when there is a lot of hype about the topic on social media, there is a lot of misinformation circulating. Managers at the highest level often come across seemingly easy-to-implement AI solutions advertised by providers with big promises. In practice, however, it often turns out that these solutions are only effective for simple use cases, do not meet the specific requirements of the respective industry, lack suitable data sources and require considerable effort to integrate. At this point, it is the task of the AI team to critically scrutinize, make the costs and benefits transparent and ensure a comprehensive view. The same applies to the workforce: here, there is often concern about changes due to AI. In this context, the role should rather be to demonstrate the possibilities of AI through practical support and to reduce fears together.[10]

D. AI platform management

In addition to managing expectations and collecting the human factor, it is important to build an infrastructure that allows AI use cases to be scaled quickly and easily.[11]

---

10 See the podcasts: Podcasts *Zimmer*, Michael, Braucht man wirklich einen CDO? Und was macht der eigentlich? Im Podcast Unf*ck your data vom 22.8.2024 und *Zimmer*, Daten & KI: Die Zukunft der Versicherungen; Im Podcast #FredWagner vom 4.11.2024.

11 *Wenzel/Haag*, Die AI Factory der ERGO, in: Gillhuber/Kauermann/Hauner (eds.), Künstliche Intelligenz und Data Science in Theorie und Praxis (2023), 187 ff.

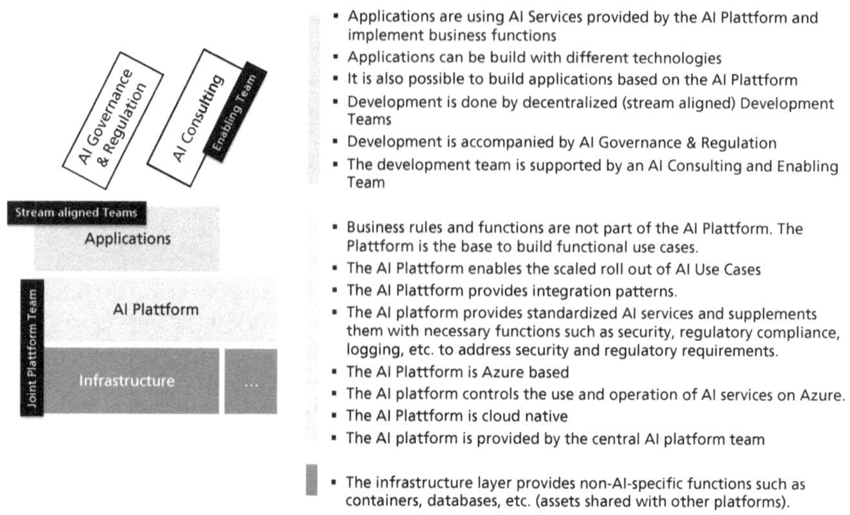

Fig. 2: Characteristics of an AI platform[12]

What is the core of such a platform? Fig. 2 shows an excerpt of the characteristics of an AI platform. The decisive factor is that the AI platform enables the development, operation, further development and maintenance of scalable AI applications. A technical architecture is not provided here.[13]

E. Identification, development and operation of AI applications

What are AI use cases that insurance companies should implement? To address this question, a central AI department is usually required as a coordinator, consultant and expert. Specialist experts from operations, for example, often see their own subjective time burden, but have no view of the underlying metrics and the overall business value.

"During job shadowing, you often hear comments like: 'I need more than 10 hours every time for this particular use case—AI could really be a relief here. However, if you ask more precisely how often this problem actually occurs and how many colleagues are affected by it, it often turns out that it only happens once a year and no one else is involved. Although the person in

12 *Zimmer*, Aufbau einer KI Organisation in Haneke/Zimmer/Trahasch (Hrsg), Künstliche Intelligenz für Business Analytics 129 Abb 9.3.

13 This can be found in *Zimmer*, Aufbau einer KI Organisation in Haneke/Zimmer/Trahasch (Hrsg), Künstliche Intelligenz.

question finds the task particularly stressful, there is no real need for action from the perspective of the entire department to automate this case with AI.[14]

To evaluate cases, a simple rule of three is useful for determining the value metric. How long does a process take, how often is it repeated and what cost rate is behind the task. In this way, a categorization can be made at the beginning using a simple metric. Once a case with value has been identified and described, an incremental approach to development with the business departments is recommended. "In order to involve and inspire the business departments in the development, the following procedure has proven to be a good start. 1) Ideation workshop to identify topics and test initial scenarios using a special AI demo environment 2) Creation of a simple business case, provision of relevant data and documents and initial iteration of a simple model. 3) Decision on how to proceed on the basis of the results and joint development as well as planning of additional services for process integration into other systems."[15]

With the help of this approach, the business department can be shown results quickly. In addition—explainable AI—the explainability of AI is part of the process. This ultimately allows solutions to be developed quickly, easily and in a targeted manner. The downstream integration efforts in peripheral systems such as host, application routes or CRM systems should not be overlooked. In practice, this is usually forgotten and the effort required for the recurring provision of necessary data and/or documents as well as the extraction from or integration into IT systems is many times greater than the development of the actual AI application. "Healthy realism and the specification of reusable integration patterns are required here.

Once an application is in production, regular monitoring and further development is required. This is where companies usually forget to plan the necessary effort. Even for small cases, 0.1 Full-Time-Equivalent per year should be planned for operation, further development and refactoring. The necessary experience also helps to realistically design the business case".[16]

14 *Zimmer*, Aufbau einer KI Organisation in Haneke/Zimmer/Trahasch (Hrsg), Künstliche Intelligenz für Business Analytics 130.

15 *Zimmer*, Aufbau einer KI Organisation in Haneke/Zimmer/Trahasch (Hrsg), Künstliche Intelligenz für Business Analytics 131.

16 *Zimmer*, Aufbau einer KI Organisation in Haneke/Zimmer/Trahasch (Hrsg), Künstliche Intelligenz für Business Analytics 131.

III. First and second line for AI

The adoption of the EU AI Act created the legal framework for the implementation of governance for AI. In the past, a second line was more likely to be designed in accordance with EU GDPR data protection law. The EU AI Act additionally brings an ethical component into play. With the entry into force of the European Artificial Intelligence Regulation (EU AI Regulation)[17], EU legal requirements now apply to the development, operation and use of AI systems and models.

But what is the nucleus for establishing a governance structure in accordance with the EU AI Act? "As a minimum, we recommend the introduction of a functional and technical owner of the use case, a governance officer (preferably also the Head of AI) and a senior data scientist as a technical supervisory authority. In addition, interfaces to IT such as IT operations or enterprise architecture as well as to the works council and data protection are required."[18] Many of these roles are nothing new for insurers from the VAIT or DORA environment. For example, even before the EU AI Act, technical and functional persons responsible for an application had to be named.

But what does cooperation between the roles involved look like within the Three Lines of Defense model?[19]

The task of the Head of AI is to ensure that the regulatory requirements of the EU AI Act are implemented and complied with. To ensure this, it makes sense to coordinate all of a company's AI initiatives via the central AI unit. The EU AI Act promotes such an approach, as the evaluation of AI cases is required in a central repository. "With increasing maturity of the AI organization, more responsibility can gradually be transferred to the business departments. However, it is advisable, in the sense of a RACI matrix, that the AI unit (or the responsible AI officer) is informed at an early stage as soon as the deployment

17 Regulation (EU) 2024/1689 of the European Parliament and of the Council of 13 June 2024 laying down harmonised rules on artificial intelligence: http://data.europa.eu/eli/reg/2024/1689/oj.

18 *Zimmer*, Aufbau einer KI Organisation in Haneke/Zimmer/Trahasch (Hrsg), Künstliche Intelligenz für Business Analytics 132.

19 This is a procedure from which risk management in the operating units (first line) is separated from controlling (second line) and monitoring units (third line). Cf. *The Institute of Internal Auditors*, The IIA's Three Lines Model. An Update of the Three Lines of Defense (2024): www.theiia.org/globalassets/documents/resources/the-iias-three-lines-model-an-update-of-the-three-lines-of-defense-july-2020/three-lines-model-updated-english.pdf (accessed 21.11.2025).

or development of a new AI system is planned. This is also important in order to fulfil the requirement of a complete inventory of deployed AI systems."[20]

Details on a concrete testing scheme for AI applications within the framework of the EU AI Act, taking into account the three lines of defense principle, can be found in Zimmer 2025. Table 2 shows regulatory requirements by line, role and task.

Table 2: Regulatory tasks and lines of defense[21]

Line of defence	Roles	Tasks in the life cycle of the AI knowledge bot
1st Line (Operational)	Technical owner	Definition of the application purpose, requirements & goals
	AI development as part of the AI organization IT Operations	Development of the knowledge bot Implementation of technical and functional measures Documentation & control of the proper functioning of the knowledge bot
2nd line (governance, control, consulting)	Governance officer & AI Governance Office	Implementation of the regulatory requirements of the EU AI Act, risk classification & assessment, advising the specialist department on the requirements & compliance with AI governance
	Data protection officer	Data protection audit
	Risk management	Review of systemic risks & mitigation measures
	Compliance department	Monitoring of company-wide compliance and ensuring embedding in the internal control system (ICS)
	Works Council	Checking the impact on employees
3rd line (independent audit)	Internal audit	Audit for proper compliance with regulatory obligations and internal regulations and guidelines

20 *Zimmer*, Aufbau einer KI Organisation in Haneke/Zimmer/Trahasch (Hrsg), Künstliche Intelligenz für Business Analytics 132. Here you will also find details on a specific testing scheme for AI applications within the framework of the EU AI Act, taking into account the three lines of defense principle.

21 *Zimmer*, Aufbau einer KI Organisation in Haneke/Zimmer/Trahasch (Hrsg), Künstliche Intelligenz für Business Analytics 133, Abb 9.2.

IV. Integration of an AI unit in the insurance organisation

AI is characterized by the fact that it is not the sole excellence of a unit such as a business department or IT, but only becomes successful through an interdisciplinary approach by all those involved from IT, departments, regulatory affairs and AI. In the recent past, insurance companies have often introduced AI labs that have attracted attention for their ivory tower-like behavior. In most cases, data scientists from outside the industry were recruited and brought together in one lab. Centralization is a good approach in principle, but the basic principles for successful AI must be observed. "AI requires direct interaction between subject matter experts, data experts and AI experts, but also centralized integration patterns and in-depth IT knowledge in order to make AI applications truly productive".[22] The tasks of an AI department presented in the previous subchapter are also important here.

As already mentioned, several times beforehand, the challenge is usually not the AI development as a kind of magic, but the procurement of the data and the integration of the services into the heterogeneous IT landscape with cloud and host. These efforts are often underestimated by data scientists. This is hardly surprising, as data scientists are not architecture and system integrators, but specific AI developers. The integration of a usable service can take several months without predefined integration patterns to the standard systems of an insurance company (website for sales, policy system, claims system, ...). In addition, ivory tower-like AI labs have often implemented complex and interesting applications. Technical excellence as an end in itself was a common pattern here. Scaling and creating value were not the focus. The current MIT study on GenAI shows that these patterns are repeating themselves. Here it was postulated that 95 % of GenAI do not generate any additional revenue[23]. Tobias Zwingmann, an AI Influencer, regularly points out that we should start simply and scale up in the long term.[24]

22 *Zimmer*, Aufbau einer KI Organisation in Haneke/Zimmer/Trahasch (Hrsg), Künstliche Intelligenz für Business Analytics 136.

23 Vgl. *Challapally/Pease/Raskar/Chari*, State of AI in Business 2025, 3: www.artificialintelligence-news.com/wp-content/uploads/2025/08/ai_report_2025.pdf (accessed 10.5.2025).

24 *Zwingmann*, The Augmented Advantage (2025) accessible via https://blog.tobiaszwingmann.com/.

But how can this problem be tackled as an organization? In organizational terms, the hub-and-spoke approach known from data architecture is of great importance. Similar to airports, there are decentralized feeders (spokes, such as Stuttgart) that are connected to a central hub (Frankfurt) as the central infrastructure. In the area of data, this approach has been established since the times of management information systems, from data warehouses to today's Lakehouse architectures, and is also of great importance in modern modelling approaches such as data vaults.

But what does this mean for an organization? Specifically, a central (data) and AI area is created. In line with the aforementioned tasks of an AI unit, this serves as a knowledge carrier, home base, platform provider for AI, control instance and AI development CoE. However, since AI is a team sport and not an individual sport[25], it is necessary to establish organizational counterparts, the spokes, in the specialist area. An example is shown in Fig. 3. When setting up the spokes, the maturity of the organization must be taken into account. Depending on the maturity, classic development scenarios with the department as the pure requester and process expert, but also self-service development by the business department based on central standards of the AI hub must be enabled.[26]

25 *Mese*, KI ist kein Einzelsport, Versicherungsmonitor 2024/09: https://versicherungsmonitor.de/2024/09/16/ki-ist-kein-einzelsport/ (accessed 21.11.2025).

26 How such a Governance can be implemented ca be found in: *Zimmer/Diemann*, Von einer Bi-Landschaft zum Data &Analytics Ökosystem. in: Haneke/Trahasch/Zimmer/Felden (Hrsg), Data Science – Grundlagen, Architekturen und Anwendungen[2] (2021) 143–160 sowie *Zimmer/Haneke*, Self-Service und Governance im Data-Science-Umfeld: der emanzipierte Anwender. in: Haneke/Trahasch/Zimmer/Felden (Hrsg), Data Science – Grundlagen, Architekturen und Anwendungen[2] (2021) 161–176.

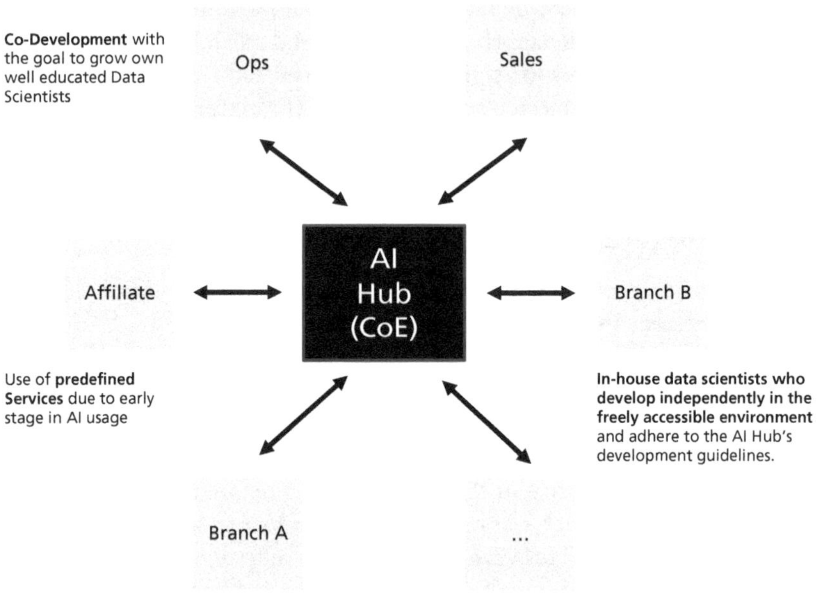

Fig. 3: Tasks of a hub and the spokes in the AI environment[27]

In the central AI department, technical and AI expertise is combined in an overarching central area. The assignment to the right C-level is certainly also crucial here. It is important that the AI area is not categorized as a sub-area of IT, but rather directly under the CEO or COO as part of the business world. As a rule, there is often an us and them mentality between IT and the specialist area, including the not invented here syndrome. By categorizing AI close to the specialist area and taking IT standards into account, trust can be built up, delivered jointly and ultimately bridges built between the units. The advantages of an integrated approach compared to an ivory tower approach are briefly described below as an example: *An ivory-tower AI unit works independently of the department on a solution that extracts key value pairs from application or claims documents for claim handlers. To do this, they only access a few randomly selected documents provided by a contact person from the departments. No questions are asked about the frequency, significance or sequence of the key value pairs to be extracted. There is also no dialogue with other stakeholders. After a short development phase, a product is ultimately created that can read*

27 *Zimmer,* Aufbau einer KI Organisation in Haneke/Zimmer/Trahasch (Hrsg), Künstliche Intelligenz für Business Analytics 136.

the content of the available documents very well, but acceptance in the specialist area is low as it only deals with low-volume documents.[28]

This contrasts with an approach in which the clerks' documents are used as a starting point to launch an initial ideation phase in collaboration with other colleagues from the operations or claims area. In this phase, questions are clarified, such as which document types and quantities are available and which key values are actually relevant. During the discussions, the AI hub makes it clear to the specialist colleagues, for example, that it does not make sense to extract all fields, as fully automated processing without human review becomes almost impossible as the number of fields and error rate increase. In one workshop, the departments also mentioned that a rule-based database and corresponding guidelines could be used for support in addition to the documents. Trust is created through several discussions, the department, IT and AI come together and there is an active exchange of knowledge. As a result, a solution can ultimately be developed that offers real added value and is also accepted by the business departments, as the explainability of the AI is an integral part of the development process. This procedure is illustrated in Fig. 4.

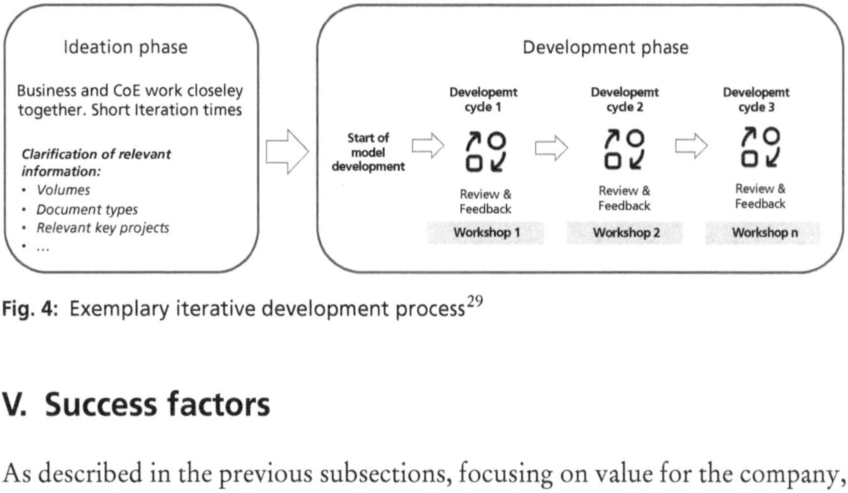

Fig. 4: Exemplary iterative development process[29]

V. Success factors

As described in the previous subsections, focusing on value for the company, a pragmatic approach between the parties involved, regulation by design and an interdisciplinary approach are critical success factors when setting up an AI unit. In concrete terms, this means

28 Such procedures are not uncommon in large international corporate structures. Here, corporate divisions try to impose solutions on the country units without having any knowledge of the specifics of the country markets.

29 *Zimmer,* Aufbau einer KI Organisation in Haneke/Zimmer/Trahasch (Hrsg), Künstliche Intelligenz für Business Analytics 138.

- Focusing on value
- Pragmatic approach between the parties involved
- Regulation by design
- Interdisciplinary positioning
- References and resources.

A. Focusing on value

"Use cases in general and AI use cases in particular should never be used as an end in themselves, to create unnecessary technical excellence or purely for fun. It is better to carry out a clear priority with value metrics. Whether these are quantitative values such as time saved, additional revenue or qualitative factors such as customer satisfaction is in principle secondary. The important thing is to consider the business value before making a case and to actively discuss them with management".[30]

B. Pragmatic approach between the parties involved

"In general, direct communication is an underestimated success factor. In line with the motto: 'we do the most extreme and talk to each other.' This promotes dialogue and interdisciplinarity. However, pragmatism also includes the will to find solutions and to take the necessary regulatory requirements into account without falling into excessive safety precautions. It is important that it is clear who bears what responsibility".[31]

C. Regulation by design

"Regulation is a critical issue, especially in larger companies. Instead of ignoring the topic until go-live, it has been shown that early involvement can not only be seen as a critical success factor, but that the inclusion of regulatory units builds trust, which in the long term leads to faster implementation, more satisfied customers and ultimately more legally compliant applications."[32]

30 *Zimmer*, Aufbau einer KI Organisation in Haneke/Zimmer/Trahasch (Hrsg), Künstliche Intelligenz 139.

31 *Zimmer*, Aufbau einer KI Organisation in Haneke/Zimmer/Trahasch (Hrsg), Künstliche Intelligenz 139.

32 *Zimmer*, Aufbau einer KI Organisation in Haneke/Zimmer/Trahasch (Hrsg), Künstliche Intelligenz 139.

D. Interdisciplinary positioning

"In a topic such as AI, which requires technology, expertise, statistics and process integration, the interdisciplinary set-up of AI teams is essential. Knowledge of data, expertise and legal knowledge from day-to-day business is combined with highly specific AI expertise to create successful cases. Each individual covers only part of the requirements. These skills come together in an interdisciplinary team".[33]

References and resources

Bischof, POC erfolgreich, doch was nun? 4 Erfolgsfaktoren, um KI-Projekte zum Erfolg zu führen (2025): www.it-finanzmagazin.de/ki-transformation-poc-218497/ (accessed 10.5.2025)

Challapally/Pease/Raskar/Chari, State of AI in Business 2025: The GenAI Divide. Project NANDA at MIT (2025): www.artificialintelligence-news.com/wp-content/uploads/2025/08/ai_report_2025.pdf (accessed 10.5.2025)

Haneke/Zimmer/Trahasch (Hrsg), Künstliche Intelligenz für Business Analytics (2026)

Haneke/Zimmer, Self-Service und Governance im Data-Science-Umfeld: der emanzipierte Anwender in: Haneke/Trahasch/Zimmer/Felden (Hrsg), Data Science – Grundlagen, Architekturen und Anwendungen[2] (2021) 161–176

McKinsey, The state of AI in 2025: Agents, innovation, and transformation (2025): www.mckinsey.com/capabilities/quantumblack/our-insights/the-state-of-ai (accessed 19.5.2025)

Mese, KI ist kein Einzelsport, Versicherungsmonitor 2024/09: https://versicherungsmonitor.de/2024/09/16/ki-ist-kein-einzelsport/ (accessed 21.11.2025)

Microsoft, Azure Open AI Dienste – Preise: https://azure.microsoft.com/de-de/pricing/details/cognitive-services/openai-service/ (accessed 21.11.2025)

The Institute of Internal Auditors, The IIA's Three Lines Model. An Update of the Three Lines of Defense (2024): www.theiia.org/globalassets/documents/resources/the-iias-three-lines-model-an-update-of-the-three-lines-of-defense-july-2020/three-lines-model-updated-english.pdf (accessed 21.11.2025)

Wenzel/Haag, Die AI Factory der ERGO, in: Gillhuber/Kauermann/Hauner (Hrsg), Künstliche Intelligenz und Data Science in Theorie und Praxis (2023) 187ff

Zimmer/Diemann, Von einer Bi-Landschaft zum Data &Analytics Ökosystem. in: Haneke/Trahasch/Zimmer/Felden (Hrsg), Data Science – Grundlagen, Architekturen und Anwendungen[2] (2021) 143–160

33 *Zimmer*, Aufbau einer KI Organisation in Haneke/Zimmer/Trahasch (Hrsg), Künstliche Intelligenz 140.

Zimmer/Haneke, Self-Service und Governance im Data-Science-Umfeld: der emanzipierte Anwende, in: Haneke/Trahasch/Zimmer/Felden (Hrsg), Data Science – Grundlagen, Architekturen und Anwendungen[2] (2021) 161–176

Zimmer, Aufbau einer KI Organisation, in Haneke/Zimmer/Trahasch (Hrsg), Künstliche Intelligenz für Business Analytics (2026)

Zwingmann, The Augmented Advantage (2025): https://blog.tobiaszwingmann.com/ (accessed 21.11.2025)

Xaver—An AI-native Fintech enabling insurers to utilize agentic AI compliant and at scale

Max Bachem
Co-founder and CEO, Xaver.com

Abstract: This section uses the Cologne-based insurtech "*Xaver*," founded in 2023, as a case study to illustrate the possibilities of an AI-native insurance platform built without legacy constraints. *Xaver* leverages an agentic AI workforce and a dual-layer architecture that combines a hyper-personalized customer experience with a regulated, BaFin-licensed infrastructure back-end. An analysis of a forward-looking milestone—the first fully compliant, end-to-end sale of a life insurance policy via ChatGPT, enabled by emerging standards like the Model Context Protocol (MCP)—demonstrates AI's transformative potential in distribution.

Keywords: Fintech, insurance platform, Personalization, Digitalization, Model Context Protocol, Insurance sales, AI, artificial intelligence, Agentic Finance, personal AI assistants, AI-based insurance advisory, KYC, Human-in-the-Loop

Contents

https://doi.org/10.33196/9783704698520-106

I. *Xaver*—An AI-native Fintech enabling insurers to utilize agentic AI compliant and at scale

A. Introduction to *Xaver*: Mission and market position

Launched in Cologne in 2023, *Xaver* was founded with the mission to address Europe's significant pension gap through AI-driven financial solutions.[1] The company operates as a business-to-business (B2B) provider, enabling banks, insurers, and brokers to offer modern, AI-enhanced pension and investment products. Rather than competing with incumbents directly, it provides them with the technology to modernize their own offerings and sales processes.

B. A dual-layer architecture: Balancing agility and compliance

At the core of *Xaver's* model is a strategic dual-layer architecture designed to resolve a central tension in financial technology: the need for rapid innovation at the customer interface versus the demand for rigorous security and compliance at the infrastructure level.

- **The Customer Experience Layer:** This front-end layer delivers hyper-personalized user journeys through generative AI. Customers and advisors interact with AI assistants that provide tailored advice, conduct needs analyses, and generate product recommendations in natural language across any channel—web, mobile, or chat. Those AI assistants also adjust online and mobile journeys in real-time to the individual user, creating a hyper-personalized ux.
- **The Regulated Infrastructure Layer:** This back-end layer handles all product management, investment execution, and compliance functions. It serves as the secure, regulated core that ensures every AI-driven interaction is grounded in approved products and compliant processes.

This separation allows *Xaver* to innovate at speed on the customer-facing side, continuously refining its AI models and user interfaces, without compromising the stability and integrity of its regulated financial core. It is a purpose-built solution to avoid the pitfalls that many incumbents face, where monolithic legacy systems make even minor changes to the customer experience slow and costly. This approach enables what *Kohury et al*, term "strategic deployment

1 www.xaver.com/about (accessed 19.11.2025).

at full scale" from the outset, bypassing the common fate of being perpetually "locked into pilots".[2]

C. A regulated, MCP-native core

A differentiator for *Xaver* is its regulated subsidiary, *Xaver Asset Management* (XAM), which was granted a license by Germany's Federal Financial Supervisory Authority (BaFin) to operate as a *Vermögensverwalter* (asset manager). This license is the foundation of *Xaver's* end-to-end capabilities. It empowers the company to develop its own white-label investment and pension products, which can be offered by its B2B partners.[3]

Crucially, both layers of *Xaver's* architecture were built to be **MCP-native**. The Model Context Protocol (MCP) is a new open standard, introduced by Anthropic in late 2024, that acts as a universal connector—like a USB-C port for AI—allowing AI agents to securely and programmatically interact with external data sources and tools.[4]

By having an MCP-enabled customer interaction layer, *Xaver* can directly interact via personal AI assistants like ChatGPT, Gemini, etc. And by designing its asset management core to be MCP-native, *Xaver* has created a financial institution designed to directly interact with AI agents—*Xaver's* enabling backend for "Agentic Finance".

This architecture enables *Xaver's* AI workforce to perform real-time, autonomous actions that are challenging or impossible to do by AI agents with traditional systems. For example, an AI agent can directly access portfolio data, execute trades, and rebalance a customer's investments based on predefined rules or market events, all without human intervention. This capability prepares *Xaver* and its partners for the emerging "agentic web" and "agentic finance", a future where customers' personal AI assistants will conduct financial transactions on their behalf. Legacy systems, which are not designed for such direct, programmatic access, cannot easily support this new paradigm of AI-to-AI commerce.

2 *Kohury et al*, Insurance Leads AI Adoption. It's Time to Scale (2025): www.bcg.com/publications/2025/insurance-leads-ai-adoption-now-time-to-scale (accessed 19.11.2025).

3 *Rathjen*, KI-gestütztes Fintech Xaver Asset Management erhält Bafin-Lizenz (2025): www.private-banking-magazin.de/xaver-asset-management-erhaelt-bafin-lizenz/ (accessed 19.11.2025).

4 *Anthropic*, Introducing the Model Context Protocol (2024): www.anthropic.com/news/model-context-protocol (accessed 19.11.2025).

II. Deploying an agentic AI workforce

A. From co-pilots to autonomous agents: A practical definition

Agentic AI can be defined as autonomous AI systems capable of perception, reasoning, planning, and execution to achieve complex goals without constant human direction.[5] Unlike a simple chatbot that reacts to queries, an AI agent can proactively take a multi-step series of actions—such as analyzing a customer's financial data, identifying a pension gap, recommend a product, and generate the application documents to process the application and open a trading account – to complete an entire workflow.[6]

Xaver employs a hybrid model built for omnichannel distribution:

- **AI Co-Pilots:** These tools augment the capabilities of human financial advisors. They can surface relevant information, perform complex calculations in real-time, and handle administrative tasks, freeing the human expert to focus on building client relationships and providing strategic counsel. This aligns with Accenture's finding that 81 % of executives believe AI will create new, augmented roles rather than simply replacing existing ones.[7]
- **Autonomous AI Agents:** These specialized agents automate entire processes in the front, middle, and back office. One agent might handle the initial customer dialogue, another might perform the financial analysis, and a third might execute the resulting investment transactions via the MCP-native core.

B. Quantifying AI-driven efficiency

AI-based insurance advisory and sales solutions can significantly increase sales efficiency. In the case of *Xaver*, this figure is not a single, monolithic improvement but rather the aggregate result of a dual-mode implementation, moving from process optimization to a fundamental restructuring of the sales model.

Mode 1: **AI as an Assistant to a human advisor (Process Augmentation).** The initial source of efficiency gain derives from augmenting existing human-led processes. In this mode, the AI functions as a sales assistant, reducing the

5 *Jothilingam*, Agentic AI in life insurance underwriting (2025): www.cognizant.com/us/en/insights/insights-blog/agentic-ai-in-life-insurance (accessed 19.11.2025).

6 *Arya*, Agentic AI in Insurance: Transforming the Industry with Enterprise AI (2025): https://hexaware.com/blogs/agentic-ai-in-insurance-transforming-the-industry-with-enterprise-ai/ (accessed 19.11.2025).

7 *Reilly*, AI Underwriting: Beyond the hype, Insurance Blog Accenture (2025): https://insuranceblog.accenture.com/ai-underwriting-beyond-the-hype (accessed 19.11.2025).

administrative and preparatory burden on human advisors. The intervention occurs across the advisory workflow:

- **Pre-Consultation:** Assisting in the research and preparation of advisory materials.
- **During Consultation:** Providing real-time support, such as live transcription, surfacing relevant data (e.g., policy details), and offering contextual prompts.
- **Post-Consultation:** Automating administrative tasks, including generating documentation and drafting the required consultation protocols.

This augmentation targets low-value, time-intensive tasks. The empirical effect is a direct reduction in the advisor's administrative workload, typically saving 5–10 hours per week. This translates to a quantifiable efficiency gain of 20–25 %, allowing advisors to reallocate that time to client-facing or revenue-generating activities.

Mode 2: **AI as an autonomous Financial or Insurance Agent/Advisor (Process Multiplication).** A more profound structural impact is achieved when the system transitions from an assistant to an autonomous agent. This second mode moves beyond mere optimization to a multiplication of the advisor's capacity by deploying a "team" of AI agents capable of executing complete tasks independently.

This represents a paradigm shift where the AI agents manage entire segments of the value chain, such as:

- **Customer Acquisition:** Active customer outreach (email, phone), lead acquisition, lead evaluation, lead management.
- **Advisory and Sales:** Executing complete, compliant financial advice sessions, customer and product evaluations, recommendations and sales. Handing over to the human advisor on a customer request or when identified that human advice would be beneficial for the customer or result in a higher probability to conduct a sale.
- **Become personal financial advisor:** Provide a always-on, 24/7 advisory via a customer's channel of choice. Promote cross- and up-selling.

In this model, the human advisor's role evolves from direct execution (a one-to-one model) to oversight (a one-to-many at the same time model) and selective, AI enhanced consultations. An advisor can manage a portfolio of AI agents, each conducting concurrent sales processes. This model enables agent to focus on the customer cases which require personal interaction, while in parallel their AI Assistant generates new leads, answer simple questions by other customers or also do full advice sessions or sales. The advisor benefits from the commission, but their income is decoupled from their direct time expenditure.

Xaver observed a blended 50–65 % efficiency gain in initial projects. It reflects the aggregate performance of sales teams in a hybrid adoption state: some advisors primarily use the AI for Mode 1 augmentation (achieving 20–25 % gains), while others leverage Mode 2 autonomy for a multiplicative effect on their sales capacity.

III. Case study: The first autonomous, compliant life insurance sale via ChatGPT—utilizing MCP

To illustrate the full potential of its platform, *Xaver* has outlined a forward-looking milestone in 2025: powering the first complete, compliant, end-to-end sale of a life insurance policy via a public generative AI interface – ChatGPT. This case study serves as a powerful demonstration of how emerging technologies are poised to fundamentally reshape insurance distribution.

A. The enabling technologies: Personal AI assistants (PAIAs) and the Model Context Protocol (MCP)

This milestone rests on the convergence of two key technological trends:

- **Personal AI Assistants (PAIs):** Consumers are increasingly using sophisticated AI assistants – *ChatGPT, Google Gemini, Apple* intelligence, etc. – to manage tasks and make decisions on their behalf. This trend is creating a new distribution channel where the primary customer interface is no longer a website or a human broker, but the user's own AI. A 2024 report by *Sexton* predicts that by 2030, customers may not interact directly with insurers at all; instead, their PAIAs will research, negotiate, and purchase policies autonomously.[8]
- **Model Context Protocol (MCP):** As previously noted, MCP provides the standardized and secure communication rails necessary for this new form of commerce. It allows a customer's PAIA to connect to *Xaver's* advisory and sales platform (which is again connected to *Xaver's* asset management backend as well as to insurers' core systems to request quotes, submit applications, and bind policies without bespoke, brittle integrations.[9] Rapid

8 *Sexton*, No more human customers (2025): www.cognizant.com/en_us/about/documents/cognizant-how-ai-could-transform-insurance-by-2030.pdf (accessed 19.11.2025). Siehe auch *MIT Technology Review Insights*, Reimagining the future of banking with agentic AI (2025): www.technologyreview.com/2025/09/04/1123023/imagining-the-future-of-banking-with-agentic-ai/accessed 19.11.2025).

9 *Collabnix*, What is Agentic AI? A Deep Dive into MCP and the Modern Agent Ecosystem (2025): https://collabnix.com/what-is-agentic-ai-a-deep-dive-into-mcp-and-the-modern-agent-ecosystem/ (accessed 19.11.2025).

adoption of MCP by major technology players like *OpenAI* and *Google* is paving the way for it to become the de facto standard for the agentic web.[10]

B. The end-to-end process: From advice to binding via AI

Xaver's life insurance sale via a PAIA demonstrates a seamless, AI-driven customer journey:

1. **Initiation:** A user issues a high-level command to their PAIA, which is running on a ChatGPT interface: "Analyze my finances, identify my pension gap, and recommend an appropriate solution."
2. **AI-to-AI Interaction:** The PAIA connects to *Xaver's* platform via the MCP. It engages in an automated dialogue with *Xaver's* AI agents to conduct an IDD-compliant financial needs analysis, if needed including a detailed pension-gap calculation.
3. **Product Selection and Quotation:** Based on the analysis, *Xaver's* system recommends a specific financial product (investment or savings plan, life insurance product, etc.), providing a real-time, personalized quote. To be able to do this in line with the EU AI Act, *Xaver* orchestrates a team of AI agents utilizing powerful LLMs as well as AI agents utilizing explainable AI and deterministic models to allow explainability and auditability of each recommendation.
4. **Binding and Documentation:** With the user's pre-authorization, the PAIA confirms the purchase. *Xaver's* system instantly opens the account or binds the policy, generates all necessary documents (policy contract, T&Cs, disclosures, consultation protocol), and delivers them digitally to the user.
5. **Human-in-the-Loop for KYC:** The only step requiring leaving the PAIA interface today is the legally mandated Know Your Customer (KYC) verification, which was triggered and supervised by the *Xaver* agent.

C. Controls, outcomes, and implications for incumbents

This autonomous process is underpinned by rigorous controls. Suitability checks are embedded into the AI's logic, ensuring all recommendations are compliant with the Insurance Distribution Directive (IDD)[11] and the EU AI

10 *Martin et al*, Put AI Agents to Work Faster Using MCP, Boston Consulting Group (2025): www.bcg.com/publications/2025/put-ai-to-work-faster-using-model-context-protocol (accessed 19.11.2025).

11 Directive (EU) 2016/97 on insurance distribution: http://data.europa.eu/eli/dir/2016/97/oj.

Act[12]. The entire AI-to-AI interaction is recorded, creating an immutable and fully auditable trail for regulators and auditors.

IV. Governance and guardrails for enterprise-grade AI

Xaver's innovative potential is enabled, not hindered, by a robust governance framework that prioritizes security, compliance, and responsible AI principles from the outset.

A. A compliance-by-design framework

Xaver has embedded Compliance into its architecture. This "compliance-by-design" approach is a direct and proactive response to Europe's complex regulatory landscape.

- GDPR: All data handling processes are designed to be compliant with the General Data Protection Regulation.
- IDD: Suitability and appropriateness checks required by the Insurance Distribution Directive are hard-coded into the AI's decision-making logic.
- EU AI Act: *Xaver's* framework anticipates the requirements of the forthcoming EU AI Act. Under this regulation, AI systems used for risk assessment and pricing in life insurance can fall under the "high-risk" level. This designation mandates rigorous data governance, continuous monitoring, human oversight, and transparency[13] – all of which are core tenets of *Xaver's* model.

B. Key governance patterns: Model risk management and human-in-the-loop

The framework is operationalized through several key patterns:

- Model Risk Management: Any changes to the AI's core advice or underwriting algorithms are subject to a formal approval process, similar to how banks manage model risk.
- Continuous Monitoring: AI models are constantly monitored for performance, accuracy, and potential bias to prevent model drift and ensure fair outcomes for consumers.

12 Regulation (EU) 2024/1689 (Artificial Intelligence Act): http://data.europa.eu/eli/reg/2024/1689/oj.

13 *Munich Re*, New EU Act Regulates AI in Insurance (2025): www.munichre.com/automation-solutions/en/resources/insights/ai/new-eu-act-regulates-ai-in-insurance.html (accessed 19.11.2025).

- Human-in-the-Loop (HITL): The system is designed with clear escalation paths. If a customer query is too complex, emotionally sensitive, or falls outside the AI's predefined capabilities, it is seamlessly handed off to a human advisor or an AI supervisor. This ensures that technology empowers, rather than replaces, human judgment where it is most needed. This approach aligns directly with the principles outlined in *EIOPA*'s August 2025 Opinion on AI governance, which emphasizes fairness, explainability, and human oversight as critical for building trust.[14]

References and resources

Anthropic, Introducing the Model Context Protocol (2024): www.anthropic.com/news/model-context-protocol (accessed 19.11.2025)

Arya, Agentic AI in Insurance: Transforming the Industry with Enterprise AI (2025): https://hexaware.com/blogs/agentic-ai-in-insurance-transforming-the-industry-with-enterprise-ai/ (accessed 19.11.2025)

Collabnix, What is Agentic AI? A Deep Dive into MCP and the Modern Agent Ecosystem (2025): https://collabnix.com/what-is-agentic-ai-a-deep-dive-into-mcp-and-the-modern-agent-ecosystem/

EIOPA, Regulatory framework applicable to ai systems in the insurance sector |(2024): www.eiopa.europa.eu/document/download/b53a3b92-08cc-4079-a4f7-606cf309a34a_en?filename=Factsheet-on-the-regulatory-framework-applicable-to-AI-systems-in-the-insurance-sector-july-2024.pdf (accessed 19.11.2025)

Jothilingam, Agentic AI in life insurance underwriting (2025): www.cognizant.com/us/en/insights/insights-blog/agentic-ai-in-life-insurance (accessed 19.11.2025)

Kohury et al, Insurance Leads AI Adoption. It's Time to Scale (2025): www.bcg.com/publications/2025/insurance-leads-ai-adoption-now-time-to-scale (accessed 19.11.2025)

Martin et al, Put AI Agents to Work Faster Using MCP, Boston Consulting Group (2025): www.bcg.com/publications/2025/put-ai-to-work-faster-using-model-context-protocol (accessed 19.11.2025)

MIT Technology Review Insights, Reimagining the future of banking with agentic AI (2025): www.technologyreview.com/2025/09/04/1123023/imagining-the-future-of-banking-with-agentic-ai/

14 *EIOPA*, Regulatory framework applicable to ai systems in the insurance sector | (2024): www.eiopa.europa.eu/document/download/b53a3b92-08cc-4079-a4f7-606cf309a34a_en?filename=Factsheet-on-the-regulatory-framework-applicable-to-AI-systems-in-the-insurance-sector-july-2024.pdf (accessed 19.11.2025). See also *Munich Re*, New EU Act Regulates AI in Insurance (2025): www.munichre.com/automation-solutions/en/resources/insights/ai/new-eu-act-regulates-ai-in-insurance.html (accessed 19.11.2025).

Munich Re, New EU Act Regulates AI in Insurance (2025): www.munichre.com/automation-solutions/en/resources/insights/ai/new-eu-act-regulates-ai-in-insurance.html (accessed 19. 11. 2025)

Rathjen, KI-gestütztes Fintech Xaver Asset Management erhält Bafin-Lizenz (2025): www.private-banking-magazin.de/xaver-asset-management-erhaelt-bafin-lizenz/ (accessed 19. 11. 2025)

Reilly, AI Underwriting: Beyond the hype, Insurance Blog Accenture (2025): https://insuranceblog.accenture.com/ai-underwriting-beyond-the-hype (accessed 19. 11. 2025)

AI in insurance broker companies: The three-lane approach

Igor Raičević
Head of Group IT, GrECo Group

Abstract: This chapter presents a comprehensive framework for artificial intelligence implementation in insurance brokerage operations, addressing the unique challenges brokers face as intermediaries in the insurance ecosystem. Drawing from practical experience at *GrECo Group*, a leading Central and Eastern European broker operating across 21 countries with over 1.400 employees, I propose a three-lane approach to AI adoption that maximizes value while respecting operational constraints.

The framework encompasses: (1) *Microsoft 365 Copilot* for universal productivity enhancement across communication, documentation, and meeting intelligence; (2) *Claude Code* for accelerating internal development teams in building custom integrations and compliance tools; and (3) bespoke AI solutions addressing core business processes including policy data extraction (MLP), client intelligence generation (PredictiveAI), and automated claims processing (ClaimsAI).

Through detailed case studies and implementation architectures, this chapter demonstrates how brokers can transform operational efficiency while maintaining their essential role as trusted advisors. Key considerations include integration complexity across disparate systems, change management strategies, data governance requirements, and regulatory compliance across multiple jurisdictions.

The chapter concludes that successful AI implementation in brokerage requires viewing technology as human capability amplification rather than replacement, enabling deeper client relationships and more sophisticated risk management while building sustainable competitive advantages in an evolving market landscape.

Keywords: Artificial Intelligence, Insurance Brokerage, Digital Transformation, Process Automation, Machine Learning, Natural Language Processing, Microsoft 365 Copilot, Custom AI Solutions, Claims Processing, Policy Data Extraction, Client Intelligence, Multi-jurisdictional Operations, Regulatory Compliance, Change Management, Human-AI Collaboration

Key Technologies: Azure AI Services, Named Entity Recognition (NER), Optical Character Recognition (OCR), Microsoft Outlook Integration, API Integration, Cloud-Native Architecture, Natural Language Processing (NLP), OpenAI

Business Applications: Document Processing, Email Intelligence, Meeting Automation, Claims Management, Client Onboarding, Risk Analysis, Market Benchmarking, Predictive Analytics, Workflow Optimization

https://doi.org/10.33196/9783704698520-107

Contents

I. Introduction

The insurance brokerage industry occupies a unique position in the insurance ecosystem. Unlike insurers who own the underwriting process or insured parties who own the risk, brokers serve as sophisticated intermediaries, creating value through expertise, relationships, and efficient process management. This intermediary role presents both distinctive challenges and opportunities when implementing artificial intelligence solutions.

GrECo Group manages 69 subsidiaries in 21 countries with more than 1.400 employees from its headquarters in Vienna and is globally represented in over 200 countries via *GrECo nova*. In 1989, we were one of the first insurance brokers and consultants to expand into Eastern Europe. *GrECo* is the leading insurance broker in the CEE region. This scale and geographic distribution creates both opportunities and complexities when implementing AI solutions across diverse markets, regulatory environments, and client requirements.

As brokers operating across multiple countries and serving diverse client portfolios, we don't control the fundamental insurance processes, we facilitate them. This reality shapes how we can leverage AI effectively. Rather than attempting to recreate insurer capabilities or compete directly with carrier technologies, successful AI implementation in brokerage requires a three-lane approach that recognizes and optimizes our unique position in the value chain.

The multi-market environment that characterizes modern brokerage operations adds layers of complexity to AI implementation. Different countries have varying regulatory requirements, language considerations, and market practices. Solutions must be robust enough to handle this diversity while remaining efficient and cost-effective to deploy and maintain.

This chapter explores how insurance brokers can strategically implement AI across three distinct but complementary lanes: general productivity enhancement, development acceleration, and custom business process solutions. Each lane addresses different aspects of broker operations while collectively transforming how we serve clients, manage relationships, and create competitive advantage across diverse geographic and regulatory environments.

In this article, I share my personal experiences from implementing AI at *Greco* and therefore refer to the specific solutions used—*Microsoft 365 Copilot* and *Claude Code*. Other products can certainly achieve similar results, but since my practical experience is limited to these applications, I can only report from their perspective.

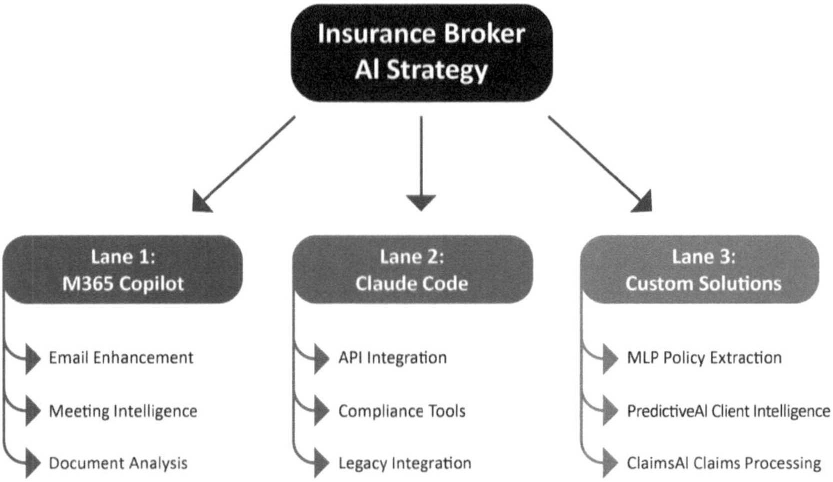

Fig. 1: Three-lane AI strategy overview

II. The broker's AI challenge: Working between systems

Before examining specific AI implementations, it's crucial to understand the unique constraints and opportunities that define the broker environment. Unlike insurers who can implement AI within closed systems they control, or corporate clients who can standardize internal processes, brokers must work across multiple, often incompatible systems and processes.

Consider a typical broker workflow: client data flows between CRM systems, insurer platforms, compliance databases, and internal management tools. Each system has different data formats, access methods, and integration capabilities. Traditional automation approaches often break down in this fragmented environment, making AI not just helpful but essential for creating coherent, efficient processes.

Furthermore, brokers must maintain relationships with multiple stakeholders, clients who demand personalized service, insurers with varying requirements and platforms, and regulatory bodies with evolving compliance standards. AI implementation must enhance these relationships rather than create barriers or reduce the personal touch that defines broker value.

III. Lane 1: *M365 Copilot* as the universal assistant

The first lane of AI implementation leverages *Microsoft 365 Copilot* as a general productivity multiplier. This approach recognizes that much of broker work involves information synthesis, communication, and task coordination across multiple platforms and relationships.

A. The power of contextual assistance

From my perspective, *M365 Copilot* fits naturally into our daily work because it's built into the *Microsoft Office* tools we already use, no extra training needed. For brokers, this means emails can be more personal, meeting notes turn into clear action items, and documents become more tailored to each client's needs.

B. Real-world applications

Meeting Intelligence: One of the most useful features for me is how *Copilot* handles meeting notes. It automatically captures key points during discussions and organizes them into clear summaries. I can also easily turn any note into a follow-up task, which helps me stay on top of next steps and makes sure nothing gets missed.

Document Intelligence: Policy documents, proposals, and compliance reports become interactive resources. *Copilot* can extract key terms, identify potential issues, and suggest improvements based on current best practices and regulatory requirements.

C. Strategic implementation

For *Copilot* to succeed, it's important to present it as a tool that boosts broker expertise, not a replacement. Training should focus on asking the right questions to get actionable insights, like identifying coverage gaps or comparing terms to industry standards, rather than just requesting generic summaries.

IV. Lane 2: *Claude Code* for internal development teams

The second lane addresses the growing need for custom technical solutions in modern brokerage operations through enhanced developer productivity. As client expectations rise and competitive pressures increase, brokers increasingly need bespoke tools and integrations that commercial software cannot provide.

However, developing these solutions efficiently requires accelerating internal development capabilities.

A. Empowering professional development teams

Claude Code has become a real partner for our development team. Our projects often involve integrating with different insurer APIs, dealing with complex regulations, and building workflows that just don't exist in off-the-shelf software. Having *Claude Code* means we get expert coding help right when we need it, which lets us solve problems faster and focus on the unique challenges of broker-specific applications.

B. Strategic development acceleration

The key to successful *Claude Code* implementation is integrating it into existing development workflows rather than replacing established practices. Development teams use *Claude Code* to accelerate research phases, generate boilerplate code, debug complex issues, and implement sophisticated algorithms.

For example, when building the MLP system described in Lane 3, *Claude Code* assisted our development team in understanding *Azure* AI service integration patterns, optimizing the NER training pipeline, and implementing robust error handling across the three-stage processing workflow. This acceleration allowed the team to focus on business logic and domain expertise rather than spending weeks researching Azure documentation and API specifications.

C. Quality and efficiency benefits

Claude Code doesn't just increase development speed, it improves code quality through several mechanisms:

Code Review Assistance: *Claude Code* can analyze proposed implementations for potential issues, security vulnerabilities, and performance bottlenecks before code reaches formal review processes.

Knowledge Transfer: When team members leave or new developers join projects, *Claude Code* can analyze existing codebases and generate explanations that accelerate onboarding and knowledge transfer processes.

V. Lane 3: Custom AI solutions for core business processes

The third lane represents the most strategic AI implementation: custom solutions that directly enhance core broker capabilities. These solutions address fundamental business processes that define broker value and competitive advantage.

A. MLP: Transforming policy data management

The Machine Learning Parser (MLP) exemplifies how custom AI can solve broker-specific challenges. Insurance policies arrive in countless formats from dozens of insurers, each with different layouts, languages, and presentation standards. Extracting critical information; policy numbers, premiums, coverage details, effective dates, traditionally requires hours of manual review that adds no strategic value.

MLP transforms this challenge into a competitive advantage through a sophisticated three-stage process:

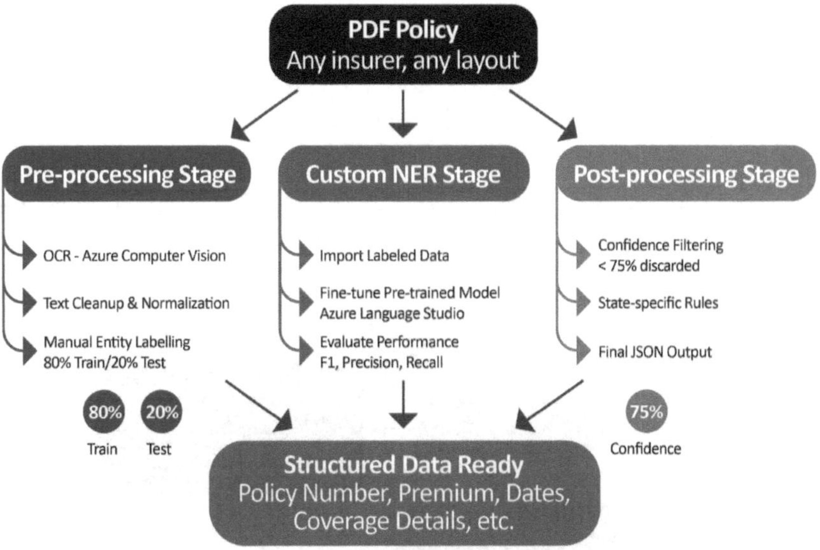

Fig. 2: MLP: Machine Learning Parser process flow

Pre-processing Stage: The system begins with diverse PDF policies, applying OCR through *Azure* Computer Vision to convert documents to text, then normalizing and cleaning the output to prepare for analysis. Critical to success is curating representative training data that includes equal coverage of different insurers and product lines, ensuring the system performs consistently across the broker's entire client portfolio.

Custom NER Implementation: Using *Azure* Language Studio, the system fine-tunes a Named Entity Recognition model specifically for insurance documents. This custom approach ensures accuracy for insurance-specific terminology and data structures that generic AI models might miss or misinterpret.

Post-processing Intelligence: The final stage applies confidence filtering, business rules, and country-specific logic to produce clean, structured JSON output. Each data point includes confidence scores and source references, enabling audit trails and quality validation.

The result is transformation of a manual, error-prone process into an automated system that delivers structured data in minutes rather than hours. This efficiency gain enables brokers to focus on analysis and client advisory rather than data extraction, while improving accuracy and consistency across all policy reviews.

B. PredictiveAI: Revolutionizing client engagement

PredictiveAI demonstrates how custom AI can transform client acquisition and relationship development. Traditional client onboarding requires extensive discovery processes, market research, and competitive analysis before brokers can provide meaningful insights. This delay often means missed opportunities and generic initial interactions.

PredictiveAI compresses this timeline dramatically by generating comprehensive business intelligence from a single input: the client's website URL. Within 3–5 minutes, the system delivers:

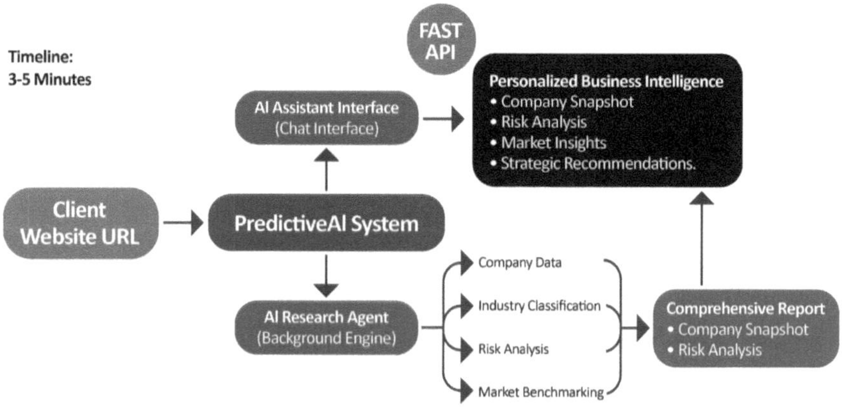

Fig. 3: PredictiveAI: From URL to business intelligence

Company Intelligence: Automated extraction of fundamental business data including industry classification, turnover estimates, employee counts, and geographic focus. This information provides the foundation for tailored service approaches and appropriate insurance program design.

Predictive Risk Analysis: Industry-specific risk profiling that identifies likely exposures based on business type, size, and market conditions. This predictive capability enables proactive risk management discussions rather than reactive problem-solving.

Market Benchmarking: Comparative analysis that positions the prospect within their industry context, highlighting areas where insurance programs might be optimized or expanded based on peer group performance and industry trends.

Strategic Recommendations: AI-generated insights that provide conversation starters and demonstrate broker expertise from the first interaction.

C. ClaimsAI: Transforming claims processing through email intelligence

ClaimsAI represents another breakthrough in custom AI solutions, addressing one of the most routine yet critical aspects of broker operations: claims processing. Traditional claims handling involves manual data entry, scattered communication channels, and administrative inefficiencies that create delays and potential errors at precisely the moment clients need responsive service.

The solution integrates directly into Microsoft Outlook as a lightweight AI-powered extension that transforms email-based claims notifications into structured data entries within the GOS|Claims core system:

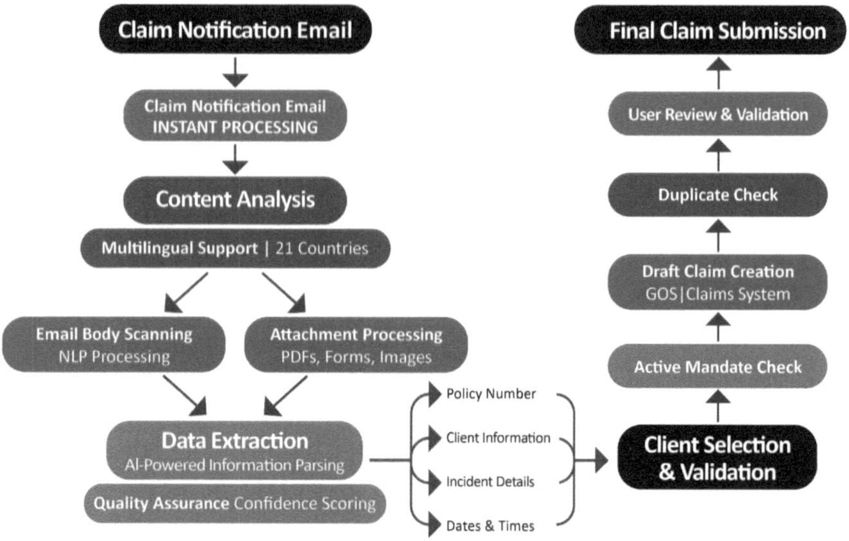

Fig. 4: ClaimsAI: Email-to-claims processing workflow

Intelligent Email Processing: When a client submits a claim notification via email, ClaimsAI automatically activates upon opening the message in Outlook. The system applies natural language processing to scan both email content and attachments, extracting key information such as policy numbers, incident descriptions, dates, and client details. This automated extraction eliminates the need for manual data transcription while ensuring no critical information is overlooked.

Structured Data Creation: The extracted information automatically populates a draft claim within the GOS|Claims system, creating a structured record that maintains consistency across the organization's claims processing workflows. All populated fields remain editable, allowing claims professionals to validate and refine the extracted data as needed.

Quality Assurance Features: ClaimsAI includes sophisticated duplicate detection capabilities that warn users if a claim has already been created from the same email, preventing processing errors while allowing legitimate multiple entries when justified. The system also validates client information against active mandates, ensuring claims processing aligns with current broker-client relationships.

Multilingual Processing: Operating across 21 countries requires handling claims communications in multiple languages. ClaimsAI's built-in language flexibility processes emails in all languages used within the *GrECo Group*, ensuring consistent functionality regardless of the communication language while maintaining localized interfaces that match user preferences.

D. Implementation architecture

MLP, PredictiveAI, and ClaimsAI demonstrate key principles for successful custom AI implementation in brokerage environments:

Cloud-Native Architecture: Leveraging *Azure* services ensures scalability and reliability while avoiding the need for internal AI infrastructure management. Each solution builds on proven cloud platforms that can scale with business growth and handle peak processing demands across multiple geographic markets.

Integration-First Design: All three solutions integrate seamlessly with existing business systems, MLP with document management workflows, PredictiveAI with client engagement processes, and ClaimsAI with core claims processing systems. This approach ensures AI enhancement rather than workflow disruption.

Audit-First Design: Every AI output includes confidence scores and source references, enabling validation and regulatory compliance. This is particularly important for ClaimsAI, where claims processing decisions must be traceable and defensible in regulatory reviews or legal proceedings.

Modular Construction: Systems are designed with discrete components that can be updated or modified without rebuilding entire solutions. This modularity is essential when operating across multiple jurisdictions with varying regulatory requirements and business practices.

Human-AI Collaboration: Rather than replacing human judgment, these systems augment broker capabilities by handling routine processing and providing enhanced information for strategic decision-making. ClaimsAI exemplifies this approach by automating data extraction while preserving human oversight for validation and final processing decisions.

VI. Strategic benefits of the three-lane approach

The three-lane AI implementation strategy creates synergistic benefits that exceed the sum of individual components:

A. Operational efficiency

Lane 1 productivity tools reduce time spent on routine tasks while improving output quality. Lane 2 development capabilities eliminate bottlenecks caused by technical limitations. Lane 3 custom solutions automate core processes that previously required manual effort. Together, these improvements free broker professionals to focus on relationship building and strategic advising.

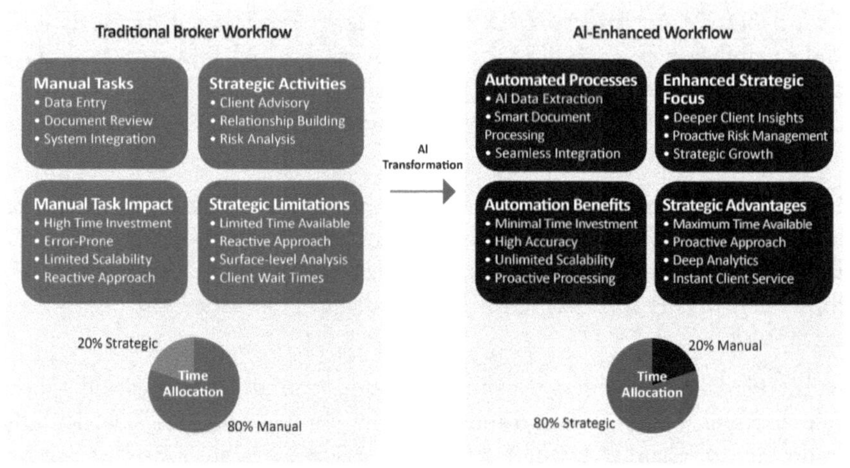

Fig. 5: Operational efficiency: Traditional vs AI-enhanced workflow. Operational efficiency transformation

B. Competitive differentiation

While competitors may implement individual AI tools, the integrated three-lane approach creates sustainable competitive advantages. Clients experience faster response times, more insightful recommendations, and higher service quality. The combination of general productivity enhancement, custom development capability, and specialized business process automation creates service levels that competitors cannot easily replicate.

C. Scalable growth

Traditional brokerage scaling requires proportional increases in staff to handle growing client volumes and complexity. The three-lane AI approach enables non-linear scaling where technology amplifies human capability rather than simply replacing it. Brokers can handle larger client portfolios while maintaining personalized service levels.

D. Risk management and compliance

AI implementations provide audit trails and documentation that enhance regulatory compliance and risk management. Automated processes reduce human error while creating detailed records of decision-making processes and data handling.

VII. Implementation challenges and solutions

A. Integration complexity

The broker technology environment involves multiple disparate systems that often lack modern integration capabilities. Success requires careful planning around data flow, authentication, and error handling across various platforms.

Solution Approach: Start with point solutions that provide immediate value while building integration capabilities incrementally. Focus on API-first architectures where possible, and develop translation layers for legacy systems that lack modern connectivity options.

B. Change management

AI implementation requires significant changes in daily workflows and professional habits. Resistance often stems from concerns about job displacement or technology complexity.

Solution Approach: Position AI as capability enhancement rather than replacement. Provide comprehensive training that emphasizes how AI enables brokers to deliver higher-value services. Start with willing early adopters who can demonstrate success and advocate for broader adoption.

C. Data quality and privacy

Broker operations involve sensitive client information that must be protected while being processed by AI systems. Data quality issues can undermine AI effectiveness and create compliance risks.

Solution Approach: Implement robust data governance frameworks that include encryption, access controls, and audit logging. Establish data quality standards and validation processes. Choose AI providers with appropriate security certifications and compliance capabilities.

D. Cost management

While AI can provide significant ROI, initial implementation costs can be substantial, particularly for custom solutions. Budget pressures may limit the scope of initial implementations.

Solution Approach: Phase implementation to spread costs over time while generating early wins that fund subsequent phases. Focus initial investments on highest-impact applications that generate measurable ROI quickly.

VIII. Future evolution and strategic considerations

The three-lane AI approach provides a foundation for continuous evolution as AI capabilities advance and market conditions change. Several trends will shape future development:

A. Enhanced integration

AI systems will become increasingly sophisticated at working across multiple platforms and data sources. Brokers should prepare for more seamless integration capabilities that reduce current technical barriers.

B. Regulatory evolution

Insurance regulation will evolve to address AI usage more specifically. Brokers should monitor regulatory developments and ensure AI implementations maintain compliance flexibility.

C. Client expectations

As AI becomes more prevalent across industries, client expectations for AI-enhanced service will increase. Brokers must stay ahead of these expectations to maintain competitive positioning.

D. Industry standardization

Market forces may drive standardization in certain AI applications, particularly around data exchange and integration protocols. Brokers should participate in industry initiatives that shape these standards.

IX. Conclusion

The three-lane approach to AI implementation recognizes the unique position and challenges of insurance brokers while providing a practical framework for strategic technology adoption. By combining general productivity enhancement through *M365 Copilot*, development acceleration through *Claude Code*, and custom business process solutions like MLP, PredictiveAI, and ClaimsAI, brokers can transform their operations while maintaining the relationship focus that defines their value.

Success requires viewing AI not as a technology solution but as a strategic capability that enhances human expertise rather than replacing it. The broker's role as trusted advisor becomes more important, not less, as AI handles routine processing and enables focus on strategic relationship building and risk management.

In my experience, AI is becoming a practical necessity in insurance. By using the three-lane approach, I've found it much easier to keep up with the growing complexity of client needs and market changes. Combining our expertise with AI tools helps us deliver better service and adapt as the industry evolves—without losing the personal touch that's so important in our work.

As we implement these AI solutions across *GrECo's* 21-country operation, we continue to learn and adapt our approach. The key insight remains constant: AI amplifies human capability rather than replacing it, enabling us to deliver superior service while building deeper, more strategic relationships with our clients. This is the essence of successful AI implementation in the insurance brokerage industry.

The digital underwriter: How AI is reshaping risk coverage

Christoph E. Nabholz/Simon Woodward
CEO RiskInsight Consulting GmbH/
Freelance author & researcher, insurance specialist

Abstract: Artificial intelligence (AI) is changing insurance underwriting. It can improve decision-making, speed, and personalization. It can further enhance productivity and support new products, such as usage-based insurance. This paper reviews how AI has developed in underwriting, from statistical models and expert systems to machine learning, generative AI, and agent-based systems.

AI helps underwriters process large volumes of data, both structured and unstructured. It can reduce fraud, improve risk assessment, and frees-up underwriters to focus on their most complex tasks. Dynamic products, such as telematics-based car insurance or health policies using wearables, show the potential of personalized pricing. Yet adoption is still limited. Regulation, legacy systems, high costs and cultural resistance all slow the pace of change.

This paper also looks at risks, including bias, fairness, and data privacy. The legal aspects of AI have yet to be fully defined, creating uncertainties, particularly around the liabilities of AI-driven decisions. Governance, accountability, and human oversight are essential to build trust.

In conclusion, AI has great potential to transform underwriting. However, change will more likely be incremental. The main barriers are not technical but human, legal, and cultural; as well as creating proven cost efficiencies. Insurers who can balance innovation with strong governance and compliance will create value while maintaining trust.

Keywords: Artificial Intelligence, Insurance Underwriting, Machine Learning, Generative AI, Agentic AI, Dynamic Underwriting, Usage-Based Insurance, Risk Assessment, Regulatory Compliance, Fairness and Bias, Governance

Contents

I. Introduction

Underwriting is fundamental to insurance, relying on statistical analysis of past data but also requiring expert judgment for future risk predictions. Underwriting takes place in a data and rules-based environment, providing potentially fertile ground for the adoption of artificial intelligence (AI). Indeed, the first use of a machine learning (ML) platforms within underwriting go back to the 1980s, enhancing the use of risk-based modelling. The sudden emergence of generative AI (GenAI) in recent years allows underwriters to potentially move beyond narrow ML functions to wider applications and a broader use of data.

There has been much excitement about how new generations of AI can further enhance, indeed even transform, the underwriting process by: (1) enhancing decision making and predictive capacities; (2) making potentially significant efficiency and productivity gains; (3) including non-traditional and recently measurable data sources, such as wearables; (4) creating new or bundled insurance products, including dynamic pricing and use-based insurance; (5) supporting greater risk segmentation and insurance personalisation; (6) using agentic AI to further enhance process automation; and (7) ultimately contributing to lower premiums through enhanced risk predictions.

However, AI does not come out the box, ready to plug-and-play. It faces significant challenges in implementation, from managerial, cultural and regulatory perspectives. Ultimately, AI must create profit at a time when questions are being asked more broadly of the ability of the technology to generate returns on investment. We suggest AI will bring change; but that change will be more incremental than transformative.

II. Using AI within underwriting

A. AI in underwriting: A long history

The insurance industry has a long tradition of using statistical models. The foundations of risk-based modelling were laid between the 1950s and 1970s in the form of generalized linear models (GLMs) and actuarial statistics.[1] These have subsequently evolved to become widespread industry practices. In the 1980s, insurers started experimenting with rule-based expert systems to assist underwriters. One leading example was MYCIN, developed by Stanford University to assist diagnosing serious bacterial infections and recommend appropriate antibiotic treatments.[2] The model was able to give judgement and explain its reasoning. The basic components of MYCIN were: (1) a knowledge base (facts, rules, etc); (2) an inference engine; and (3) a user interface (knowledge acquisition and explanation subsystem). MYCIN inspired insurers to move away from purely statistical models to ML-driven decision support.

One of these rule-based decision engines, Magnum, was launched in 1995 by *Swiss Re*. It was a rule-driven configurable system still in use today by over 70 life & health insurers across the globe to take automated underwriting decisions. Today Magnum can provide policy judgements for up to 90 % of applications in less than 4 minutes. In the last 5 years alone, it has provided decisions for 50 million life insurance policies.[3]

Despite the arrival of neural networks in the 1990s, which provided the foundations for the first AI-based predictive models in the 2000s, it was only in the 2010s that insurers widely adopted advanced ML solutions.[4] As large, structured datasets became more accessible, insurers focused on helping underwriters make smarter decisions, improve efficiency, and offer personalized services. Key AI applications included streamlining contract wording, enhancing risk scoring, and improving fraud detection.

AI further allowed new data sources to be used in underwriting, notably from Internet of Things (IoT) devices, which allowed for the creation of new or enhanced products. Notable examples included wearable data in life and health lines of business; and telematic devices in cars to monitor driving. However, while some insurers developed a specialist niche with new offerings, these products never went mainstream (see below Dynamic Underwriting).

1 *Bohn J*, Machine intelligence in insurance, Swiss Re sigma (2020).
2 *Wikipedia*, https://en.wikipedia.org/wiki/Mycin (accessed 27.1.2026).
3 *Swiss Re*, Swiss Re's Magnum: Automated underwriting platform (accessed 27.1.2026).
4 *Loveland*, A brief history of ai in the P&C insurance industry (accessed 27.1.2026).

A significant growth in patent filing demonstrated the interest of insurers in AI innovation during the late 2010s. The major difficulty, however, was to have a production-ready data strategy with an end-to-end enterprise process.[5] Some data – application forms, motor vehicle records – could be combined relatively easily with external sources, such as credit scores. However, it was a far greater challenge to integrate data with higher compliance and regulatory thresholds, such as electronic health records, telematics or wearables data.

In the 2020s, regulators developed guidelines for the use of AI within the insurance industry, centred around fairness, ethics, accountability, and transparency.[6] These regulatory constraints slowed development of AI in underwriting; up until the launch of ChatGPT in November 2022, when industry attention suddenly shifted to GenAI. In practical terms, this meant less focus on improving risk forecasting and bringing greater efficiency to the underwriting workflow.

One early example of this shift is *Swiss Re's* Life Guide[7], an underwriting tool first launched in 2004, which provides rating guidelines of medical conditions differentiated by products and regions. *Swiss Re* launched the product in 2024 as Life Guide Scout, a GenAI powered underwriting agent.[8] This enhanced release enables thousands of underwriters at more than 800 client companies to consult the Life Guide and obtain guidance and ratings for complex medical conditions in seconds, rather than searching for each risk factor individually. Notably, the agentic-AI tool draws exclusively on the Life Guide manual and never consults external web sources. We will likely see similar agents soon supporting underwriters across all product lines and the entire underwriting workflow. However, high regulatory hurdles mean core underwriting functions, such as risk forecasting and pricing, will transform only slowly.

B. Adoption of AI in underwriting: Where are we?

Survey data suggests the adoption of AI in underwriting may be at an inflexion point. According to a 2022–23 survey by the National Association of Insurance Commissioners (NAIC), 88 % of auto insurers used or planned to explore the use of AI, followed by 70 % home insurers and 58 % of life insurance companies.[9] In 2025, a further NAIC survey revealed that 92 % of health insurers planned to use or explore AI.[10] In 2025, 70 % of insurance companies were

5 *Bohn J*, Machine intelligence in insurance, Swiss Re sigma (2020).
6 *MAS*, Methodologies for responsible use of AI by financial institutions (2022).
7 *Monks K et al*, New business and underwriting systems, CELENT (2024).
8 *Swiss Re*, Life Guide: moving forward in life (accessed 27.1.2026).
9 *NAIC*, Big data and artificial intelligence working group meeting (2025).
10 *NAIC*, Big data and artificial intelligence working group meeting (2025).

actively testing AI solutions but only 22 % had fully advanced AI projects into their workstreams.[11]

Specifically in underwriting, the NAIC reported that 47 % of home insurers and 18 % of auto insurers reported using AI tools.[12] Moreover, underwriting (34 %) and marketing (36 %) were the most common AI use cases in life insurance in 2023. The three largest use cases of AI in auto and home insurance were underwriting, rating and fraud prevention.

Key targets for underwriters in 2025 was to use AI to drive premium growth (75 %), followed by increasing speed to quote (54 %) and lowering loss ratios (43 %).[13]

A recent insurance industry survey by *Roots* in 2025 revealed the following AI priorities for underwriting:[14]
- **Workflow processes (61 %):** AI to automate key workflow processes using agents.
- **Processing unstructured data and documents (59 %):** AI to process PDF files, emails, or images.
- **Processing structured data and documents (45 %):** AI to analyse numerical data in data bases or *Excel* sheets.
- **Risk assessment and/or scoring (40 %):** predictive AI to assess risks associated with insuring a policyholder.
- **Premium determination (15 %):** AI to assist more accurate premium calculations.

Cost reduction through efficiency gains has been the key driver for recent AI investments. Insurers report AI-powered underwriting systems dramatically reducing processing times. Hiscox claimed AI enabled it to cut underwriting times, in some cases, from 3 days to 3 minutes through the following efficiencies:[15]
- **Fraud detection and prevention:** Identifying fraudulent client behaviour during the application process and enhancing truthful declaration.
- **Efficiency increases to free-up underwriters:** Automating the most time-consuming processes with AI agents, freeing-up underwriters for more complex cases, strategic decision making and product innovation.
- **Increase accuracy:** Enhancing predictive modelling capacity through collecting, processing, and analysing data.

11 *Roots,* State of AI Adoption in Insurance 2025 (2025).
12 *Todoroff N et al,* How your insurance company is using AI, Bankrate (2024).
13 *Roots,* State of AI Adoption in Insurance 2025 (2025).
14 *Roots,* State of AI Adoption in Insurance 2025 (2025).
15 *INSLY,* Artificial intelligence in insurance underwriting (accessed 27.1.2026).

- **Risk assessment:** Automating feedback loops between claims and underwriting to produce new insights and efficiencies.

Current use cases of AI in underwriting include:[16]

- **Underwriting & pricing**: AI automates risk assessment through analysing medical records, lifestyle or telematic data, customer behaviour data, and other third-party data such as credit scores or other sources.
- **Fraud detection & prevention**: AI analyses unusual behaviours (such as multiple policies for a single person, client onboarding behaviour, missing submission data) to reduce fraud.
- **Onboarding clients**: Chatbots and virtual assistants provide personalized support, helping customers select policies, fill out underwriting questionnaires, and obtain customer consent in accessing relevant data.
- **Risk management**: AI identifies emerging risks, including health and environmental trends, which can influence pricing and reserving strategies.
- **Legal policy wording**: Underwriters are supported by an AI assistant to review policy terms, flag critical legal wordings, provide standardized clauses, and suggest how exclusions are drafted, explained and enforced.

C. The rise of AI powered dynamic underwriting products

AI can support and enhance dynamic underwriting, enabling usage-based insurance (UBI) products that do not rely on traditional rules-based one-time risk assessments. UBI can be particularly beneficial in capturing granular data in life and health product lines. One health insurer saw a reported claims reduction of 28 % following the integration of health wearables with an insurance product.[17] UBI further provides greater personalisation, with data correlated to health and mortality outcomes, as confirmed by large longitudinal cohorts such as the UK Biobank. There is clear medical evidence of how wearables can help achieve better outcomes. One paper suggested increasing daily step counts to 4000 a day by less active adults would result in lowering the risk of some cancers.[18] Several insurers are using dynamically underwritten programmes encouraging life-style improvements, as measured by steps, heart rate and sleep, including *John Hancock* Vitality[19] and *Manulife* MOVE.[20]

16 *Zych J*, AI in insurance, Guidehouse (2024).
17 *Klintworth K*, Rethinking health insurance, Vitality (2024).
18 *Shreves AH et al,* Amount and intensity of daily total physical activity (2025).
19 *Vitality*, Our mission in action (accessed 27.1.2026).
20 *MOVE*, ManulifeMOVE, inspiring your every step, every move (accessed 27.1.2026).

UBI can also be used in motor or pay-how-you-drive products.[21] UBI uses telematics to capture driving behaviour, which can be assessed by AI to detect patterns and to potentially adjust premiums. Several telematic products are on the market, including Progressive Snapshot, Allstate Drivewise, and State Farm Drive Safe & Save.[22]

The use of UBI affords several potential advantages to customers and insurers:

- Reducing premiums for individuals who can prove they are better-than-average risks.
- Greater segmentation of risk pools and underwriting personalisation, helping insurers reduce adverse selection and contributing to a stronger underwriting book.
- Creating incentives for policy holders, rewarding better behaviours such as exercise and careful driving.
- Providing personalised feedback and advice to policy holders to reduce their risk.
- The potential to bundle services together with insurance, such as a common health ecosystem platform with insurance, medical services and exercise data.
- Greater customer engagement.

However, despite being on the market for some years, UBI is still niche within the larger insurance market. Telematic driving solutions are most frequently purchased by younger, careful drivers, to lower otherwise high premiums. Health UBI products are predominantly purchased by fit individuals who might monitor key vital statistics anyway. The reasons for UBI products struggling to gain traction include: (1) consumer distrust at the perception of being tracked by their insurer; (2) fears that technology may provide incorrect data; (3) uncertainty at what else data might be used for, including being sold to data brokers;[23] (4) the knowledge that premiums could rise as well as fall; (5) regulatory concern, particularly what happens to higher risk individuals if risk pools are more segmented; and (6) competition concerns around ecosystem exclusivity.

Nonetheless, the UBI market has expanded over recent years from a small base; and some suggest growth could be significant in coming years.[24]

21 *Philips B*, Telematics and usage-based insurance (accessed 27.1.2026).
22 *Philips B*, Telematics and usage-based insurance (accessed 27.1.2026).
23 *Rajamohan W*, What went wrong with data-driven car insurance (accessed 27.1.2026).
24 *Global Market Insights*, UBI Market Size, 2024.

D. A glimpse into the future of AI in underwriting

The adoption of AI in underwriting has been a slow process. It took regulators over a decade to develop guidelines for the compliant use of AI and ML.[25] It was only in 2018, for example, that the Monetary Authority of Singapore (MAS) developed the FEAT (Fairness, Ethics, Accountability and Transparency) principles: fairness (consistency, equity, fairness, bias minimization), ethics (human oversight, right to human review, monitoring), accountability (risk ownership, lawful basis, reliability), and transparency (explainability, disclosure to users, purpose).[26] Transparent ML (such as GLMs) are widely accepted today for life and property and casualty underwriting, while deep learning models face higher scrutiny unless accompanied by explainable AI (XAI) tools. Given the time and effort it has taken underwriters to explain AI capabilities, there has been a tendency to stick to the simpler, more easily explainable models. Underwriters seeking to use predictive AI models have found regulators a significant hurdle.

Established large insurers, who often grew through historic mergers and acquisitions, frequently have operations spread across fragmented legacy systems that were never designed to work together. This creates inefficiencies, slows data integration, and makes real-time insights difficult. By contrast, recent market entrants, such as US insurer Lemonade, can expand on unified digital platforms, a significant advantage when deploying AI.[27] Since its 2016 launch, Lemonade has scaled rapidly from 14,000 customers in its first six months to 2.69 million today. At the core of its model are AI-powered applications: Maya, a chatbot that can collect up to 100 times more data per customer than traditional insurers, guiding onboarding and underwriting; while Jim, a claims bot, autonomously resolves 27 % of claims in seconds using natural language processing (NLP) and behavioural analytics. These systems streamline interactions, reduce overheads, and deliver a 92 % customer satisfaction rate.

Moreover, *Lemonade's* underwriting models now integrate telematics, real-time data, and, since 2025, catastrophe-risk modelling through its partnership with *ZestyAI*. Together, these innovations cut the company's gross loss ratio to 67 % in Q2 2025, a 12-point year-on-year improvement, and better than many established property and casualty (P & C) providers.[28] However, the AI strategy also comes with risk. In 2021, a Lemonade customer filed a lawsuit alleging mishandling of biometric data, which damaged customer trust.[29]

25 *Noordhoek D*, Regulation of AI in insurance, Geneva Association (2023).
26 *MAS*, FEAT Principles (accessed 27.1.2026).
27 *Boguslawski G et al*, Lemonade: Mini-Case Study Report, UNL Raikes (2025).
28 *Lemonade*, Lemonade delivers AI-powered insurance (accessed 24.9.2025).
29 *TopClassActions*, Lemonade insurance biometric privacy (accessed 27.1.2026).

While companies like Lemonade demonstrate how domain-specific AI can deliver tangible gains in underwriting performance, the industry is now entering a new phase shaped by Gen AI and foundation models. Unlike purpose-built ML systems, these large, general-purpose models raise fresh questions about transparency, accountability, and regulatory acceptance.

New foundation models are neural-based systems trained on large datasets, making their internal processes more opaque and harder to explain. Foundation models are owned by third parties, such as Meta, Anthropic or OpenAI; and there remains a lack of clarity as to whether the responsibility for decision making lies with the model, the prompt or the entire pipeline. At a minimum, insurers will need to ensure they take consistent and fair underwriting decisions. This requires documentation for: (1) the prompting strategy (effectively this is now part of the model design); (2) the justification (model testing for bias); and (3) risk management controls (independent evaluation and human-in-the-loop checks for high-impact underwriting decisions). Without clear guardrails, the pressure to adopt GenAI could see it channelled into unofficial or poorly governed workflows, creating 'shadow AI' risks that undermine consistency and compliance. Given these demands, underwriters are more likely to refine other parts of the underwriting process before employing GenAI. GenAI may instead be deployed in functions perceived as lower risk, such as document summarization, automated risk reporting (including fraud detection) and customer communications. It may take years to embed foundation models in end-to-end underwriting platforms.

Following GenAI, the next major wave of AI technology will be agentic. Agentic AI could enable the orchestration of underwriting workflows, with a central controller bot prompting services from other AI applications. A hypothetical AI multiagent could begin by ordering a data ingestion agent to extract relevant underwriting data and automatically request information to fill data gaps found in medical records or engineering reports.[30] A compliance and fairness agent could review the process to ensure auditability. A triaging agent could label cases with higher fraud potential and escalate cases that need senior underwriting review. A feedback agent could link claims experience with underwriting decisions and propose model adjustments or workflow optimizations.[31] The human-in-the-loop principal would remain critical to build trust and transparency with regulators and clients. The key challenge in such solutions, however, is as much change management as technology (see IV: Considerations before fully integrating AI in underwriting).

30 *Milinkovich N et al*, The future of AI in the insurance industry, McKinsey (2025).
31 *Milinkovich N et al*, The future of AI in the insurance industry, McKinsey (2025).

III. Underwriting AI risk

As well as using AI in underwriting, underwriters will need ways and means to insure AI, as it spreads through the risk landscape and into their portfolios. In underwriting AI, insurers will want to consider: (A) how regulatory structures treat AI and what impact that may have on risk; (B) how the legal character of AI is evolving and how that may impact liability in particular; (C) the transparency of AI use among insured parties; (D) the danger of tail risks and their potential spillover; and (E) how insurers can respond to the widespread adoption of AI.

A. Regulatory requirements and AI

Regulators already have an oversight of known AI risks they are seeking to regulate and police (see below, Section IV). These include:

- **Bias, indirect discrimination and fairness:** AI has the potential to embed and propagate inherent data biases. To prevent bias, regulators require regular testing, auditing, and governance frameworks.
- **Data privacy and security:** AI specific legislation builds on already existing data privacy measures to further protect end users.
- **Explainability and transparency:** As decisions and processes become more automated, regulators will insist on being able to open black boxes.
- **Accountability and governance:** Regulators seek clear internal accountability for AI systems, together with resilient risk management.

Within these overriding principles, there is considerable scope for shaping regulations that reflect the overall ideological outlook of the particular regulatory authority. The European Union has placed consumer protection at the forefront of its 2024 EU AI Act[32]. The act is a single rights-based piece of legislation, incorporating a risk-based approach that sees certain sectors – including insurance – being judged as 'high risk'. The United States, by contrast, has a principles-based regulatory regime, divided across federal government, states and industry sectors. The approach is designed to foster innovation and growth in emerging AI technology, with emphasis put on voluntary codes and informal guidance. Globally, more governments have leaned towards the US rather than the EU model. Singapore, for example, prioritizes voluntary frameworks, guidance and toolkits over rigid legislation. China, by contrast,

32 Regulation (EU) 2024/1689 laying down harmonised rules on artificial intelligence (Artificial Intelligence Act) http://data.europa.eu/eli/reg/2024/1689/oj.

regulates AI products individually based on how they both support national security and the governing ideology.[33]

B. Legal evolution of AI

Whilst regulation provides a framework in which to use AI, the dynamic and emergent nature of the technology means its legal identities are still evolving. This legal uncertainty particularly affects insurance liability lines, establishing where responsibility for any potential faults lies between: (1) the foundational model (where applicable); (2) the AI app; (3) the contracting company; and (4) the end-user. Court cases, regulatory rulings, precedents and further legislation will all continue to define the AI space. The US is main theatre in which these cases will be played out; but other jurisdictions will also shape the legal character of AI.

Although this is far from an exhaustive list, key recent cases that will influence the legal development and evolution of AI include:

- **AI liability in services:** In 2023, a chatbot provided an *Air Canada* passenger information that differed from what was stated elsewhere on the website. The passenger sued. *Air Canada* suggested the customer should not have relied solely on a chatbot. A Canadian tribunal flatly rejected defence, stating the airline was inferring the chatbot was a 'separate legal entity'. Air Canada was held unambiguously responsible for the content of all its website, including chatbots.[34]
- **AI liability in health:** Legal opinion largely accepts the use of AI as an assistant to the practicing professional, who is ultimately liable for patient outcomes. This does not absolve the AI entirely. If there is fault with the product, or a failure to warn users about its limitations, the AI could become subject to a lawsuit. This occurred in 2024, when AI provider Pieces Technologies was sued by the State of Texas for exaggerating the accuracy of its GenAI services.[35] Model-accuracy overestimation was also found in the widely used Epic Sepsis Model.[36]
- **AI liability in transport:** In 2019, a *Tesla* operating in autopilot mode caused a fatal crash. *Tesla* maintained a driver should remain attentive and ready to assume control even when a car is in autopilot. However, a jury in 2025 found Tesla partly responsible for the crash, with total damagers set at USD243 million. *Tesla* stated it would appeal the verdict.[37] Both the

33 *Noordhoek D*, Regulation of AI in insurance, Geneva Association (2023).
34 *Forbes*, Air Canada Lost in 'Remarkable' Lying AI Chatbot Case (2024).
35 *Paxton K*, Attorney General Settlement in Healthcare GenAI Investigation (2024).
36 *Smith D*, Widely used AI tool for early sepsis detection (2024).
37 *Kolodny L*, Tesla must pay $329 million after fatal Autopilot crash, CNBC (2025).

nature of the settlement (the partial culpability of AI) and the size of the settlement (significantly exceeding personal auto insurance limits) could set precedents. *Tesla* has defeated previous lawsuits and settled others, while still facing claims in a number of jurisdictions related to autonomous driving.[38]

- **Shifting AI liability from service to product:** A Florida court ruled in 2025 that *Character.ai* should be treated as a product, rather than a service, in the case of the suicide of a 14-year-old, opening the company to a strict and potentially more expensive defective product claim.[39] Also of significance, the court ruled it was 'too early' to rule on whether a chatbot's output qualifies as freedom of speech under the First Amendment of the US Constitution.
- **AI, intellectual property law and fair use:** Multiple intellectual property (IP) laws suits have been filed against GenAI providers, focusing on model training, plagiarism and what constitutes 'fair use'.[40] These legal cases, mostly but not exclusively in the US, could redefine the parameters of intellectual property (IP),[41] focused on: (1) data ingestion for model training without permission; (2) content creation differing little from original texts/audio/image/video without recognition; and (3) imitation of artistic style/voice/appearance.[42] Few expect resolution of these questions to be quick, and many judge the genie to already be out of the bottle, with some content providers signing agreements with GenAI providers rather than contest their rights. Moreover, the status of materials produced by AI is also not clear, the US insisting on human involvement to earn copyright protection.

C. AI transparency

As AI adoption accelerates, transparency will become critical. Insurers, regulators, and customers alike need clarity on where AI is being used, how decisions are made, and who remains accountable. Outside of the hype, the scale of AI use in the economy is uncertain. There are forecasters who see AI as a truly transformative technology, poised to provide an unprecedented boost to productivity and growth.[43] Others are more circumspect. One prominent economist suggested (in 2023) the gains of generative AI will be "non-trivial, but modest, resulting in no more than a 0.66 % increase in total factor productivity over 10 years".[44] It could also be that AI becomes a wide spread technology without being a catalyst for productivity gains, an updated version of the 1980s

38 *Vigliarolo B,* Tesla facing another Autopilot fatality lawsuite, The Register (2024).
39 *Social Media Victims Law Center,* AI Chatbot Lawsuit (2025).
40 *Wired,* Every AI Copyright Lawsuit in the US Visualised (2024) (accessed 27.1.2026).
41 *Reuters Institute,* How AI is reshaping copyright law (2025).
42 *Ctech,* The King and AI: Elvis vs copyright infringement (2024).
43 *Shrier D et al,* AI could add 10 % to global GDP by 2032, Chatham House (2023).
44 *Acemoglu D,* The Simple Macroeconomics of AI, NBER (2024).

Solow paradox, where the mass adoption of computers did little to positively impact underlying growth.

The quantitative use of AI will need to be combined with an understanding of where and how it is being used. Certain sectors will be more transparent than others. Healthcare, for example, is a relatively transparent sector, where regulators require the declaration and risk assessment of many AI products.[45] This is not the case in many industry sectors. GenAI use in software development, for example, is almost ubiquitous; but frequently poorly declared or documented.[46] Where there is less transparency, there will be fewer guarantees that AI solutions will be properly calibrated, assessed and validated. Indeed, individual employees may use AI solutions without the knowledge of their managers.[47]

This combination of a rapidly spreading technology with limited transparency could see risk accrue in traditional business and casualty lines not designed with AI in mind. This exposure has been described as 'silent AI', in part a homage to the phenomenon of silent cyber, when cyber claims began appearing in traditional lines in the 2000s.[48]

D. Tail risks

Many prominent AI entrepreneurs and researchers believe unchecked AI development could pose extreme, even civilisation-ending risks.[49] In some cases, the motivation behind such warnings may be for tech companies to have a strong role in regulating their own technology[50]; and some of these doomsday scenarios are too extreme to be easily captured by risk managers.

Nonetheless, it is possible to imagine tail risk scenarios, in which AI may pose a systemic risk that leads to possible exposure over a range of insurance lines. These could include:

- **Rogue AI:** AI could overstep weak guardrails in pursuit of an overriding goal in an unforeseen fashion – for example, being told to maximise marketing publicity for a product and doing so by drawing on sensationalist or unsuitable content. Continual human oversight in processes will provide one means of control.

45 *FDA*, AI-Enabled Medical Devices (accessed 27.1.2026).
46 *Nguyen-Duc et al*, Generative Artificial Intelligence for Software Engineering – A Research Agenda, arXiv:2310.18648 (2023).
47 *Krantz T et al*, What is shadow AI, IBM (2024).
48 *Swiss Re Institute*, AI – silent cyber (2024).
49 *The Future of Life Institute*, Pause Giant AI Experiments (2023).
50 *Thales*, How AI affect Security Risks, Cloud Security Alliance (2024).

- **AI and systemic risk:** As black box AI systems become more stacked and more agentic, faults in one AI service could cascade across systems and be difficult to identify or control. AI owners will need to identify potential dependencies, create effective firebreaks and necessary kill switches.
- **GenAI vendor diversity:** As foundation models are dominated by a relatively small number of major providers, there could be significant knock-on effects should one of these providers be compromised, as well as lock-in dependencies.
- **AI and infrastructure:** Cloud based hosting is central to many AI providers; but this opens vulnerabilities to model theft and data poisoning.[51]
- **AI and cyber risk:** AI provides many new attack surfaces and vectors for cyber attackers. Cyber risk is a growing threat for insurers, with ransomware attacks reported up around 25 % in 2025 over 2024.[52] Equally, AI can also be used as a defensive tool against cyber risk.[53]
- **AI and deep fakes:** As attackers are aware, humans are often the weak link in cyber defences and can be fooled by sophisticated deep fakes.[54] Equally, fake content generated by AI could be an exceptionally powerful propaganda tool, as already seen in the Ukraine conflict.[55]
- **AI and robotics:** As AI breaks out of virtual systems into robotics and the IoT, it has the potential to cause real-world damages. Nowhere is this more the case than with autonomous vehicles, where a nightmare scenario could be the cyber hijacking of a car, or fleet of cars, by a hostile actor.
- **AI weaponry:** Extensive use of AI drones and other AI technologies in the Russia-Ukraine conflict is redefining many of the rules of warfare and potentially of terrorism.[56] Whilst war and terrorism are largely excluded by insurers, a major AI-enabled terrorist attack could spill into lines such as workers' compensation or political risk.
- **AI societal impact:** There is considerable potential for AI to have a societal impact that would affect our environment, democracy, governance and economy. Researchers have attempted to frame these into a wide-reaching taxonomy, much of which could have a longer tail impact on insurers.[57]

51 *Thales*, How AI affect Security Risks, Cloud Security Alliance (2024).
52 *Knesebeck von dem A et al*, Cyber Insurance Risk and Trends 2025, Munich Re (2025).
53 *Greis J et al*, Making AI safer, McKinsey (2024).
54 *Chen H et al*, Finance worker pays out $25 million, CNN (2024).
55 *Bronovytska Y*, Deepfakes: The Russian Case, Conflict Justice Decolonisation (2024).
56 *Geneva Centre for Security Policy*, Ten Lessons from the Russia-Ukraine War (2025).
57 *Uuk R et al*, A Taxonomy of Systemic Risks from General-Purpose AI (2024).

E. Insurance responses

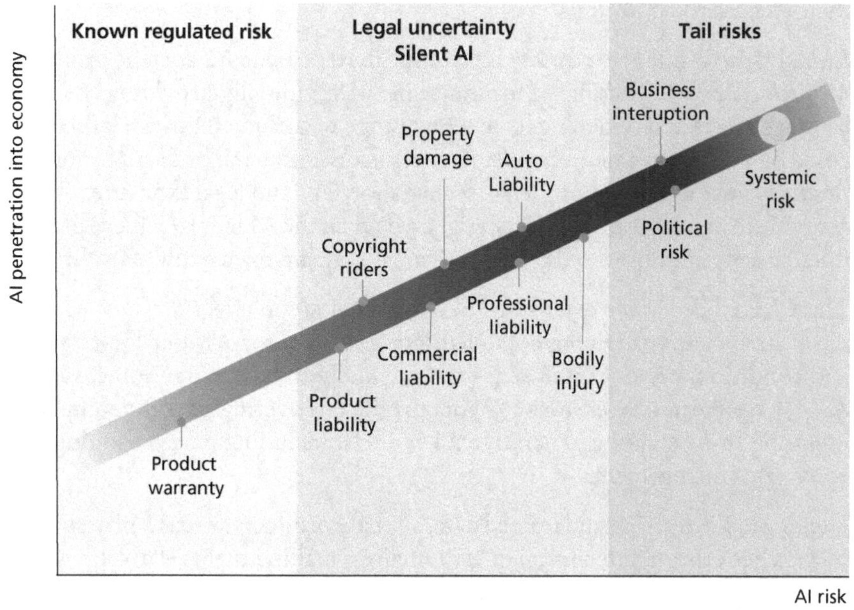

Fig. 1: Illustrative sketch of impact of AI on insurance lines

Put all these different factors together—(1) known AI risks and current regulatory structures; (2) silent AI and the lack of legal certainty around many AI products; and (3) the unknown potential of tail risk—and it is no wonder that many insurers are seeking to actively understand and control the AI risk they might be exposed to on their underwriting book. As can be seen in the above sketch, many insurance policies fall in a corridor of legal uncertainty and silent AI.

The quickest means for insurers to control AI exposure is to write exclusions on existing policies. Individual companies have reportedly started this process, with both broad and narrow exclusions.[58] However, exclusions will not be welcome by brokers or clients; and could be legally challenged in a claim. Exclusions become more feasible when the market moves collectively, as it ultimately did with cyber (see below).

To some degree, GenAI providers are creating their own risk solutions. *Amazon*, *Adobe* and *OpenAI* provide copyright protection for selected (but not all) product users.[59] *Microsoft* and *Google* provide assurances of copyright protection,

58 *Hunton*, How Insurance Policies are Adapting to AI Risk (2025).
59 *Magnusson*, OpenAI's Copyright Shield (2023).

but their legal framings are less clear. Equally, several generative AI providers specifically exclude copyright infringement liability from their products in their terms and conditions.

Equally, the insurance industry is stepping in to provide AI-specific products. *Munich Re* began offering AI insurance in 2018,[60] initially providing coverage for developers and widening its product range to include AI users, largely focused on AI performance. *Armilla Insurance*, operating out of *Lloyds*, similarly provides guarantees against performance shortfalls and legal exposures. These are typically parametric products, triggered when the AI fails to achieve pre-defined targets and thresholds. They are most suitable for narrow AI solutions.

There have been some extensions beyond what are in effect product warranties. Carriers are providing some liability coverage for AI, but limits, terms and conditions are not disclosed – and are likely to be narrow. Some, such as *AXA*, have created extensions to cyber products, covering risks for companies investing in or creating generative AI models, including data poisoning and copyright infringement.[61]

Lacking historical or standardized data, all these products are currently tailored to the client through technical questionnaires, making them relatively expensive and slow to underwrite (although AI may make such coverage quicker and easier). Both the need for technical expertise and the lack of appetite by insurers – shaped by legal and technical uncertainties – means AI coverage is currently a niche market, with only around half a dozen providers. *Deloitte* projects the global market could grow to USD 4.7 billion by 2032, which would assume significant annual growth figures from a currently low base.[62]

Whilst no one would doubt the potential for AI coverage, if cyber serves as a forerunner, expansion may not prove rapid. While cyber coverage was on the market in the mid 1990s, demand only really picked up in the 2010s, driven by (1) major cyber incidents, such as the WannaCry attack; (2) changing regulatory requirements, most notably the EU's GDPR[63]; and (3) insurers moving consistently to exclude cyber from traditional lines. A similar combination of learning from major incidents and clearer regulations or precedents could boost demand and supply of AI specific coverage.

60 *Devrise I et al*, Insuring Generative AI: Risks and Mitigation Strategies, Munich Re (2024).

61 *Rodriguez Sanz C et al*, Generative AI: An insurer's perspective, AXA (2025).

62 *Suhrada S et al*, Providing insurance coverage for AI, Deloitte (2024).

63 Regulation (EU) 2016/679 of the European Parliament and of the Council of 27 April 2016 on the protection of natural persons with regard to the processing of personal data and on the free movement of such data (General Data Protection Regulation): https://eur-lex.europa.eu/eli/reg/2016/679/oj.

Nonetheless, risk coverage could be a valuable support in encouraging the use of AI into the broader economy. Regulatory measures, such as greater disclosure requirements of AI use in production processes, could help reduce silent AI. Greater AI product standardization would make for an easier underwriting process. Creating an architecture where AI risks and losses were more transparent would further enhance the ability of insurers to provide coverage.

IV. Considerations before fully integrating AI in underwriting

A. Data quality

AI in underwriting depends on accurate, representative, and unbiased data. Maintaining data quality requires continuous cleaning, annotation, and validation. This process is resource-intensive and demands long-term organizational commitment. Poor data quality introduces bias, leading to underfitting or overfitting, and undermines both pricing accuracy and regulatory compliance. Sustainable value creation from AI requires treating data as a core strategic asset.

B. Data systems and infrastructure

Legacy systems remain a critical barrier in insurance. Many insurers still rely on fragmented IT architectures and paper-based processes, which limit data accessibility and interoperability. Modern AI requires scalable, integrated platforms capable of handling high volumes of structured and unstructured data. Building such infrastructure is costly but essential. Without robust systems, even high-quality data cannot be effectively leveraged, and AI solutions will fail to scale.

C. Skills, expertise and change management

The skills required for AI integration in underwriting have shifted. In the 2010s, success depended on technical experts and data scientists able to code bespoke AI solutions. With the advent of foundation models and GenAI, the emphasis has moved to professionals who combine business process knowledge with an understanding of digital capabilities and their application to underwriting challenges. Technical skills remain important but must be complemented by domain expertise and strategic vision. Equally important is structured change management. Insurers must invest in reskilling and upskilling staff, enabling them to adopt AI tools, develop relevant solutions, and adapt to new workflows. Organizational readiness and workforce transformation are as decisive as the technology itself.

D. Regulatory compliance and ethics

Meeting regulatory requirements in AI-enabled underwriting demands dedicated expertise. A small specialist team should oversee validation studies, ensure explainability, and build robust process frameworks. These structures provide guidance for business experts and support consistent compliance. The industry has made progress with transparent ML models, as demonstrated by regulators providing guidance to the financial sector,[64] but adoption remains limited as the regulatory approval burden is still too cumbersome. For LLMs and GenAI, regulatory adaptation is at an early stage. Key regulatory issues[65] include cross-border data compliance for multinational insurers, adherence to data protection frameworks such as the EU GDPR or California CCPA (California Consumer Privacy Act), and alignment with emerging requirements under the EU AI Act or the Colorado AI Act. Proactive governance, such as the OECD AI Principals,[66] is essential to reduce compliance risks and maintain trust with regulators and customers.

E. Bias, fairness and risk of exclusion

AI in underwriting raises profound concerns about fairness and inclusivity. Poorly designed models can unintentionally create "insurance deserts",[67] excluding entire groups based on geography, socio-economic status, or proxy variables. This amplifies social and ethical debates around equitable access to coverage. Moreover, an increased use of AI may lead underwriters fearing job losses due to automation.

Bias is challenging to detect and mitigate. Historical and sampling biases, as well as hidden correlations in proxy variables, can distort outcomes. Back-testing requires substantial manual effort, as validating machine decisions over large datasets often takes weeks. Although synthetic datasets may help, they too carry risks of embedded bias.

Mitigation requires systematic governance: fairness metrics, representative training data, synthetic augmentation with caution, and transparent validation frameworks. Global standards, such as the IEEE 7003-2024[68] standard on algorithmic bias or the AI Risk Management Framework by NIST[69], provide guidance for building inclusive and trustworthy AI models.

64 *MAS*, Methodologies for responsible use of AI by financial institutions (2022).
65 *Noordhoek D*, Regulation of AI in insurance, Geneva Association (2023).
66 *OECD*, AI Principles (2024).
67 *Mills E*, What are insurance deserts? WEF (2025).
68 *IEEE*, IEEE Standard for Algorithmic Bias Considerations (accessed 27.1.2026).
69 *NIST*, AI Risk Management Framework (accessed 27.1.2026).

F. Security and data privacy

Robust security and privacy are non-negotiable in AI-enabled underwriting. Systems must be protected against hacking, data breaches, and algorithmic manipulation. Data privacy requirements, including rights such as the "right to be forgotten", demand careful implementation to safeguard customer information. The insurance industry has a long tradition of prudent data stewardship, built on decades of regulatory compliance and customer trust. This foundation must not be compromised in the pursuit of AI innovation. Strong encryption, continuous monitoring, and privacy-by-design principles are essential to maintain integrity and trust in underwriting processes.

G. Creating governance and accountability frameworks

Effective governance structures are essential to ensure compliance, transparency, and sound risk management in AI underwriting. A central inventory of AI use cases provides oversight and enables consistent reporting. Clear guidance must define responsibilities, documentation standards, and monitoring practices.

ML models and GenAI foundation models present different governance needs. Traditional ML models are typically transparent, well-documented, and reusable when validated. They can be trained and maintained internally, supporting trust and operational consistency. By contrast, GenAI foundation models function as black boxes. Their training demands are enormous, often require supercomputer-scale infrastructure, ultra large datasets analysing hundreds of billions of parameters, and expenditures that can easily exceed USD 10 million in computer and data acquisition. As a result, most insurers do not build these models in-house, instead, they typically buy them from a small number of external vendors (such as *OpenAI, Anthropic, Google, Meta*), then adapt or fine-tune them for sector-specific applications. This creates dependency risks, including vendor lock-in and operational disruption if a provider fails. Mitigation requires contingency planning, such as backup deployment options or multi-vendor strategies.

Governance should also extend to ethical oversight. Establishing an ethics board can help ensure that AI use cases are socially responsible and aligned with corporate values. Model lifecycle management, covering development, validation, deployment, monitoring, and retirement, is necessary to sustain accountability. Independent certifications and third-party assurance reports can provide further transparency and support regulatory trust.

V. Conclusion for risk and underwriting

There has long been the belief that – by AI or other means – underwriting is a highly automatable process. *Frey* and *Osbourne* had it as one of the most vulnerable professions to 'computerisation' in 2017;[70] in 2021 *McKinsey* suggested that by 2030 underwriting could cease to exist across most personal and small business lines.[71] This change would be transformative.

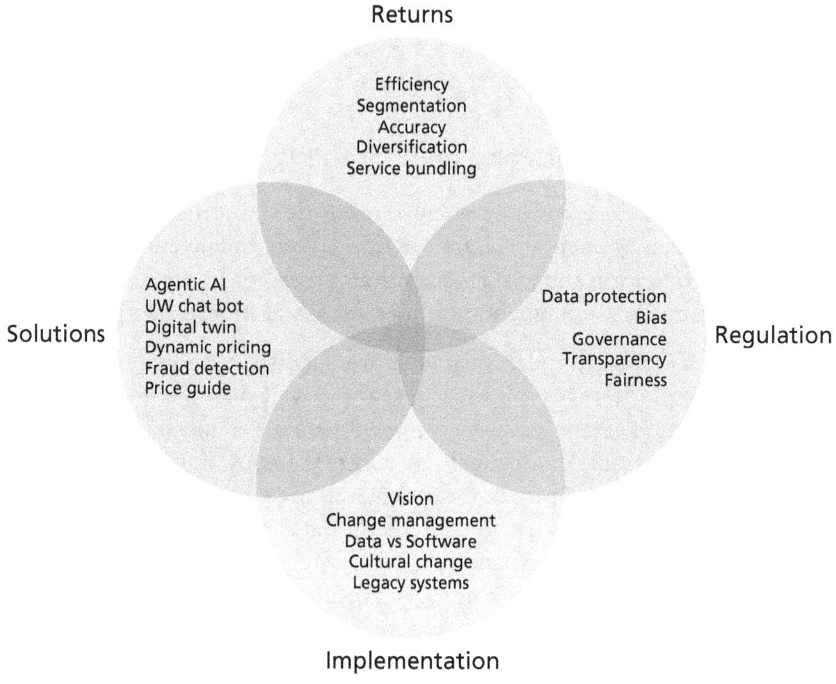

Fig. 2: AI in underwriting: Balancing the impact of technology

However, as discussed in the introduction, AI is not an out-of-the-box technology. For all the solutions that AI, in a narrow or broad sense, can bring to the table, insurers must balance innovation in underwriting with implementation, regulation and ultimately the profitability of the technology. For all the great potential of GenAI, for example, regulators will have to be convinced of its use in decision-making processes; underwriters must have the skills to fully utilise the technology; and returns from efficiencies, better decisions or new income streams need to exceed investment costs. Technology is only one of

70 *Frey KB et al,* The future of employment (2017).
71 *Balasubramanian R et al,* Insurance 2030 – The impact of AI (2021).

the factors at play. It will certainly bring change and contribute to the modernisation of the underwriting process—our conclusions suggest this change will be incremental rather than transformative.

VI. Appendix: A practical guide to implement AI into underwriting

The successful integration of AI into underwriting requires balancing strategic enabling capacities with steps in practical execution. Insurers who build strong data, governance and skill foundations while carefully executing targeted use cases will achieve sustainable value, compliance, and customer trust.

A. Strategic enablers (what to build)

- **Data quality:** Reliable, representative, and unbiased data must be continuously cleaned and validated.
- **Data systems and infrastructure:** Scalable, integrated platforms are essential to handle diverse data and support AI at scale.
- **Skills, expertise, and change management:** Success depends on blending business process knowledge with digital fluency, supported by reskilling and organizational readiness.
- **Regulatory compliance and ethics:** Dedicated teams and robust validation frameworks are needed to meet evolving requirements (GDPR, EU AI Act).
- **Bias, fairness, and risk of exclusion:** AI models must be governed to avoid exclusionary practices and systemic bias.
- **Security and data privacy:** Protect systems from breaches and ensure compliance with privacy rights and frameworks.
- **Governance and accountability:** Maintain inventories of AI use cases, ensure lifecycle management, plan for vendor dependency risks, and establish ethical oversight boards.

B. Practical execution steps (how to build)[72]

- **Start small:** Define and rank use cases, beginning with quick wins.
- **Set objectives:** Clarify whether AI is intended to speed decisions, reduce loss ratios, or achieve other outcomes.
- **Define clear KPIs:** Use measurable benchmarks and align stakeholder expectations.

72 *INSLY*, Artificial intelligence in insurance underwriting (accessed 27.1.2026).

- **Embed risk management:** Identify risks early and implement mitigation strategies from the outset.
- **Digitise relevant data and processes:** Ensure the right data sources and governance is in place to feed AI models.
- **Invest in specialist skills:** Upskill staff, hire expertise, or collaborate with universities and external partners.
- **Maximise off-the-shelf tools:** Leverage proven AI solutions rather than reinventing them from scratch.
- **Test, and test again:** Apply iterative testing and validation, recognising AI deployment as a process of trial and refinement.

References and resources

Acemoglu D, The Simple Macroeconomics of AI, NBER (2024)

Balasubramanian R et al, Insurance 2030 – The impact of AI on the future of insurance (2021)

Bohn J et al, Machine intelligence in insurance: insights for end-to-end enterprise transformation, Swiss Re, sigma, no 05 (2020)

Boguslawski G et al, Lemonade: Mini-Case Study Report, UNL Raikes Seniors (2025)

Bronovytska Y, Deepfakes as Digital Propaganda: The Russian Case in the War in Ukraine, Conflict Justice Decolonisation (2024)

Chen H et al, Finance worker pays out $25 million after video call with deep fake CFO, CNN (2024)

Ctech, The King and AI: Elvis vs copyright infringement (2024)

Devrise I et al, Insuring Generative AI: Risks and Mitigation Strategies, Munich Re (2024)

FDA, AI-Enabled Medical Devices (accessed 27.1.2026)

FootAnstey, Like Company v Google Ireland: Copyright law at technological crossroads (2025).

Forbes, What Air Canada Lost in 'Remarkable' Lying AI Chatbot Case (2024)

The Future of Life Institute, Pause Giant AI Experiments: An Open Letter (2023)

Frey KB, et al, The future of employment: How susceptible are jobs to computerisation? Technological Forecasting and Social Change, vol 114, pp 254–280 (2017), https://doi.org/10.1016/j.techfore.2016.08.019

Fullbrook D, AI Summit brings Elon Musk and world leaders to Bletchley Park, BBC (2023)

Geneva Centre for Security Policy, Ten Lessons from the Russia-Ukraine War (2025)

Greis J et al, The cybersecurity provider's next opportunity: Making AI safer, McKinsey (2024)

Hunton, How Insurance Policies are Adapting to AI Risk (2025)

IEEE, IEEE Standard for Algorithmic Bias Considerations (accessed 27.1.2026)

INSLY, Artificial intelligence in insurance underwriting – a revolution is underway (accessed 27.1.2026)

Klintworth K, Rethinking health insurance: vitality health claims insights, Vitality (2024)

Knesebeck von dem A et al, Cyber Insurance Risk and Trends 2025, Munich Re (2025)

Kolodny L, Tesla must pay portion of $329 million in damages after fatal Autopilot crash, jury says, *CNBC* (2025)

Krantz T et al, What is shadow AI, IBM (2024)

Lemonade, Lemonade delivers AI-powered insurance (accessed 27.1.2026)

Loveland Innovations, A Brief History of AI in the P&C Insurance Industry (accessed 27.1.2026)

Magnusson, OpenAI's Copyright Shield – Peace of Mind for Some from Something (2023)

MAS, MAS-led Industry Consortium Publishes Assessment Methodologies for Responsible Use of AI by Financial Institutions, Monetary Authority of Singapore, Media Release (2022)

MAS, Principles to Promote Fairness, Ethics, Accountability and Transparency (FEAT) in the Use of Artificial Intelligence and Data Analytics in Singapore's Financial Sector (accessed 27.1.2026)

Milinkovich N et al, The future of AI in the insurance industry, McKinsey (2025)

Mills E, What are insurance deserts and what are their implications for business and people? WEF (2025)

Monks K et al, New business and underwriting systems: North America life insurance edition, CELENT (2024)

MOVE, ManulifeMOVE, inspiring your every step, every move (accessed 27.1.2026)

Munich Re, Cyber Insurance Risk and Trends 2025 (2025)

NAIC, Big data and artificial intelligence working group meeting (2025)

NIST, AI Risk Management Framework (accessed 27.1.2026)

Noordhoek D, Regulation of Artificial Intelligence in Insurance, The Geneva Association (2023)

OECD, AI Principles (2024)

Paxton K, Attorney General Ken Paxton Reaches Settlement in First-of-its-Kind Healthcare Generative AI Investigation (2024)

Philips B, Telematics and usage-based insurance: what's changing and what consumers really think, The Zebra (accessed 27.1.2026)

Rajamohan W, What went wrong with data-driven car insurance—and how to fix it, Smartcar (2024) (accessed 24.9.2025)

The Register, Tesla facing another Autopilot fatality lawsuite (2024)

Reuters Institute for the Study of Journalism, How AI is reshaping copyright law and what it means for the news industry (2025)

Rodriguez Sanz C et al, Generative AI: An insurer's perspective on the promises and perils, AXA (2025)

Roots, State of AI Adoption in Insurance 2025, Roots.ai (2025)

Shrier D et al, AI could add 10% to global GDP by 2032, Chatham House (2023)

Shreves AH et al, Amount and intensity of daily total physical activity, step count and risk of incident cancer in the UK Biobank, British journal of sports medicine vol. 59,12 839–847 (2025), doi:10.1136/bjsports-2024-109360

Smith D, Widely used AI tool for early sepsis detection may be cribbing doctors' suspicions, University of Michigan News (2024)

Social Media Victims Law Center, AI Chatbot Lawsuit Clears Key Legal Hurdle in Landmark Case (2025)

Suhrada S et al, Providing insurance coverage for artificial intelligence may be a blue ocean opportunity, Deloitte (2024)

Swiss Re, Swiss Re's Magnum: Automated underwriting platform (accessed 27.1.2026)

Swiss Re, Life Guide: moving forward in life (accessed 27.1.2026)

Swiss Re Institute, AI—unintended insurance impacts and lessons from silent cyber, Swiss Re (2024) (accessed 27.1.2026)

Thales, How do AI and Cloud Computing affect Security Risks, Cloud Security Alliance (2024)

Todoroff N et al, How your insurance company is using AI (and why you should care), Bankrate (2024)

TopClassActions, Lemonade insurance biometric privacy USD4 million class action settlement (2022) (accessed 27.1.2026)

University of Michigan News, Widely used AI tool for early sepsis detection may be cribbing doctors' suspicions (2024)

Uuk R et al, A Taxonomy of Systemic Risks from General-Purpose AI (2024)

Vigliarolo B, Tesla facing another Autopilot fatality lawsuite, The Register (2024)

Vitality, Our mission in action (accessed 27.1.2026)

Wikipedia, Mycin, https://en.wikipedia.org/wiki/Mycin (accessed 27.1.2026)

Wired, Every AI Copyright Lawsuit in the US Visualised (accessed 27.1.2026)

Zych J, AI in insurance: developing a robust AI/ML strategy, Guidehouse (2024)

Artificial intelligence as a lever for "inclusive insurance": How AI can improve access to insurance coverage

Thomas Münkel
Insurance Manager

Abstract: This article discusses the use of AI as a lever to improve access to insurance coverage for disadvantaged population groups, i. e. AI for improving inclusive insurance. The potential customer groups are described and the main barriers to the implementation of inclusive insurance are examined. It becomes clear that AI can make an important contribution to overcoming all these barriers, enabling people, especially in developing countries, to gain better access to often urgently needed insurance cover. Numerous examples are used to describe use cases that demonstrate the successful implementation of such AI solutions in practice.

Keywords: Digitalisation, artificial intelligence, inclusive insurance, financial inclusion, access to insurance cover, Sustainable Development Goals, Geneva Association, International Association of Insurance Supervisors, risk prevention, awareness, accessibility, availability, affordability, microinsurance, gig economy, insurtech, embedded insurance, pay-per-use, peer-to-peer

Contents

https://doi.org/10.33196/9783704698520-109

I. Introduction: What is "inclusive insurance"?

One aspect that rarely comes up in current discussions about AI is its potential to make it easier for disadvantaged groups to access insurance cover, thereby making a significant contribution to a better and safer life. The term "inclusive insurance" is regularly used in this context. What does it mean? Since the term "inclusive insurance" is used in different contexts, let's start by explaining what it does not mean: it does not refer to additional coverage in an insurance policy, the bundling of insurance policies in a single policy, or a package of insurance with other services. Rather, inclusive insurance focuses on enabling or at least facilitating access to insurance coverage for underserved populations. In this sense, inclusive insurance is part of financial inclusion, which aims to give all population groups access to basic financial services regardless of their socio-economic or socio-demographic status. In a 2015 paper on inclusive insurance[1], the International Association of Insurance Supervisors (IAIS) highlighted its core areas:

- The specific customer profile for inclusive insurance.
- The country-specific context and market conditions.
- The various forms of distribution for inclusive insurance.
- The digitisation of transactions in inclusive insurance.

This article aims to show that artificial intelligence (AI) can make an important contribution in these areas, enabling underserved populations to gain better access to insurance protection and close important gaps in coverage. Who are these customer groups?

II. The customers of inclusive insurance

For most people in wealthy countries, insurance is probably more of a necessary evil than a welcome safeguard.[2] In many poorer countries, however, insurance cover is a barely attainable commodity for the majority of people, one that could protect them from the ravages of severe natural events (e.g. storms, heavy rain, floods, earthquakes, droughts) and make their lives a little more predictable

1 *International Association of Insurance Supervisors (IAIS)*, Issues Paper on Conduct of Business in Inclusive Insurance (2015): https://uk.practicallaw.thomsonreuters.com/2-619-4406?transitionType=Default&contextData=(sc.Default)&firstPage=true (accessed 21.11.2025).

2 The often underestimated potential of insurance solutions for achieving the UN's goals for general sustainable development should be mentioned here; see, for example, *L. Hall/P. Walsh*, Insurance and Sustainable Development: Partnering on Risk, Resilience, and Transformation (2025): DOI:10.25546/111474.

and secure—if only they had access to it. People in developing countries are certainly the largest potential customer group worldwide for inclusive insurance.

But inclusive insurance is also an increasingly important issue in wealthy countries: in a representative survey conducted in 2024, the *Geneva Association*[3] examined seven economically strong countries, focusing on six population groups for whom inclusive insurance could be important: older people, Generation Z, the chronically ill, the self-employed, people on low incomes and immigrants. One finding was that Generation Z and poorer population groups in particular tend to have insufficient[4] insurance cover, especially in terms of (private) health insurance and home insurance. So even in wealthy Europe, inclusive insurance is a relevant issue!

And (affordable) insurance cover against natural disasters such as storms, droughts or floods is becoming an increasingly serious problem for almost all population groups in many countries, driven in part by the consequences of climate change. So how can AI help in these different areas?

According to the *Geneva Association*[5], the following "4 A's" describe the biggest barriers to implementing inclusive insurance:

- **Awareness**: Problems arise from a lack of information or financial education, as well as a lack of risk awareness. AI is a good tool for improving knowledge transfer.
- **Accessibility**: Problems arise due to complex products, a lack of (financial) education or a lack of distribution structures. AI can enable or at least simplify access to insurance cover in the first place.
- **Availability**: Problems with a limited product range due to asymmetric information, lack of data, complex insurance regulations. AI facilitates the availability of insurance cover.
- **Affordability**: Probably the biggest hurdle to inclusive insurance. AI is an important lever for reducing costs.

Let's take a closer look at the AI solutions for these barriers:

3 *Geneva Association,* Inclusive Insurance in Advanced Economies (2024): www.genevaassociation.org/sites/default/files/2024-11/inclusive_report_1911_digital.pdf (accessed 21.11.2025).

4 "insufficient" is derived here from the difference between the average insurance coverage of a country and the coverage of certain population groups (Gen Z, poor people, migrants, etc.) in that country.

5 Inclusive Insurance in Advanced Economies (2024) 28 ff: www.genevaassociation.org/sites/default/files/2024-11/inclusive_report_1911_digital.pdf (accessed 21.11.2025).

A. "Awareness": Better information through the use of AI

Before we can think about inclusive insurance offerings, people first need the necessary information: What risks can I protect myself against with insurance? What is insurance? What is risk prevention? What do I really need? Are there suitable, affordable insurance solutions? Can I trust these offerings? etc.

Even if there are suitable products at affordable prices, people still need to know about them and understand what they involve. Take **agriculture**, for example: in the poorer countries of the Global South in particular, a functioning local agricultural sector is a basic prerequisite for sheer survival. Local farmers face multiple challenges here:

Frequent natural disasters: Droughts, floods and storms have been a constant threat capable of destroying entire harvests in a short space of time, and not just since the acceleration of climate change.

Lack of knowledge about risks and insurance options: This is not just a matter of general, theoretical knowledge, but also of practical information about flood risks, weather developments and the consequences of pesticide use. It is also about (permitted) access to this information.

Lack of language skills: If the local smallholder does not understand the offer because he only speaks a local dialect or cannot read, what use is the offer?

The extent of the need for insurance can be seen from the fact that 90 % of all farms in Asia (excluding India and China), Africa and Latin America are uninsured.[6] Can AI really help here? Well, the non-profit tech organisation *Digital Green*, for example, has developed FarmerChat, an AI-powered chatbot[7] that enables farmers to receive information in their local dialect and in everyday language about risks to their crops (e.g., impending droughts or the consequences of using various pesticides) and possible remedies: AI, combined with local expertise and feedback from farmers, helps to prevent risks.

Digital Green is also attempting to reduce the problem of discrimination against women: although women are often the actual drivers of agriculture, they regularly face disadvantages in terms of access to information and decision-making[8].

---

6 *Salman/Shastri/Fernandez Vidal*, The Role of Data in Inclusive Insurance (2024) www.cgap.org/research/role-of-data-in-inclusive-insurance.

7 *Digital Green*: https://digitalgreen.org/farmer.chat/ (accessed 21.11.2025).

8 See, for example, *Microinsurance Network*, The Landscape of Microinsurance (2024): www.rfilc.org/wp-content/uploads/2025/03/The-Landscape-of-Microinsurance-2024.pdf (accessed 21.11.2025) according to which women are significantly less likely to be reached if insurance is provided through traditional agricultural cooperatives, for example. Or the current legislation in Mali, according to which the

FarmerChat aims to remedy this situation as well. The bot is mostly used through speech rather than text. The organisation also cooperates with local communities and women's organisations.

And the result? *Digital Green* reports on a study finding that 96 % of women report greater confidence in decision-making after using FarmerChat. Impact according to *Digital Green*: 8.2 million farmers reached (43 % women), 80 % implementation of recommendations, 17 % higher crop yields, 24 % increase in income.[9]

B. Accessibility: Improved access to insurance coverage with inclusive insurance through AI

This opens up a wide field for the use of AI across all insurance sectors and countries. Due to the wealth of topics, only a few examples will be briefly outlined here to illustrate the diverse range of possible applications:

Case-study 1: Overcoming the distribution problem through digital platforms in conjunction with AI-supported customer interfaces (e.g., voice bots (text to speech, etc.)), as well as simplifying and improving the product range: In a systematic experiment in Mali[10], using an approach similar to FarmerChat, it was demonstrated that small farmers are willing (and able) to take out crop failure insurance if they receive an easy-to-understand product offering via mobile phone that combines insurance cover with weather information and advice on improving maize cultivation.

Case-study 2: Improved monitoring of potential flood areas with more precise sensors, mapping, evaluation of historical data, etc.[11] In this area, AI can fully exploit its strengths in evaluating huge and complex data structures. This makes risks more insurable (residential buildings, fields, commercial properties, etc.) in areas that were previously classified as uninsurable across the board. This is also an important issue in many places in Europe, such as the flooding

husband is the head of the household by law (No. 2011-087) and the wife must be subordinate to the husband: *FIDH (Fédération internationale des ligues des droits de l'Homme),* Le nouveau Code de la famille au Mali: une véritable régression pour les droits des femmes (2012): www.fidh.org/fr/regions/afrique/mali/Le-nouveau-Code-de-la-famille-au (accessed 21.11.2025).

9 *Digital Green*, https://digitalgreen.org/global-impact/ (accessed 21.11.2025).

10 *Kirchner/Musshoff*, Digital opportunities for the distribution of index-based microinsurance: Evidence from a discrete choice experiment in Mali, Journal of Agricultural Economics, 75/2/2024: https://doi.org/10.1111/1477-9552.12584.

11 *Liu/Coleman et al*, Artificial Intelligence for Flood Risk Management: A Comprehensive State-of-the-Art Review and Future Directions, International Journal of Disaster Risk Reduction, Vol 117 (2025): https://doi.org/10.1016/j.ijdrr.2024.105110.

in the Ahr Valley in Germany, heavy rainfall events in northern Italy or the flood areas of the Danube, to name just a few examples.

Case-study 3: Improved access to insurance cover for small businesses: In Malaysia, *VSureTech* has developed an app-based insurance platform for various insurance lines, all of which aim to enable micro and small businesses to insure themselves through flexible and affordable "pay-per-use" or "on-demand" package solutions. This platform (which also offers Sharia-compliant peer-to-peer solutions) was recognised as the best digital innovation by the United Nations Development Programme (UNDP) at the end of 2024[12] because it gives small business operators in Malaysia a new kind of access to insurance cover that was previously almost unthinkable. *VSureTech* uses AI for automated risk assessments, fraud detection, real-time claims processing and, of course, customer service (chatbots, etc).

C. "Availability": How AI can increase the availability of insurance coverage

The lack of health insurance coverage is perhaps the biggest problem worldwide when it comes to inclusive insurance across all insurance sectors. Examples come to mind in the USA, Europe and, of course, especially in developing countries. The issue is addressed in the UN's 17 Sustainable Development Goals[13], but so far, multiple obstacles have prevented better availability of health insurance in many regions: lack of hospitals, lack of staff, difficult transport conditions, inadequate technical equipment, etc. As a result, more than half of the population on the African continent, for example, has no health insurance coverage. AI can help on many fronts here[14]: AI-supported risk assessment, AI-automated claims processing, AI for fraud detection to expose cases of abuse and thus conserve resources in rural regions, personalised insurance offers, AI-supported direct contact with doctors and specialists, etc.

People in the gig economy make a living by repeatedly taking on short-term, flexible jobs (gigs), which they usually find via digital platforms. These are not only "IT migrant workers," but also drivers for delivery services or ride-hailing services such as *Uber*. Their access to insurance cover is often very limited, as

12 *UNDP*, UNDP and Generali Announce the Winning Solution of the SME Insurance Innovation Challenge in Malaysia (6.11.2024): https://irff.undp.org/news/undp-and-generali-announce-winning-solution-sme-insurance-innovation-challenge-malaysia (accessed 21.11.2025).

13 UN Sustainable Development Goals: https://sdgs.un.org/goals (accessed 21.11.2025).

14 See, for example *Adewole et al*, Leveraging AI to improve health insurance access and address disparities in rural Africa, Journal of Medicine, Surgery, and Public Health, Vol 5 (2025): https://doi.org/10.1016/j.glmedi.2024.100172.

their risk profile is difficult to assess (frequently changing activities, places of residence, general conditions). Here as well are insurtech companies that use AI to make insurance cover available to this target group in a new form: the insurtech company *Zego*[15], for example, offers motor insurance cover via its platform for couriers, driving and delivery services, among others. In order to provide solutions that are individualised, risk-appropriate and affordable, it uses the motion sensors of smartphones via smartphone apps. Zego collects data on braking behaviour, acceleration, cornering, etc. *Zego's* use of AI is similar to the examples mentioned earlier: AI-supported risk modelling and pricing. AI for claims settlement and fraud detection. AI-based customer service.

So we can see that providers in many markets and regions are essentially using a similar set of AI solutions to make inclusive insurance available to new and particularly affected target groups.

D. Affordability: cost reduction through AI in inclusive insurance

Excessive costs are almost always cited as the main reason[16] why people cannot afford the insurance cover they urgently need. Here, digitalisation, including the use of AI, can help to significantly reduce costs, e.g., in terms of sales and marketing costs, operating costs or claims settlement costs. This works particularly well when digitalisation is being promoted comprehensively in a country or region, as this further reduces the costs of unavoidable external services and enables, for example, the widespread use of mobile phones with AI solutions. Think of Scandinavia or the example of India described in the next section, but also of sub-Saharan African countries, where good mobile phone coverage and access to smartphones must compensate for the otherwise often inadequate infrastructure. This book discusses the potential for cost reduction through AI in many places. Therefore, only a few areas that are particularly relevant for inclusive insurance are briefly highlighted below:

- **Acquisition costs:** Elimination or reduction of acquisition costs through direct AI-supported interaction between provider and end customer, without intermediaries[17], but also a significant reduction in the time required for intermediaries or other costs associated with the conclusion of a contract[18].

15 Zego: www.zego.com/.

16 See, for example *Geneva Association,* Inclusive Insurance in Advanced Economies (2024) 25: www.genevaassociation.org/sites/default/files/2024-11/inclusive_report_1911_digital.pdf (accessed 21.11.2025).

17 See also the India example in the next section.

18 See again the example of India for KYC costs.

- **Marketing costs:** Reduction of costs through much more targeted, tailored marketing, often directly to potential end customers.
- **Risk costs:** Reduction through better data analysis (data quality, data scope), more targeted risk profiles — see examples from *Zego* or *VSureTech*.
- **Administrative costs:** Especially in the back office — see Brian Walsh's comments in this book.[19]
- **Claims settlement costs:** Reduction of claims processing costs through complete automation, often in real time. Reduction of claims costs through fraud detection, which is often only possible on a large scale and cost-effectively through AI, etc.

The total cost reduction potential is estimated at a minimum of 25–40 %, with economies of scale having a particularly strong effect in the case of AI-supported platforms in conjunction with mobile devices.

III. The country-specific context and market conditions

The country-specific context has already been addressed in several examples in the previous sections. Therefore, only two further particularly comprehensive approaches will be listed here:

A. Example: India

India is a huge country with massive challenges, but also remarkable progress in improving financial inclusion — through digitalisation. In a working paper published in 2023, the *International Monetary Fund* (IMF)[20] reported that closing costs for financial institutions (including insurers) in India have fallen dramatically thanks to a universally accessible platform for instant digital payments and a biometric ID system. For example, KYC costs[21] fell from USD 12 to USD 0.06, a reduction to 0.5 % of the initial value!

This was made possible by a government initiative for a digital public infrastructure (India's DPI), which gave millions of Indians access to financial services, as the DPI drastically reduced costs for providers and these savings were passed on to customers. AI further reduces these costs by automating processes, enabling cost-effective analysis of large amounts of data and thus simpler and more targeted underwriting.

---

19 *Walsh*, AI in Back Office Automation and Regulatory Reporting (in this volume) 143 ff.

20 *Alonso et al*, Stacking up the Benefits: Lessons from India's Digital Journey", IMF Working Papers 2023, 078 (2023): https://doi.org/10.5089/9798400240416.001.

21 KYC = "Know Your Customer", i. e. necessary information about the customer.

Another special feature of India is its linguistic diversity, with 22 official languages and over 2,200 dialects. Here, AI-supported multilingualism is being used in a targeted manner[22] to promote access to inclusive insurance and other services in general by responding very specifically to the individual (language) needs of potential customers.

B. Example: Brazil

Brazil is systematically promoting the use of AI[23], with a clear focus on using AI to improve financial inclusion. The digital payment system *PIX* introduced by the central bank has already proven to be a successful tool for this purpose[24]. And the introduction of the "digital real"[25] announced in October 2025, with its offline functionality, is being hailed as a "breakthrough" for access to financial services for previously underserved populations, especially in Brazil's many hard-to-reach areas.

In this context, it is hardly surprising to find providers of AI-supported solutions for inclusive insurance. For example, *Justos*, an insurtech company acting as an MGA, offers AI-based motor insurance, whereby driving behaviour is monitored by smartphone sensors and more cautious driving is rewarded with lower premiums. T*hinkseg* from Sao Paulo offers similar services, including pay-per-use insurance.[26] The insurtech company *Azos* offers AI-supported life insurance. *Icatu Seguros*,[27] on the other hand, is the largest independent life insurer in Brazil with 2.5 million customers. *Icatu* uses deep learning models for risk analysis in micro life insurance and health insurance, focusing on small businesses, women and families in rural areas of Brazil.

22 *Priyanka/Westley/Jagdish*, Multilingualism as strategy, Marketing Strategy Journal, Volume 4 (2025): https://doi.org/10.1016/j.msj.2025.100011.

23 See, for example, the Brazilian government's AI strategy published in June 2025 which appears to be published only in Portuguese: www.gov.br/mcti/pt-br/acompanhe-o-mcti/noticias/2025/06/plano-brasileiro-de-inteligencia-artificial-pbia-_vf.pdf (accessed 21.11.2025). A helpful summary is available at Brazil—Launches the Brazilian Artificial Intelligence Plan 2024–2028 | Investment Policy Monitor | UNCTAD Investment Policy Hub (accessed 21.11.2025).

24 *Germer*, The Pix Effect: How It's Driving Financial Inclusion and Boosting Brazil's GDP (2025) www.pagbrasil.com/blog/experts-point-of-view/the-pix-effect-how-its-driving-financial-inclusion-and-boosting-brazils-gdp/ (accessed 21.11.2025).

25 *Eberle*, Brasiliens digitaler Real vor dem Durchbruch: DREX soll das Bargeld für über 200 Millionen Menschen ablösen (2025): https://maresmedia.se/brasiliens-digitaler-real-vor-dem-durchbruch-drex-soll-das-bargeld-fuer-ueber-200-millionen-menschen-abloesen/ (accessed 21.11.2025).

26 See also the "Zego" example above.

27 Icatu Seguros: www.icatu.com.br/index_en.html.

The list could go on and on for other countries. But the two examples mentioned should give a sufficient idea of where the potential and focus for AI-promoted inclusive insurance is seen, especially in developing countries.

IV. The distribution problem with inclusive insurance

In many use cases, AI is the decisive lever for bridging the gap between the insurer with its offerings and the potential end customer. This distribution gap is very often closed by reaching end customers directly via their mobile phones. Not only in Europe, but especially in the countries of the Global South, this is often the only (and very good) solution[28] to the distribution problem.

But AI is also being used successfully to support sales units in brokering inclusive insurance policies. One example is Lami, an insurtech company from Kenya[29], which uses its AI-supported digital platform in a B2B2C business model to enable intermediaries to sell insurance policies. The intermediaries in this case are local banks, retailers or logistics companies that integrate insurance coverage into their existing offerings. This may sound very familiar, as such business models are well known in Europe. But such approaches are much more important for the success of inclusive insurance in developing countries: Of course, *Lami's* success is not only based on its sales approach and broad network of partnerships, but also on AI-supported solutions for tailor-made and affordable products, innovative products for the specific needs of African markets (e.g., inexpensive per-trip transit insurance for transport companies) and an API-based platform.

Other sales models particularly suited to the distribution of inclusive insurance using AI include:

- Embedded insurance, with offers personalised by AI.
- Chatbot-based distribution (see, for example, FarmerChat above).
- Mobile and IoT-based microinsurance (see the examples from the motor insurance sector)
- AI-supported peer-to-peer and community models, in which AI manages collective risk pools and organises payouts in microinsurance groups. (Example: Insurtech *Loovi* from Brazil[30]).

It is therefore clear that AI solutions can reduce the distribution problem precisely where inclusive insurance offerings are particularly important.

28 Of course, access to smartphones is a challenge in itself for people in these countries.
29 Lami: www.lami.world/.
30 Loovi: Motor insurance with community pooling: https://loovi.com.br/.

V. Conclusion

Artificial intelligence is often perceived as a threat or something negative[31]. However, AI can fully exploit its positive aspects in the area of inclusive insurance: AI can make a valuable contribution and help insurance fulfil its core task of providing protection and assistance via a risk community where individuals are overwhelmed, particularly where previous insurance solutions have failed and there are large, often existential gaps in coverage for large sections of the population.

References and resources

Adewole, Akingbola, et al.: Leveraging AI to improve health insurance access and address disparities in rural Africa, Journal of Medicine, Surgery, and Public Health 5/2025, doi.org/10.1016/j.glmedi.2024.100172

Alonso et al, Stacking up the Benefits: Lessons from India's Digital Journey", IMF Working Papers 2023, 078 (2023): doi.org/10.5089/9798400240416.001

Digital Green: https://digitalgreen.org/ (accessed 21.11.2025)

Eberle, Brasiliens digitaler Real vor dem Durchbruch: DREX soll das Bargeld für über 200 Millionen Menschen ablösen (2025): https://maresmedia.se/brasiliens-digitaler-real-vor-dem-durchbruch-drex-soll-das-bargeld-fuer-ueber-200-millionen-menschen-abloesen/ (accessed 21.11.2025)

FIDH (Fédération internationale des ligues des droits de l'Homme), Le nouveau Code de la famille au Mali: une véritable régression pour les droits des femmes (2012): www.fidh.org/fr/regions/afrique/mali/Le-nouveau-Code-de-la-famille-au (accessed 21.11.2025)

Geneva Association, Inclusive Insurance in Advanced Economies (2024): /www.genevaassociation.org/sites/default/files/2024-11/inclusive_report_1911_digital.pdf (accessed 21.11.2025)

L. Hall/P. Walsh, Insurance and Sustainable Development: Partnering on Risk, Resilience, and Transformation (2025): DOI:10.25546/111474

Germer, The Pix Effect: How It's Driving Financial Inclusion and Boosting Brazil's GDP (2025): www.pagbrasil.com/blog/experts-point-of-view/the-pix-effect-how-its-driving-financial-inclusion-and-boosting-brazils-gdp/ (accessed 21.11.2025)

International Association of Insurance Supervisors (IAIS), Issues Paper on Conduct of Business in Inclusive Insurance (2015): https://uk.practicallaw.thomsonreuters.com/2-619-4406?transitionType=Default&contextData=(sc.Default)&firstPage=true (accessed 21.11.2025)

31 The risks of AI are by no means overlooked or ignored!

Kirchner/Musshoff, Digital opportunities for the distribution of index-based microinsurance: Evidence from a discrete choice experiment in Mali, Journal of Agricultural Economics, 75/2/2024: doi.org/10.1111/1477-9552.12584

Liu/Coleman et al, Artificial Intelligence for Flood Risk Management: A Comprehensive State-of-the-Art Review and Future Directions, International Journal of Disaster Risk Reduction, Vol 117 (2025): doi.org/10.1016/j.ijdrr.2024.105110

Microinsurance Network, The Landscape of Microinsurance (2024): www.rfilc.org/wp-content/uploads/2025/03/The-Landscape-of-Microinsurance-2024.pdf (accessed 21.11.2025)

Priyanka/Westley/Jagdish, Multilingualism as strategy - AI-enabled STP for inclusive market development in emerging economies, Marketing Strategy Journal, Vol 4 (2025): doi.org/10.1016/j.msj.2025.100011

Salman/Shastri/Fernandez Vidal, The Role of Data in Inclusive Insurance (2024): www.cgap.org/research/role-of-data-in-inclusive-insurance (accessed 21.11.2025)

UNDP, UNDP and Generali Announce the Winning Solution of the SME Insurance Innovation Challenge in Malaysia (6.11.2024): https://irff.undp.org/news/undp-and-generali-announce-winning-solution-sme-insurance-innovation-challenge-malaysia (accessed 21.11.2025)

AI in the insurance industry—myth or already part of the daily business of an insurer

Michael Zimmer
Chief Data and AI Officer, W&W Group

Abstract: This chapter examines the use of Artificial Intelligence (AI) in the insurance industry and illustrates, through practical examples, how AI is already integrated into various processes today. After a brief introduction to the specifics of the main insurance segments, the lifecycle of an insurance product is presented to facilitate the classification of AI use cases. The examples range from product development to underwriting, policy administration, and claims handling. Both traditional descriptive methods and modern approaches such as Generative AI are discussed. The chapter highlights that AI not only contributes to automation but also serves as an assistive system for complex decision-making. Finally, opportunities, challenges, and regulatory aspects essential for the successful implementation of AI in insurance companies are addressed.

Keywords: Artificial Intelligence, Insurance Industry, Product Lifecycle, Underwriting, Claims Handling, Generative AI, Document Extraction, Voicebots, Fraud Detection, Automation, Augmentation

Contents

https://doi.org/10.33196/9783704698520-110

I. Introduction

Artificial intelligence (AI) has been seen by companies as a solution to almost all challenges for several years now. The miraculous hype about almost magical technological has reached conservative areas such as the insurance sector. While big data[1] used to be the hype in the past, today it is about AI[2], GPT[3] and Agentic AI[4]. Nevertheless, it seems that only a few players are using AI consciously, purposefully and successfully. There is a need for improvement in order to highlight the existing potential of AI in the insurance industry and to show the path already taken by insurers to optimise existing business models with AI.

The chapter briefly presents the specifics of different insurance sectors and relates them to the possibilities of AI. Furthermore, a generic insurance process is introduced, on the basis of which AI use cases are presented and categorized as brief case studies.

II. Insurance is insurance, isn't it?

If we consider insurance as a product, people outside the insurance industry usually have an existing view on the insurance industry that is characterised by the products of personal lines. However, the heterogeneity of our industry

1 "Big data is traditionally characterized by the "three V's": volume, velocity, and variety. Volume naturally refers to the large size of such datasets; velocity refers to the speed with which such data are produced and analyzed; and variety refers to the many different types of data, which can be in text, audio, video, or other forms. (Two further V's are sometimes added: value, referring to the usefulness of the data; and veracity, referring to the data's truthfulness.)" *Gregersen, E.*, "big data." Encyclopedia Britannica (2025): www.britannica.com/technology/big-data (accessed 24.11.2025).

2 "artificial intelligence (AI), the ability of a digital computer or computer-controlled robot to perform tasks commonly associated with intelligent beings." *Copeland*, B., "artificial intelligence." Encyclopedia Britannica (2025): www.britannica.com/technology/artificial-intelligence (accessed 24.11.2025).

3 "Generative Pre-trained Transformer (GPT) represents a notable breakthrough in the domain of natural language processing, which is propelling us toward the development of machines that can understand and communicate using language in a manner that closely resembles that of humans. GPT is based on the transformer architecture, a deep neural network designed for natural language processing tasks." *Yenduri/Ramalingam/Selvi/Supriya et al*, IEEE Access, Vol. 12, pp. 54608–54649, (2024): https://ieeexplore.ieee.org/document/10500411.

4 There is no fixed definition. Most commonly it is used for assistants based on LLMs. In the future there will be agents for tasks that act independently.

is often forgotten. All insurance products have the collective concept to share risks in common, but otherwise they can differ essentially. Life insurance, for example, is a long-term investment and financial security product with few points of contact with the customer. What is important here is solid growth of the invested amount over the years. A motor vehicle tariff, on the other hand, is renewed annually. The unique selling point here is a favourable price and good claims handling.

In general, a distinction can be made between life insurance, (private) health insurance, property/casualty insurance and reinsurance based on the products[5]. In addition, there is a further differentiation based on the customer relationship between personal customers and corporate customers.

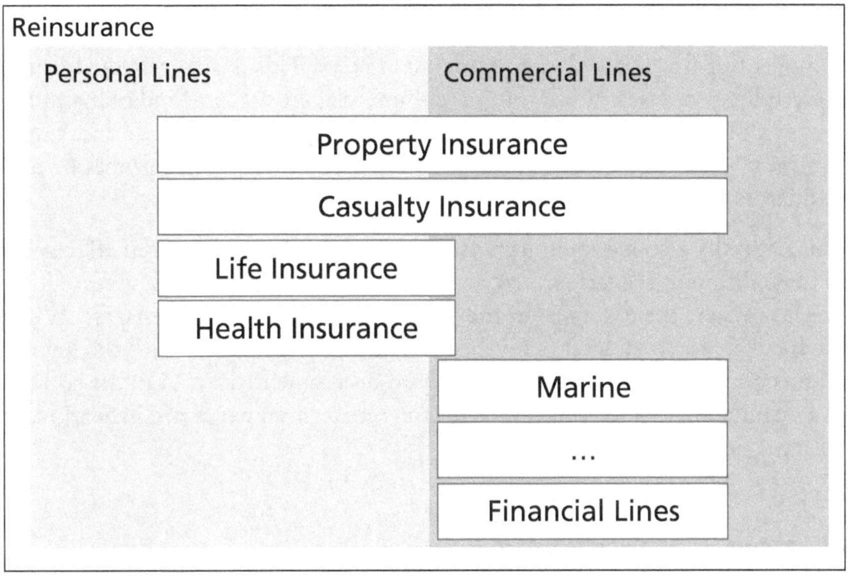

Fig. 1: Differentiation of insurance products

Fig. 1 shows this situation graphically. In general, it can be said that classic insurance products in property and casualty, such as motor vehicle and liabilities, insurance of property and buildings, are used in both personal lines as well as in commercial lines. The difference here, however, is the scope. While personal insurance covers a single vehicle or a single building, industrial insurance covers entire fleets or the entire production facilities of a company.

5 See *Koch*, Versicherungswirtschaft, Chapter 1 or *Oftermatt*, Versicherung, Chapter 2 to Chapter 6.

Life and health insurance is seen here more as traditional personal lines insurance, even if companies insure their employees with occupational disability, occupational pension or private health insurance benefits via framework agreements.

In addition to these product categories, commercial lines also covers other issues such as supply chains or production or harvest failures.

Reinsurance contracts run in the background for all scenarios in order to share risks and ensure protection against major events.

But what is the potential for AI within these lines of business and products? In general, it can be said that large volumes of standardized contracts are processed in the traditional personal lines insurance business, whereas the commercial lines insurance and reinsurance business is dominated by a small number of complex but financially large-volume contracts. This is also reflected in the underlying processes. While (larger) commercial is usually a kind of manufactory with personal relationships, highly specific underwriters and individual contracts, personal insurance is more focused on throughput, automation and standardisation.

This naturally also has an impact on the use of AI. Can AI be used effectively in these different scenarios? The answer to this question is clearly yes. However, it reflects the diversity in the possible AI deployment scenarios. While the focus in personal lines is on the automation of processes with the help of AI, in commercial lines it is more likely to be augmented by AI in the context of a manufactory. What this means in concrete terms is explained in Section IV with the help of case studies.

III. Basic insurance process

Simplified, the life cycle of an insurance product can be mapped with the following core processes.[6]

1) The actuarial department uses historical data to create risk models for the design of new insurance products or services.
2) Once these have been approved by the regulator, they are mapped in the operational portfolio systems and the sales organization is trained.
3) On this basis, agencies, brokers or partners sell the actual insurance product.
4) In the course of this, the steps of application, contract and portfolio management as well as benefits and claims settlement are completed.
   a) As part of the application, basic information is provided by the customer.

6 *Koch*, Versicherungswirtschaft, Chapter 1.

b) This information is checked by the underwriting department in order to be able to submit an offer with a customised price to the customer.
c) Once the contract has been concluded, premiums are calculated and the portfolio is managed.

5) In the event of a claim or the occurrence of a payment, the claim is settled and paid out. Checks are also carried out here. However, these are not carried out by underwriters, but by highly specialised experts.
6) The data obtained in steps 3) to 5) are in turn used to manage the portfolio and result in the recalculation of products, price adjustments and, if necessary, the reorganisation of the portfolio.

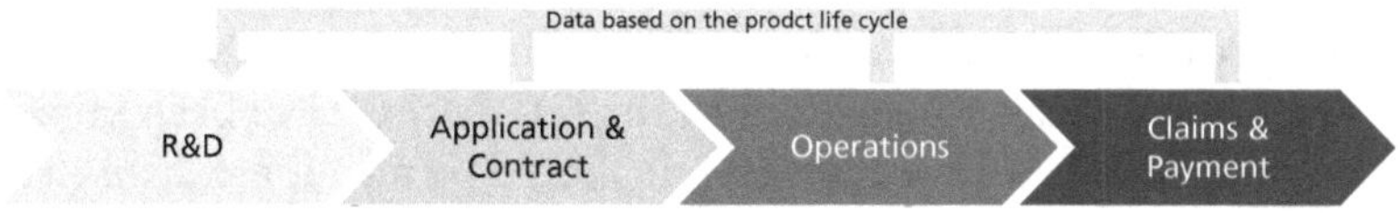

Fig. 2: Product life cycle of an insurance product

This procedure is repeated regularly as part of the product life cycle and cyclical contract renewals. This situation is illustrated in Fig. 2.

The structures in Fig. 2 are used below to illustrate examples of AI use cases and categorise them within the product life cycle.

IV. AI in insurance—some case studies

The following chapter introduces nine examples that present AI within the insurance industry. These are methods of classic descriptive AI, but also generative AI.

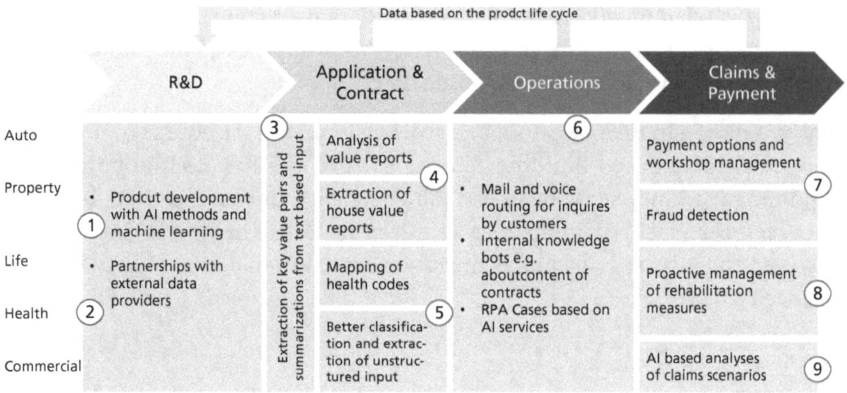

Fig. 3: AI examples in the product life cycle

A. Product development with AI

Mathematical methods have always been used in traditional product development by actuaries to map risks, price models or products. Until this decade, however, linear methods known as simplified linear models (General Linear Models – GLMs) were used here. These are and were explainable and still delivered good results. With the spread of AI, descriptive AI methods have been trialled in the actuarial field in recent years. One example is the use of neural networks in the creation of a pricing model. This shows that AI-based methods can be applied quickly and easily to existing data. AutoML[7] methods in particular, in which different models are automatically applied to existing databases, are of great interest to actuaries. Within a few days or weeks, a model with similar performance compared to the GLMs that have been improved over decades can be created. However, it should be mentioned here that explainability suffers in comparison to a GLM. However, this is essential in our regulated industry. For this reason, neural networks have been used less in the past and linear regressions or tree structures have been expanded with the help of machine learning. This makes it possible to achieve a compromise between explainability and modern models.

B. Partnerships with external providers

External data is of great importance for product design. For example, weather data, sensor data or data on driving behaviour can significantly influence the development of a pricing model. In this context, external partners can help to obtain such information. AI is often used for this purpose.

When processing weather data, providers use AI to create risk maps or predict weather events, for example. This helps not only with product development, but also with claims processing. These providers also create building maps with building fabric, type of use, coverage-relevant properties of the building such as solar systems or socio-demographic data.

Sensor data can in turn help to make risks insurable in the course of industrial insurance. Networked building sensors for fire are now commonplace as a requirement in industrial business. The exchange of machine data between manufacturers, insured companies and insurers is also being discussed. Here, however, the insurance products must be adapted to include predictive maintenance clauses.

7 AutoML is seen here as an approach were all kind of modles can be trained on an existing data sets to compare which model performs best.

Another use of sensor data is already possible today in motor vehicle insurance. However, this product is still a niche in the German market. Nevertheless, even in this niche market it is already possible for some players to calculate the expected claims expenses based on driving behaviour.

C. Extraction services as part of input management

The insurance industry can be characterised as a document-based industry due to the large number of application, contract, product description and claims documents used. Incoming mail with more than 10 million documents is not the exception, but the rule. Historically, these documents are often digitised and stored as images (Tiff process). Digitalized extractions are still not the rule here, especially not for smaller insurers. This is problematic, especially as there is a lot of hidden information in these documents that can be of great value while processing the relevant tasks. It also can keep the clerk busy for a long time when searching this kind of information manually. Extraction and digital filing is therefore essential as a hygiene factor for good data quality. But what does this mean in concrete terms? With the help of modern OCR engines, documents can not only be digitised, but also extracted cost-effectively. This information helps with specialised data extraction and correct routing. If this information is stored centrally, it can also simplify back-office processing. Search engines based on this data instead of PDF forensics is the motto here. But what does a document extracted by OCR really mean in comparison to a scanned document? In a scenario without OCR, the clerk manually searches for documents and reads the content until they find the right one. Prior specialist knowledge of products and filing systems is essential here. Especially in times of demographic change, however, such knowledge is becoming increasingly rare. With the help of a search engine and fully digitised documents, however, the clerk performs a kind of Google search and is shown the results with a direct jump to the document. If you put this in relation to the average search effort for coverage checks, there is immense potential here.

D. Analysing of invoices or expert opinions

A large number of different documents end up in the inbox of an insurance company. As part of the specialised data extraction process, the relevant content has always had to be extracted from these documents. In the past, this was a complex manual process. In the last ten years, however, the topic of descriptive AI has also become established here and, in the last two years, the topic of generative AI.

But what is behind such an extraction? An Invoice of a car repair shop needs to be separated in key value pairs and needs to be verified. Relevant information that needs to be extracted is for example the paid tax, spare part numbers or working hours. In a vehicle certificate or value report, on the other hand, car identification numbers, condition, value and the like are of interest. Standardised templates, such as for a vehicle registration document, could already be trained in the past using OCR engines, templates or ML processes. However, this was always document specific and a slightly differently structured document could not be read with in the same quality. The challenge here is the diversity of the documents. Valuation reports, for example, have the same content but look completely different from different providers or local authorities.

Before GenAI[8], this meant that training was carried out on volume-rich documents, but a small number of other documents were still processed manually. With GenAI, these can now also be read out in an appropriate quality, as the text is analysed generically and not the properties of a document type as part of an ML process. The only thing to note at is that GenAI can hallucinate. It is therefore important to query clearly defined key-value pairs and use automatic test cases to check whether the values really exist. A combination of OCR engines and several language models is essential here.

E. Structuring applications

In the underwriting of industrial business, brokers or the insured companies often hand over many documents to the insurance company that are not very standardised. These include lists of locations or buildings, reports on branches, histories of previous claims and much more. It is essential for the underwriter to gain an overview here. In this scenario, AI-based analyses with the help of AI are essential. GenAI-based solutions can help here:

- Read out the locations of the branches and store them in standard format for further processing.
- Search appraisals for anomalies such as structural risks
- Check damage histories for plausibility and point out clusters
- And to supplement these results with external databases, e.g., NatCat.

Within this application scenario, the underwriter is given an interface for analysis with which he can carry out his analyses ad hoc – supported by AI. The decisive factor here is that the underwriter still makes the decisions and AI only acts as an assistant.

8 Generative AI (GenAI) is based on large language models and can be used to extract information, summarize content or generate output based on spoken or written language.

F. AI applications in operations

In policy processing, it is essential that the right documents reach the right department in a timely manner. It is also important to understand that application documents, for example, need to be processed quickly. A false positive application that ends up in the wrong inbox usually leads to a missed sales situation. It is therefore important to utilise all AI methods here in order to proceed correctly.

In the meantime, it is not only the mailbox that is relevant in this context, but also the telephone queue. With modern voicebots, waiting times can be used for authentication and classification based on the customer's spoken content instead of the obligatory "dial one, two or three". What might something like this look like?

Customer: *"I want to report a claim"*

Voicebot: *"Tell me your policyholder number"*

Customer: *"I have a claim and don't have a number"*

Voicebot: *"Please tell me your licence plate number and the licence plate number of the person insured with us"*

Customer: *"AB-CD-123 is mine, EF-GH-123 is the licence plate number of the person who caused the accident, Manfred Müller"*

This short fictitious snippet of a conversation shows how a voicebot responds to the classification (no insured person) and records the licence plate number and the name of the person who caused the damage. Of course, more information is added here. In the end, the customer ends up with the claim handler, who can already access all this information in his cockpit and can ultimately provide advice instead of making enquiries.

In addition to recording the concerns, a knowledge database is also essential for the clerk. Here, GenAI-based Retrieval Augmented Generation solutions (RAG) have quickly become a de facto standard. Especially as contracts in the industry are often not stored as digital images in databases, but have to be searched through as documents by the clerk. The knowledge bot directs the clerk to the right contract for questions about cover and the answer is found quickly. It is important here that the clerk remains in the process as a control instance and does not blindly rely on the AI. Depending on the process and the number of different documents, hallucinations are the rule rather than the exception at 10 % and 30 %.

G. Analysing claims cases

As part of claims processing, there are a large number of cases that need to be analysed. For example, it is relevant when reporting a motor vehicle claim:

- to enable the claims system to provide an easy to access notification process where modern voicebots can be of great use
- make a decision regarding an offer for a fictitious payout based on the information available
- to steer the claim to the right workshop if possible
- and recognise fraud.[9]

Here too, AI can help to prepare the right information in order to initiate dark processes or involve the relevant clerks. For a fictitious payout, for example, it is relevant to have quick access to information on the age and condition of the damaged vehicle from the damage report, expert opinion or police report and to enrich it with the relevant customer data or socio-demographic data. In this way, it is ultimately possible to decide whether or not to offer a fictitious payout. GenAI-based extraction processes and ML processes for classification are again used here.

Workshop management, on the other hand, quickly requires the relevant information on the location of the damage and the damage in order to enable standardised processes for transport, appraisals and processing of the damage in a partner workshop as quickly as possible.

In the context of fraud identification, AI in turn helps to record the large number of documents such as expert reports, police reports, statements or damage reports and make them comparable. Keywords such as "The car came out of nowhere" in connection with recently registered older but expensive cars are, for example, an indication of what clerks see per se. However, this can also get lost in the multitude of documents that are often provided with a delay. This is why AI processes are also very important as a supplement in cases of fraud.

H. Proactive control of rehabilitation measures

In health and life insurance, too, it is important to provide customers with the best possible treatment quickly. In the context of disability insurance, for example, it is a win-win for both the insurance company and the insured person if they are quickly referred to the best clinics in order to contribute to their health in difficult times and thus shorten the disability period. This requires

9 See also *Zimmer/Narr/Horbach/Hatterscheid,* Künstliche Intelligenz bei der Zurich Versicherung – Anwendung und Beispiele, in Haneke/Trahasch/Zimmer/Felden (Hrsg), Data Science. Grundlagen, Architekturen und Anwendungen[2] (2021).

the relevant findings to be recorded in the inbox and made available to the specialists in the benefits area. Ultimately, they can help to identify the right clinic, provide the customer with household services and ultimately ensure a good and speedy recovery.

I. AI-based analyses of loss scenarios

Industrial insurance often involves complex loss scenarios. This starts with complex fire or flood scenarios and ranges from simulating supply chains to analysing reputational risks. AI is already being used in all scenarios today. Based on 3D spatial images, experts are already using AI to analyse the causes of fires or re-inspect the site of damage that has already been demolished. AI can also help to draw conclusions about the condition of buildings in flooding scenarios, for example due to burst pipes. Supply chains, on the other hand, are analysed using classic ML methods to determine which failures are considered realistic.

Here too, AI is already in use today, albeit less as a commodity and more as an application used by highly specialised service providers to support insurance companies.

V. Conclusion

AI is not uncharted territory within the insurance industry, but depending on the size of the company, the degree of penetration varies from sparing use with initial prototypes to a commodity that is already scaling today. Large insurance companies invest in ecosystems, while small niche providers tend to become partially active via service providers. What both scenarios have in common is the great importance of AI for our industry (see also the theses in the introduction). Thanks to generative AI in particular, we are now able to read, summarise and analyse documents with impressive quality. This is a strategic asset. However, it is also a fact that AI often hallucinates or is susceptible to cyber scenarios. It is therefore essential for our industry to establish the necessary guardrails, regularly monitor AI and build up our own expertise in relation to AI, fraud, cloud and AI regulation.

References and resources

Copeland, B., "artificial intelligence." Encyclopedia Britannica (2025): www.britannica.com/technology/artificial-intelligence (accessed 24.11.2025)

Gregersen, E., "big data." Encyclopedia Britannica (2025): www.britannica.com/technology/big-data (accessed 24.11.2025)

Koch, P., Versicherungswirtschaft – Ein einführender Überblick (2013)

Oftermatt, J., Versicherungen – Kurzlehrbuch mit eLearning-Kurs (2025)

Yenduri/Ramalingam/Selvi/Supriya et al, GPT (generative pretrained transformer): A comprehensive review on enabling technologies, potential applications, emerging challenges, and future directions, IEEE Access, Vol. 12, pp. 54608–54649, (2024): https://ieeexplore.ieee.org/document/10500411

Zimmer/Narr/Horbach/Hatterscheid, Künstliche Intelligenz bei der Zurich Versicherung – Anwendung und Beispiele, in Haneke/Trahasch/Zimmer/Felden (Hrsg), Data Science. Grundlagen, Architekturen und Anwendungen[2] (2021)

AI in back office automation and regulatory reporting

Brian Walsh
CEO and Co-founder, Resolve

Abstract: Insurance companies are, at their core, data factories, transforming raw information from policyholders, intermediaries, and regulators into structured outputs such as financial reports, regulatory submissions, and policy documents. Yet the actuarial and finance functions driving these processes remain dependent on fragile End User Computing tools. Generative AI brings the opportunity to automate unstructured data processing, enhance governance, and accelerate transformation across the insurance back office.

This chapter examines how Large Language Models can extract structured data from documents, interpret product specifications, and support sustainability reporting. It explores how GenAI mitigates bottlenecks caused by scarce Subject Matter Experts while maintaining oversight and regulatory compliance. The discussion addresses operational and governance challenges, including hallucinations, explainability, and human-in-the-loop validation.

Emerging themes include the rise of Agentic AI, enabling workflow orchestration across enterprise systems, and vibe coding, which empowers non-developers but risks creating a new layer of ungoverned EUCs. The chapter argues that AI adoption in insurance must be treated as a strategic issue, integrating IT, risk, and business leadership.

Keywords: End User Computing (EUC), Subject Matter Experts (SME), CSRD, Sustainability Reporting, Artificial Intelligence, Insurance, Brokers, LLM

Contents

https://doi.org/10.33196/9783704698520-111

I. Insurance as a data factory

An insurance company is, at its core, a data factory. Raw information flows in from policyholders, intermediaries, markets, and regulators. The insurer then validates, transforms, and integrates this data, much like materials moving through an assembly line. These processes may involve actuarial models, underwriting rules, or compliance checks, but all serve a common purpose: converting inputs into structured, reliable outputs.

What emerges at the other end is not a physical product, but regulatory submissions, financial reports, policy documents, and claims decisions. These deliverables are essential: regulators depend on them for oversight, and policyholders rely on them as evidence of trust and solvency. Data is therefore not a by-product of activity, but the fundamental input, process, and output of the entire enterprise.

The actuarial, finance, and investment functions form the engine of this data factory. Yet, from a technology perspective, these areas receive less funding in comparison to functions closer to the sales and commercial arms of the insurer. As a result, these functions are frequently required to independently resolve processing challenges. This dynamic has fuelled the widespread reliance on End User Computing (EUCs).

EUCs often involve highly skilled actuaries, accountants, and business analysts creating 'systems' in Excel or Access. These tools are widely available, easy to use, and familiar. However, they are typically loosely coupled, reliant on extensive manual copy-and-paste processes, and lack the governance, oversight, and auditability required in a regulated environment.

While EUCs are not new, the regulatory and audit scrutiny they receive is growing. This is particularly true with the advent of the Digital Operational Risk Act[1] ("DORA") in the EU, which has placed significantly more focus on operational resilience for insurers. Therefore, unsurprisingly, EUCs frequently appear on Risk Registers and are a recurring source of operational errors. The manual nature of these processes means that small mistakes can propagate into large ones, sometimes resulting in significant financial loss[2].

1 Regulation (EU) 2022/2554 on digital operational resilience for the financial sector ("DORA"): http://data.europa.eu/eli/reg/2022/2554/oj.

2 JP Morgan's "London Whale" incident in 2012, which saw them lose $6.2 billion, was partially due to an error in their risk management VaR calculations. A manual change to the calculation spreadsheet resulted in dividing by the sum of a set of rates instead of their average, significantly reducing the reported volatility, and allowing the trader to take on more risk than allowed: *Pollock*, A tempest in a spreadsheet,

Generative AI ("GenAI") presents a unique opportunity to address these issues. However, it also introduces new risks that must be carefully managed. Furthermore, institutional and cultural hurdles must be overcome if adoption is to succeed. This chapter explores both the potential benefits of applying GenAI to these challenges and the ways in which risks can be mitigated, quantified, and governed.

Insurers are reaching a turning point. The old toolkit of spreadsheets and manual workarounds is ill-suited to today's regulatory and operational demands. GenAI offers an alternative, but only if insurers are prepared to rethink governance, workflows, and access to data.

II. Subject Matter Experts (SMEs) as the bottleneck

Budgetary constraints are rarely the main obstacle to implementing change in the back office of an insurance company. The real challenge is typically access to the Subject Matter Experts (SMEs) who possess the critical knowledge of how processes actually operate.

This issue is particularly acute in life insurance, due to the long-tail nature of the business. Many insurers still carry policies in-force that were written 40 to 50 years ago. As a result, even a relatively small insurer may have an in-force book encompassing hundreds of product iterations and reinsurance agreements. Each of these products will have been designed under different market conditions, by different teams, and in line with prevailing product design trends of the time. For example, an insurer may no longer offer products with capital/initial units or whole-of-life policies with investment units, but if such products were sold post circa 1980, they will still form part of today's in-force portfolio[3].

When insurers are required to abide by a new regulation, or attempt to modernise back-office operations, they face two broad options:

1) Account for historical complexity – adapting new processes and requirements to accommodate the wide range of product features that exist in the legacy book.

Financial Times vom 17.1.2013: www.ft.com/content/80bc5046-6ed2-30ef-b31a-bcbeac55d8bb (accessed 24.11.2025).

3 In the UK, the FCA brought in requirements on firms to maintain a process of ongoing analysis their closed book identify whether there are aspects of the design of the product or service which are not meeting Consumer Duty's cross-cutting rules: *Financial Conduct Authority*, FG22/5 Final non-Handbook Guidance for firms on the Consumer Duty (2022): www.fca.org.uk/publication/finalised-guidance/fg22-5.pdf (accessed 24.11.2025).

2) Simplify and standardise operations – which requires detailed assessment of policyholder fairness, as well as alignment with reinsurers, regulators, auditors, and other stakeholders.

Both approaches demand significant input from SMEs who understand the detailed workings of the insurer's products and processes. Their limited availability is therefore often the primary bottleneck to delivering change.

That said, insurers are often diligent in documenting their processes. They typically maintain detailed process maps and procedural manuals covering back-office functions, along with libraries of product specifications and terms and conditions. In addition, much of the source code or configuration logic that underpins key systems, including quotation engines, charging systems, and document generation platforms, remains accessible.

In other words, the knowledge required to support change initiatives is written down, but it is dispersed across vast amounts of documentation, specifications, and system code. For an individual, or even a team, assimilating this information is prohibitively time-consuming.

GenAI offers a compelling opportunity to relieve pressure on SMEs. Large Language Models (LLMs) are adept at interpreting both natural language and programming code, and at converting unstructured information into structured outputs. By 'reading' manuals, product specifications, configuration files, and system logic, LLMs can provide answers and insights that would previously have required lengthy consultations with SMEs. This allows change professionals to move faster, relying less on scarce SME capacity, while still grounding decisions in the insurer's accumulated knowledge base.

While AI can significantly accelerate knowledge capture, change management remains a major challenge. Regulators, auditors, and reinsurers are unlikely to accept AI-generated interpretations of product or system rules without clear SME validation. SME endorsement is still essential to building confidence and securing sign-off for change. Therefore, using AI is not about removing SMEs from the process, but rather elevating their role to that of reviewer rather than doer.

There are also cultural and political dynamics to consider. SMEs may be protective of their expertise or cautious about the implications of automation for their roles. Even when technical barriers are reduced, resistance from within the organisation can slow progress and must be managed with care. To address this, clear, open and honest communication from senior management to SMEs is of paramount importance.

III. Turning documents into data

Financial services companies are rarely at the forefront of technological change. The highly regulated nature of the industry, coupled with strong risk aversion, has often positioned them as laggards in adopting new technologies.

The rise of GenAI has been a notable and welcome exception. Financial services firms have emerged as early adopters, driven by the enormous volume of documents underpinning their operations. These documents, authored by multiple parties over several years, and lacking standardised formats, pose significant challenges for traditional computing techniques. Conventional parsing methods rely on document layout and structure, which makes them poorly suited to extracting information in a consistent manner from such sources.

LLMs remove this dependency on structure. Rather than relying on where words appear, LLMs interpret meaning by evaluating the probabilistic relationships between words.

Consider the following example of an insurance contract's Policy Specification. Text extracted from such a document can be presented to an LLM and transformed into a structured format, regardless of how the original terms were phrased or arranged:

> *Given that I have an insurance contract with the following terms and conditions, answer questions that follow:*
>
> - *Unit Linked Investment Contract with an initial commission of 3 %, trail commission of 0.5 %, annual management charge of 1.5 %*
> - *Minimum investment amount of €5,000*
> - *Maximum term of 10 years*
> - *1 % protection on death, subject to a minimum of premiums being returned if death occurs in the first 5 years and the value of units is less than premiums paid.*
>
> *Produce an output containing only a table showing: Product Code, Product Type, Initial Commission, Trail Commission, AMC, Minimum Investment, Max Term*

The LLM will return a structured table like the following:

Table 1: Structured Output from the LLM

Product Code	Product Type	Initial Commission	Trail Commission	AMC	Minimum Investment Amount	Max Term
AB123	Unit Linked Investment	3 %	0.50 %	1 %	€ 5,000	10

The precise formatting of the input text does not matter. Even if the Policy Specification were written using different words, structures, or even in another language, the LLM could return the required data in the same structured format.

This capability can be applied at scale across all Policy Specifications and similar documents, automating what has traditionally required significant manual review by SMEs. By instantly producing standardised outputs from unstructured text sources, whether PDFs, contracts, or emails, LLMs accelerate downstream processing and analysis.

The value extends beyond insurance contracts. The same technique can be used to extract structured insights from a wide range of natural and computer languages, significantly reducing reliance on SMEs for repetitive tasks. In turn, this accelerates change within back-office processes and regulatory reporting, areas where speed, accuracy, and auditability are critical.

IV. Meeting the sustainability reporting challenge

The EU has introduced a range of sustainability reporting requirements for insurers, including the Sustainable Finance Disclosure Regulation ("SFDR")[4] and the Corporate Sustainability Reporting Directive ("CSRD"). In the UK, similar requirements exist under the Task Force on Climate-related Financial Disclosures ("TCFD") and the Streamlined Energy and Carbon Reporting ("SECR") regime. These frameworks demand "look-through"[5] reporting of an insurer's environmental, social, and governance (ESG) impacts on a supplier and investment basis. For instance, insurers are required to assess all suppliers and investments in order to produce a Principal Adverse Impact (PAI) Statement, disclosing ESG characteristics across their portfolios. Pension trustees under the Institutions for Occupational Retirement Provision (IORP) framework must also explain how ESG factors are integrated into their investment decision-making processes.

4 Regulation (EU) 2019/2088 on sustainability-related disclosures in the financial services sector ("SFDR"): http://data.europa.eu/eli/reg/2019/2088/oj.

5 Look-through refers to a requirement to analyse and calculate values where they have invested in packaged investment products, like collective investment vehicles. For example, an insurer might operate a fund called "Global Equity Fund", where this fund holds a range of funds from a variety of asset managers, who may in turn, also invest in other external collectives. The look-through calculations mean including emissions from all vehicles, until you have arrived at the raw unpackaged investments at the end of the trail.

This task is particularly challenging for insurers who delegate investment management to multiple sub-investment managers ("Sub-IMs") or invest via a wide array of external collective investment schemes. Each Sub-IM or external collective typically produces documentation on their sustainable investment practices. However, these reports are usually delivered in bespoke PDF formats with lengthy narratives. Where standardisation efforts exist, such as the United Nations Principles for Responsible Investment ("UNPRI") reporting framework, these disclosures often lack the granularity required for regulatory submissions.

Most insurers currently address the problem by issuing due diligence questionnaires to Sub-IMs and the asset managers promoting the external collectives. However, even when responses are received, they typically consist of qualitative information that is difficult to aggregate using traditional computational approaches. For example, if an insurer receives fifty different responses to a question such as, "How is executive compensation linked to ESG performance?", how can those responses be standardised and aggregated across a portfolio?

Here, LLMs provide a valuable opportunity for automation and efficiency. SubIMs and collective investment vehicles publish large amounts of material on their sustainable investment practices. Instead of relying on manually completed questionnaires, LLMs can be deployed to analyse this publicly available information, extract relevant insights, and synthesise it into coherent, auditable disclosures. By applying advanced document extraction techniques, insurers can transform unstructured sustainability reporting into structured inputs for regulatory compliance.

While LLMs offer significant value in processing unstructured sustainability data, regulators demand a high level of explainability and auditability. Any AI-driven synthesis must therefore be transparent, with clear documentation of the sources used and the reasoning paths taken. Human oversight remains essential to validate the accuracy of outputs and ensure compliance with regulatory expectations. Moreover, inconsistencies in source documents, such as variations in disclosure quality or even deliberate "greenwashing"[6] by some SubIMs and asset managers, can limit the effectiveness of AI models and introduce risks if not properly managed.

6 Greenwashing is where a product is given the appearance of being ESG friendly, for example by including the word 'sustainable' in the name of the product, while not actually following through on those promised. For example, *Bank of New York* was fined in 2022 by the SEC for representing that potential investments underwent an 'ESG Review' prior to purchase, where they could not provide documentary evidence for this.

Beyond technical challenges, insurers must also consider the political and cultural implications of adopting AI in sustainability reporting. If stakeholders perceive AI-generated disclosures as insufficiently rigorous or overly reliant on unverified data, insurers could face reputational damage. In a domain as sensitive as ESG, trust in both the methodology and the integrity of the underlying information is critical.

V. The human role in AI governance

It is important to recognise that an LLM does not "understand" the meaning of words in the way a person would when reading a document. Instead, an LLM has a probabilistic understanding of how words are related to one another. This statistical mapping of word relationships is the "Model" in Large Language Model. The probabilities are derived from analysing vast quantities of text, much of it drawn from the internet, hence the "Large Language" part of the definition.

In practice, this means the LLM does not truly grasp the meaning of terms such as "Commissions" or "Charges". Rather, it draws upon probabilities based on how those terms have appeared in its training data. Because the model is probabilistic, errors are inevitable. These are commonly referred to as "hallucinations". Hallucinations are a core concept that must be understood before deploying GenAI or LLMs in a production setting.

Traditional programming techniques, by contrast, rely on deterministic parsing of inputs. While such methods deliver consistent and reliable outputs, they can only process inputs that conform to predefined formats. LLMs, however, can handle a far wider variety of inputs, albeit at the cost of occasional inaccuracies. As a result, there is a trade-off: deterministic methods are consistent within strict boundaries, whereas probabilistic methods offer flexibility but at the risk of error.

The standard mitigation for hallucinations is to ensure a human reviewer oversees the LLM's output and validates its accuracy, also know as placing a "human in the loop". For high-risk use cases, the EU AI Act makes human oversight a legal requirement. In addition to the EU AI Act, firms must also consider the GDPR's provisions[7] on automated decision-making, which mandate mean-

7 In particular, Article 22 GDPR gives individuals the right not to be subject to a decision based solely on automated processing, including profiling, that produces legal or similarly significant effects on them, unless specific safeguards and exceptions apply.

ingful human oversight as a safeguard whenever such decisions significantly affect individuals.

A common approach is to present the reviewer with a side-by-side interface: the extracted information on one side, and the source document with the relevant text highlighted on the other. This functionality also provides fine-grained data lineage, linking each extracted data point to its source.

However, challenges emerge when LLMs are tasked with extracting structured information across many decision points if a human is required to validate the correctness of each field being extracted. Research has shown that people struggle to repeatedly validate outputs where an overwhelming majority are correct. If a model is 98 % accurate, a reviewer may have to mark 49 items as "correct" for every 1 they flag as "incorrect". At 99.5 % accuracy, this ratio grows to 199 to 1. Because LLMs will never achieve 100 % accuracy, this dynamic makes oversight increasingly unsustainable.

Beyond the cognitive limitations of reviewers, there are material costs associated with maintaining a large-scale human review process, including salaries, training, and opportunity costs. These overheads can quickly erode the efficiency gains promised by automation, making the case for selective or augmented oversight rather than blanket review.

A more effective approach is to rebalance the adjudication process so that human review is focused where it adds real value. This can be achieved by validating outputs deterministically wherever possible and applying heuristic checks elsewhere, categorised through a Red-Amber-Green (RAG) confidence score. For example, extracted commission rates can be compared against the policy administration in-force data or the quotation system source code. If the extracted rate matches both systems, it can be deemed highly reliable. Conversely, if a "charge rate" is returned as 10 % or as a non-numeric value, it can confidently be flagged as incorrect.

Human-in-the-loop should not be seen as a binary choice between validating every output and none at all. Alternative models, such as human-on-the-loop (where oversight is triggered only in exceptional or edge cases) or human-in-command (where humans retain strategic override authority), are increasingly recognised as more sustainable approaches. When choosing business areas in which to apply LLMs for automated data extraction, organisations should prioritise contexts where such automated validation is feasible, limiting the extent to which humans are required in the loop.

VI. AI as the workflow conductor

Since the launch of ChatGPT by OpenAI in November 2022, people have grown accustomed to experiencing GenAI primarily through a chat interface, where they can ask questions and receive answers. The capabilities of these models have advanced significantly, particularly with the introduction of Chain of Thought[8] techniques in 2025. These developments have enabled models to pass complex professional examinations, such as those of the *Institute and Faculty of Actuaries* (IFoA) and the CFAs.[9]

Despite these advances, the chatbot model has inherent limitations. In particular, it is not capable of directly interacting with enterprise systems or effecting tangible change in the real world. For example, a chatbot might provide a detailed response on how to conduct a policyholder fairness impact analysis during a policy administration system migration. However, it cannot generate customer correspondence, execute scripts to analyse the in-force business, or estimate the cost implications of policy changes.

The conventional chatbot, familiar from ChatGPT, exists largely in isolation, capable of reasoning about complex topics but unable to act. To unlock real automation value in back-office processes and regulatory reporting, GenAI must be able to orchestrate actions across systems. This is where Agentic AI comes in.

Agentic AI extends LLM capabilities by enabling them to invoke processes within other applications such as email servers, databases, or policy administration systems. The most widely discussed mechanism for enabling this today is the Model Context Protocol ("MCP"), developed by Anthropic. MCP shifts the responsibility for integration to the system provider. A policy administration system vendor, for example, would need to provide an MCP server that

8 Chain of Thought is the internal reasoning process by which the LLM generates intermediate steps or explanations in a "scratchpad". This allows it to tackle complex, multi-step problems by simulating human-like logical reasoning.

9 The Chartered Financial Analyst (CFA) Program is a graduate-level, self-study curriculum and examination program for investment specialists. The author demonstrated an LLM achieving passing grades in SA2 – the final Life Specialist actuarial exam from the IFoA in his ProActuary talk: https://aiactuary.proactuary.com/talks/ai-actuarial-intelligence-from-workbooks-to-workflows/ (accessed 24.11.2025). Researchers from New York University Stern School of Business have demonstrated an LLM passing the CFAs: *Picker*, AI can now pass the hardest level of the CFA exam in a matter of minutes, CNBC 24.9.2025. See also *CFA Benchmark*, Benchmarking AI in Finance. Comprehensive evaluation of language models across multiple reasoning strategies, from zero-shot to advanced chain-of-thought techniques (2025): www.cfabenchmark.com/ (accessed 24.11.2025).

exposes the functions available within their software, along with how an LLM can invoke those functions. In this model, a natural-language instruction from an end-user is translated and executed through the MCP server of the target system.

When a chatbot is connected to multiple MCP servers, it ceases to be an isolated conversational tool and instead becomes an orchestrator. It can determine which systems to engage, what actions to perform, and in what sequence. For back-office automation and regulatory reporting, this means end-users drive full end-to-end workflows where the LLM determines the necessary steps dynamically, without predefined process scripts.

A key design consideration is the level of autonomy granted to such an orchestrator. System designers must decide whether the LLM may invoke actions fully autonomously or whether every action requires human approval. This mirrors the debate around "human-in-the-loop" oversight in data extraction: if human intervention occurs in 98 % of cases, the added value may be negligible, while the time delays are considerable.

A more balanced approach is to allow autonomous execution where deterministic validations confirm the activity, or where heuristic scoring assigns a positive RAG status. Activities marked Green can proceed automatically, while Red-flagged actions are surfaced for human review.

While orchestration expands automation opportunities, it also introduces new risks. A single faulty instruction could propagate errors across multiple connected systems, magnifying operational impact. In addition, every new integration point creates a potential attack surface, raising questions around security, resilience, and regulatory accountability.

For regulatory reporting in particular, auditability is non-negotiable. Any orchestration framework must generate a complete, verifiable trail of system interactions and outcomes, so that decisions and data flows can be explained to auditors and regulators. Without this, automation may reduce efficiency but undermine compliance.

In addition, orchestration is not only a technical challenge but also a cultural one. IT departments may be wary of introducing autonomous processes that bypass traditional controls, and regulators may resist systems that appear to dilute human oversight. Building trust and demonstrating control mechanisms will therefore be as important as the technology itself.

The potential of Agentic AI to transform back-office automation and regulatory reporting is considerable, but realisation depends on software providers engaging with MCP or similar frameworks. At present, few insurance platforms offer such integration, though the direction of travel suggests this will become increasingly common in the years ahead.

VII. Managing complexity at scale

A frequent critique of using GenAI to automate back-office processes and regulatory reporting is that it will lead to a “brain drain”, i. e. a loss of understanding among team members as to how these processes actually work. The concern is that, without this knowledge, staff will be unable to meaningfully validate or challenge the outputs of an LLM, undermining the value of human oversight.

In practice, this concern is not new and is by no means unique to GenAI. Many insurers rely on EUCs, painstakingly built and maintained by actuaries, accountants, and business analysts. These tools often require manual inputs, copy-paste operations, and ongoing adjustments. This involvement gives team members an intimate knowledge of the process, but it also creates operational risks: manual intervention inevitably increases the likelihood of error.

Automation can be viewed as “putting complexity into a box”. The operator’s role is to provide inputs and retrieve outputs, without requiring a detailed understanding of the mechanics inside. Expert knowledge remains necessary, but only for exceptional cases when the system behaves unexpectedly.

The analogy of driving a car illustrates this point well. A driver only needs to press the accelerator to increase speed. They do not need to understand the gearbox or engine mechanics. If something goes wrong, however, say pressing the accelerator fails to make the car speed up, a mechanic is called upon to investigate. While drivers today may have lost mechanical expertise compared to earlier generations, this design reduces both the skill threshold required to operate a vehicle and the risks associated with untrained individuals interfering with complex machinery.

The same logic applies to GenAI-driven automation. Although fewer people will need to be experts, expertise is not eliminated altogether. The result is that back-office processes and regulatory reporting become cheaper to produce, while simultaneously reducing the risk of human error.

Nevertheless, challenges of model risk and system opacity remain. For regulatory reporting, “the box” cannot remain a black box: it must be transparent, fully auditable, and subject to resilience testing to meet supervisory expectations. Regulators are increasingly demanding explainability and end-to-end audit trails, meaning that governance frameworks around automation are as important as the automation itself.

Cultural resistance also plays a role. Teams accustomed to detailed manual control may be reluctant to cede oversight to an automated system, particularly in highly regulated contexts where professional judgement carries weight. Overcoming this resistance requires not only robust governance but also change management and trust-building measures.

VIII. A new breed of EUCs

The term Vibe Coding, coined by *Andrej Karpathy*, describes how GenAI allows individuals with little or no coding expertise to generate working code. A non-developer can now describe the functionality they require in natural language, and an LLM will produce executable code in their language of choice.

Even before LLMs, there was a growing trend of employees within insurance companies, particularly actuaries, writing code. In 2019, the IFoA introduced a mandatory exam in R, formalising coding skills within actuarial training. Actuaries have long written VBA[10] within Excel, which was constrained by Excel's technical limitations: a maximum of one million rows per sheet and poor performance on datasets of even moderate size. By contrast, scripting languages such as R and Python do not suffer these restrictions and have therefore become widely adopted in actuarial departments.

The term citizen developers is often used to describe actuaries who code, distinguishing them from professional developers in IT teams with formal training in software engineering principles. Vibe Coding extends this further, lowering the barrier so dramatically that even those without Python or R skills can now produce functional applications. In practice, anyone in the back office of an insurance company can provide an LLM with a natural language prompt and receive code to solve their immediate problem.

The attraction is obvious: it is relatively easy to obtain working code that appears to solve the task at hand. For ad hoc or one-off needs, this is often efficient and effective. The challenges emerge when such code is embedded in production processes that must endure over the long term, potentially for the life of an insurance product, which may exceed 40 years.

Initial script creation may be straightforward, but managing change is significantly harder. With Vibe Coding, the difficulty is compounded because even the creator often does not understand the mechanics of the code themselves.

10 VBA (Visual Basic for Applications) is a programming language built into Excel that enables users to automate tasks, manipulate data, and control Excel's features through custom scripts and macros.

Typically, they iterate prompts until the code produces the desired output, but when requirements evolve, data volumes increase, or performance degrades, the absence of documentation or retained prompts makes updating the script risky and complex.

Another concern is duplication of business logic. In a well-architected system, common functions are centralised and reused, so that changes need to be implemented only once. By contrast, Vibe Coding generates isolated scripts without reference to shared libraries, often duplicating functionality inconsistently. This leads to fragmentation and operational risk: when business logic changes, updates must be applied across numerous scattered scripts.

This phenomenon represents a new form of EUC. However, unlike Excel-based EUCs, which were at least constrained by technical limits of Excel and usually well-understood by their creators, Vibe Coding outputs may run at scale, lack human comprehension, and yet appear deceptively correct. Over time, hundreds or even thousands of such scripts could accumulate across business processes, forming a hidden, ungoverned layer of infrastructure. This poses a systemic risk akin to a ticking time bomb, primed to detonate when conditions shift.

This is not to dismiss the value of LLMs in generating code. Used appropriately, they can greatly accelerate solution development. But sustainability demands governance. Generated code should be reviewed by experienced developers who understand the full Software Development Lifecycle ("SDLC"). Insurers must take care to avoid constructing a fragile patchwork of scripts on which they become dependent, but which proves impossible to maintain.

IX. From business workarounds to IT strategy

EUC tools continue to play a central role in back-office automation and reporting within insurers. Actuaries, accountants, and business analysts rely heavily on Excel spreadsheets and Access databases executed on their own desktops. These activities typically operate outside the scope of IT governance, with little oversight or even awareness from the IT department, and are often labelled as "shadow IT"[11].

11 Shadow IT refers to the use of software, devices, or systems within an organisation that are deployed without formal approval or oversight from the IT department. It is problematic because it creates security, compliance, and data governance risks. Unapproved tools may bypass organisational controls, expose sensitive data, and lead to inconsistent or unreliable information across systems.

The introduction of GenAI into transformation projects changes this dynamic fundamentally. Unless fully deployed as a local model, GenAI requires prompts and data to be transmitted to a cloud based API endpoint, even when using private connections arranged under enterprise agreements with providers such as Microsoft. Because data and systems in the regulated insurance space are sensitive and subject to strict requirements under GDPR[12], Solvency II[13], and DORA[14], IT departments must inevitably be involved to ensure compliance, security, and resilience.

Furthermore, GenAI-enabled processes typically run on servers rather than end-user machines. This means IT is required not only to configure connectivity (e.g., firewall rules and access policies), but also to provision and support the infrastructure on which the automation executes. This brings with it operational risks: the propagation of untested code in production environments, potential data exfiltration to external providers, and the need for resilience testing and monitoring. Regulators increasingly expect insurers to demonstrate robust auditability, traceability, and governance for all critical processes. Failure to address these risks exposes insurers to material consequences, ranging from regulatory fines and supervisory interventions to reputational damage and operational disruption.

This shift often creates tension between business units and IT. While some IT departments position themselves as enablers of change, others act as gatekeepers, exercising veto power over new technologies. In gatekeeper cultures, IT teams may prefer to leave EUCs running on desktops, as these are perceived to fall outside their remit. Yet this distinction masks a serious misalignment. The risks associated with shadow IT including, manual errors, inconsistent and duplicated logic, and lack of auditability, remain systemic, even if not formally acknowledged within IT's domain.

12 Regulation (EU) 2016/679 of the European Parliament and of the Council of 27 April 2016 on the protection of natural persons with regard to the processing of personal data and on the free movement of such data (General Data Protection Regulation): https://eur-lex.europa.eu/eli/reg/2016/679/oj.

13 Directive 2009/138/EC on the taking-up and pursuit of the business of Insurance and Reinsurance (Solvency II): https://eur-lex.europa.eu/eli/dir/2009/138/oj/eng. Under Solvency II, the Head of Actuarial Function (HoAF) is required to ensure that the data used in the calculation of technical provisions is accurate, complete, and appropriate. This responsibility includes reviewing the insurer's data governance processes, identifying material data limitations, and providing an independent opinion on data quality as part of the annual Actuarial Function Report. See Article 48(1)(c).

14 Regulation (EU) 2022/2554 on digital operational resilience for the financial sector ("DORA") http://data.europa.eu/eli/reg/2022/2554/oj.

Recognising these dynamics highlights an important lesson. AI adoption should not be treated as a purely technological matter. The question of how AI is deployed, and how it reshapes core business processes, is inherently strategic. Responsibility for AI strategy therefore lies with the insurer's senior leadership, ideally the CEO and executive committee, rather than being delegated solely to the CIO or CTO. In practice, governance works best when shared across functions: IT, risk, compliance, actuarial, investment, and finance. Without such cross-functional oversight, insurers risk underinvesting in AI, perpetuating fragmented EUCs, and allowing misaligned goals between business and IT functions to persist.

A more constructive approach is to establish sanctioned frameworks for innovation, such as controlled EUC sandboxes, IT-approved data pipelines, and federated AI governance models. These structures balance agility for business users with the control, auditability, and resilience demanded by regulators. Ultimately, framing AI as a board-level issue ensures that strategic objectives, regulatory obligations, and operational risks are addressed in a coherent way, rather than left to piecemeal technology decisions.

X. Data democratisation in practice

One of the key challenges in producing regulatory outputs is understanding why certain values deviate more than expected. This typically requires a detailed examination of the inputs, calculation processes, and outputs to determine whether an unusual movement is valid or the result of an error. Such analysis often demands access to significant volumes of data and the underlying calculation logic.

In practice, business users in actuarial, finance, or investment functions frequently need to raise requests with IT teams to extract information from systems where this data is managed. This separation, between domain experts who understand the business and insurance context, and IT specialists who understand the systems and data landscape, creates a persistent bottleneck. The resulting resistance can cause delays in identifying root causes and generate frustration on both sides.

GenAI-enabled tools are emerging to address this issue by democratising access to data for business users. These solutions allow professionals to articulate requests in natural language. For example, a user might ask: "Provide all claims greater than € X million" or "List all funds where the price moved more than Y % over the last month, and the policyholders who held those funds during that period."

Historically, whether due to limited access rights or the complexity of querying data warehouses, such requests depended heavily on IT involvement. Investigations are often iterative, with follow-up queries only becoming clear once initial results are reviewed. When each iteration involves a wait of several hours or days, the investigative process becomes especially inefficient.

GenAI solutions are beginning to ease this friction. For instance, Microsoft Fabric enables end users to write requests in natural language, which are automatically converted into SQL queries, executed against the database, and returned as results. Importantly, users can inspect and edit the generated query, correcting inaccuracies and refining results. While most business users lack the expertise to write SQL from scratch, many are capable of adjusting near-correct queries to achieve their desired outputs. Similar advances exist in visualisation tools such as Power BI, where natural language interfaces allow users to generate dashboards and reports without mastering the technical details of data modelling. Comparable capabilities are also being developed across the ecosystem, including *Snowflake's* Cortex and *Google's* BigQuery natural language tools, demonstrating that this trend is industry-wide rather than product-specific.

The democratisation of access to information represents a significant shift in capability within insurance companies. It empowers knowledge professionals, actuaries, finance teams, and investment analysts, who previously relied on IT mediation, enabling them to self-serve and iterate at speed. Pre-LLM, such independence was largely unattainable; with GenAI, it is rapidly becoming the norm.

However, alongside these benefits, several risks and challenges must be managed. Data governance and security remain paramount: uncontrolled access could expose sensitive personal data, triggering breach confidentiality obligations. Auditability and regulatory expectations also need to be considered, as regulators increasingly require evidence that outputs are correct, traceable, and compliant. Organisations must ensure that self-service queries leave a defensible audit trail, especially when used for official reporting.

Finally, training and upskilling are essential. While GenAI simplifies technical interactions, business users still need the skills to interpret outputs responsibly, understand data limitations, and avoid misapplication of results. Without adequate training, there is a risk of misinterpretation or overreliance on AI-generated queries.

When combined with strong governance, robust audit frameworks, and a commitment to upskilling, the democratisation of data access has the potential to transform insurance companies' ability to investigate issues, respond to regulatory demands, and empower business teams to act with speed and confidence.

XI. Fragmented data estate

Most insurers are operating with a significantly fragmented IT estate, where data is siloed in a number of different applications and EUCs, and processing logic is duplicated across these systems.

One claim that is often heard is that this separation of data must first be rectified before any AI projects can proceed. Attempting to fix all data challenges with an organisation is a significant undertaking and essentially means an organisation will fall behind the curve. Such an approach also completely ignores the possibility that there is low-hanging fruit available where implementing a GenAI solution could be used to assist in standardising and normalising the data maintained by the insurer.

GenAI can be used to accelerate the mapping and standardisation of data. There are often multiple sources of data in different formats, for example, Excel, CSV and API. An LLM can be used to map these disparate sources together and generate a homogenised view of the data, thus speeding up processing and eliminating challenges due to data being in different formats.

The importance of data lineage and reconciliations is paramount. Here an LLM is making decisions around what data gets assimilated together where, both the logic and resulting data transformations need to be logged in an immutable event log, so that these modifications can be reviewed and analysed in the future.

While GenAI can accelerate progress, it should not be seen as the sole solution; traditional approaches such as ETL pipelines, data virtualisation, and metadata-driven frameworks remain powerful, often complementary. Overlooking them risks an overly "AI-centric" strategy. Insurers need to be careful to avoid having everything starting to look like a nail when they are wielding an AI hammer.

Rather than trying to get all data correct from day one, insurers need to adopt an antifragile approach, where there is a best efforts endeavour from all sides to achieve data correctness, but that the overall strategy is to iteratively improve data quality, and to stop new data errors from being introduced over time.

XII. When machines speak the same language

We have already discussed how GenAI enables insurers to automatically read and extract information from unstructured text, as well as to generate both natural and computer language. A logical, though not entirely healthy, extension of this trend is the increasing use of natural language as the medium for machines to communicate with one another.

For example, in sustainability reporting, due diligence questionnaires are often distributed to asset managers and SubIMs by the insurer to learn how those entities are managing their assets and making investment decisions in line with sustainability goals. Increasingly, such questionnaires may be answered automatically by an LLM, drawing on historic responses previously provided by that organisation. In turn, when the (re)insurer receives these responses, they may also be analysed and assimilated by LLMs.

This dynamic is not limited to due diligence but extends to RFPs, questionnaires, and a wide range of structured information requests. The risk is that both the requests and responses are generated and processed by machines, with no direct human authorship or interpretation. In this sense, information is exchanged in natural language for the sake of interoperability, even though no human ever reads or writes the text.

There is, however, a more efficient method for systems to communicate: APIs. APIs avoid the ambiguities inherent in natural language and enforce stricter access control models, since users require explicit authorisation to retrieve data. By contrast, natural language exchange can introduce risks of misinterpretation, redundancy, or security gaps.

At present, it is difficult to see this trend reversing. Not all parties will have the technical capacity or willingness to adopt API-based integration. Natural language therefore remains the lowest common denominator for information exchange, meaning that LLM-mediated communication may continue to grow despite its inefficiencies and risks.

XIII. Where next for AI in the back office?

We have explored a variety of ways in which back-office processing and regulatory reporting can be automated using GenAI and LLMs, along with the associated challenges, risks, and safeguards that must be considered.

Under the EU AI Act[15], many forms of back-office automation may be categorised as low risk, since they do not directly determine policyholder outcomes. However, this categorisation is not absolute. Where personal or sensitive financial data is involved, insurers must address obligations around data protection, security, auditability, and explainability to ensure compliance with both regulatory expectations and broader governance standards.

15 Regulation (EU) 2024/1689 laying down harmonised rules on artificial intelligence (Artificial Intelligence Act) http://data.europa.eu/eli/reg/2024/1689/oj.

Much of the current attention on GenAI is marked by hype. Back-office functions, being relatively contained and insulated from direct customer interactions, provide an ideal testbed for experimentation. This environment allows organisations to address technical and operational challenges in a lower stakes setting before extending automation to more complex and sensitive domains such as claims or underwriting.

There is a growing expectation from boards and executive teams that insurers demonstrate a pragmatic understanding of GenAI's potential applications. While the opportunities for cost reduction and efficiency are considerable, GenAI should not be seen as a silver bullet. Rather, it must be integrated carefully with existing automation frameworks, data management strategies, and governance controls.

Beyond efficiency, GenAI is beneficial for employee satisfaction. Many of the tasks suited to automation, such as manual data transfer between spreadsheets, are repetitive and unfulfilling for qualified actuaries and accountants. Automating these activities can improve retention by enabling skilled professionals to focus on higher-value work such as oversight, strategy, and business decision-making.

Looking ahead, back-office automation should be viewed not as an endpoint but as a foundation for broader transformation. It allows insurers to build the operational confidence, governance maturity, and technical capabilities required for more ambitious deployments. While some may argue that the greatest value lies in customer-facing applications, such initiatives carry greater risks, both reputational and financial, and demand higher levels of oversight and control. By beginning in the back office, insurers can create a measured, evolutionary path towards adopting GenAI at scale.

References and resources

www.accenture.com/content/dam/accenture/final/a-com-migration/r3-3/pdf/pdf-178/accenture-wealth-management-ai-all-systems-go.pdf#zoom=40 (accessed 24.11.2025)

Basler Ausschuss für Bankenaufsicht, Grundsätze für die effektive Aggregation von Risikodaten und die Risikoberichterstattung (2013): www.bis.org/publ/bcbs239_de.pdf (accessed 24.11.2025)

CFA Benchmark, Benchmarking AI in Finance. Comprehensive evaluation of language models across multiple reasoning strategies, from zero-shot to advanced chain-of-thought techniques (2025): www.cfabenchmark.com/ (accessed 24.11.2025)

Financial Conduct Authority, FG22/5 Final non-Handbook Guidance for firms on the Consumer Duty (2022): www.fca.org.uk/publication/finalised-guidance/fg22-5.pdf (accessed 24.11.2025)

Panko, What We Know About Spreadsheet Errors, Journal of Organizational and End User Computing 2005/10(2): DOI:10.4018/joeuc.1998040102

KPMG, Insurance Transformation: The new Agenda. How leading insurers are driving successful operational and cost transformation (2025): https://kpmg.com/sg/en/insights/business-transformation/insurance-transformation-the-new-agenda.html (accessed 24.11.2025)

Kwak, The Importance of Excel (2013): https://baselinescenario.com/2013/02/09/the-importance-of-excel/ (accessed 24.11.2025)

McKinsey, The future of AI in the insurance industry (2025): www.mckinsey.com/industries/financial-services/our-insights/the-future-of-ai-in-the-insurance-industry (accessed 24.11.2025)

Picker, AI can now pass the hardest level of the CFA exam in a matter of minutes, CNBC vom 24.9.2025: www.cnbc.com/2025/09/24/ai-cfa-exam-pass-minutes-study.html (accessed 24.11.2025)

Pollock, A tempest in a spreadsheet, Financial Times vom 17.1.2013: www.ft.com/content/80bc5046-6ed2-30ef-b31a-bcbeac55d8bb (accessed 24.11.2025)

Customers as drivers of AI transformation in the insurance industry

Max Bachem
Co-founder and CEO, Xaver.com

Abstract: This contribution explores how digitalization and AI are reshaping consumer behavior in insurance, requiring insurers to adapt to meet customer demands. We first examine the major drivers of digital-first behaviour and rising expectations. We then discuss how digital channels have become the first point of contact for financial questions and the importance of hybrid omnichannel advice. Next, we cover customers' expectation of 24/7 availability and near-instant service, a standard increasingly met by AI-driven solutions. Finally, we delve into the rise of AI assistants in personal finance—from consumers using chatbots as comparison tools and second opinions, to the emergence of fully autonomous AI advisors that can research options and even complete purchases on a customer's behalf. Each of these trends highlights a profound shift: in the age of AI, the balance of power has tilted toward digitally savvy consumers, and insurers must adapt or risk irrelevance.

Keywords: consumer behavior, digital claims management, AI-Chatbot, policyholder, insurance, Chatbots, AI-Assistant, AI-Agent, Insurance and financial services, customer expectation

Contents

While technology is the enabler of transformation, the true driving force comes from customers themselves. Today's insurance customers' behaviour is evolving faster than ever. Empowered by digital technology and fueled by artificial intelligence, consumers have new expectations for how they discover, evaluate, and engage with financial services. They demand seamless digital experiences, personalized interactions, and immediate responses that match the best of Big Tech.

I. Drivers of digitalization in consumer behavior

Multiple forces have converged to make today's insurance customers "digital-first" in their expectations. One key driver is cross-industry influence. Consumers now compare their insurance experience to the gold-standard digital experiences they enjoy elsewhere – whether streaming personalized content on *Netflix*, one-click shopping on *Amazon* or a great, nearly instant answer to basically every question from your favorite LLM.

In fact, over 70 % of insurance customers expect their digital interactions to be as intuitive and personalized as those offered by leading tech and e-commerce brands.[1] This means an insurer's website or app is subconsciously benchmarked against the convenience of a *Google* search or the personalization of a *Facebook* feed. Insurers who fail to meet this high bar risk losing customers to more agile, digitally native competitors.

When today's consumers have a finance-related question, many turn first to search engines. In Germany, also digital comparison platforms have become especially influential. A 2025 *Bitkom* survey found 83 % of Germans have purchased an insurance policy online, with 62 % using comparison portals (e.g., *Check24, Verivox*) to do so.[2] These aggregator websites – along with online forums, fintech apps, and *Google* itself – now *"vie for the customer interface"*, offering convenient tools and transparency that attract consumers away from traditional agents. Banks have seen a similar shift: customers who once walked into branches now primarily use mobile apps and web banking, consulting branch staff only for complex needs. In short, the first stop for financial information is usually digital – a fundamental change from a decade ago. Today, an increasing number of consumers are skipping conventional search engines in favor of AI-powered assistants and LLMs to answer financial questions.

Another driver is the ubiquity of smartphones and internet connectivity. Mobile technology has put information and services at consumers' fingertips 24/7. Customers have grown accustomed to researching and transacting on the go, whether it's booking travel or managing finances. In insurance, this translates to a willingness – even a preference – to handle tasks digitally that were once the domain of agents. The modern consumer feels empowered to gather information independently in a way that simply wasn't possible a generation ago.

1 *Walker*, Personalization Is Now the Core of Insurance Customer Strategy (2025) Personalization Is Now the Core of Insurance Customer Strategy (accessed 18.11.2025).

2 *Bitkom*, Versichert per Klick: 83 Prozent schließen Versicherungen online ab, Presseinformation Bitkom e. V. (12.11.2025): www.bitkom.org/Presse/Presseinformation/83-Prozent-schliessen-Versicherungen-online (accessed 18.11.2025).

Generational shifts are accelerating these trends. Millennials and Gen Z, who grew up in an era of instant answers and on-demand services, are now a large segment of the insurance market. These digital natives have little patience for cumbersome paperwork or long wait times. They expect the same ease in buying an insurance policy as they experience ordering a ride through a mobile app. This cohort is also more open to using new technologies in financial decision-making, as we'll explore with AI assistants. Meanwhile, even older generations have adapted to digital convenience — often prodded by experiences during the COVID-19 pandemic — making online engagement mainstream across age groups. The net effect is a customer base that broadly prefers digital self-service for many tasks, from initial research to routine service queries, while having a seamless hybrid omnichannel experience, starting digitally and transferring to a human agent, for more complex tasks.

Crucially, personalization and data-driven insights have become central to customer expectations. People are willing to share personal data if it leads to tangible benefits. A 2025 consumer report showed 76 % of customers expect personalized interactions, and 82 % are willing to share data in exchange for more customized experiences.[3] Insurance buyers no longer seek one-size-fits-all policies; they want recommendations and pricing tailored to their unique needs and behaviors. They've seen how streaming platforms serve up "just for you" suggestions, or how fintech apps proactively alert them to savings opportunities. Now they expect the same individualized treatment from insurers. This is a major reason AI has gained prominence — advanced analytics can segment customers of one, powering the "hyper-personalization" that today's consumers crave. The flip side is that tolerance for generic mass marketing or impersonal service is at an all-time low. If an insurer's engagement feels irrelevant or untimely, customers will quickly look elsewhere.

In summary, the biggest drivers of digitalization in consumer behavior are the desire for convenience, control, and customization. Seamless digital experiences in other industries have raised the bar for insurance. Ubiquitous connectivity and smarter devices have made digital engagement second nature. And a new generation of consumers is pushing insurers to deliver faster, friendlier, more tailored service. These forces set the stage for the specific behavioral shifts we examine next: from the rise of digital-first touchpoints, to expectations of always-on service, to consumers embracing AI assistants as their first or even only interaction point to insurers.

---

3 *Walker*, Personalization Is Now the Core of Insurance Customer Strategy (2025) Personalization Is Now the Core of Insurance Customer Strategy (accessed 18.11.2025).

II. Digital-first contact: The new normal for financial questions

One of the clearest outcomes of these digital drivers is that customers now tend to start their financial journeys online. The digital channel has become the *first* point of contact for questions about insurance and other financial products, often replacing what would have been an in-person meeting or phone call in years past. Whether a consumer is curious about life insurance options, looking to get an auto insurance quote, or trying to understand retirement planning, their instinct is to begin with a Google or LLM search, visit a website, or open a mobile app – not to call an agent right away.

This "digital-first" behavior isn't limited to shopping for new policies – it also applies to general financial questions and education. Need to understand what a deductible is, or how disability insurance works? Most consumers will search for an explanation online or use an insurer's self-help knowledge base before they consider reaching out to an advisor. In many cases, consumers arrive at that first conversation with an agent *armed with information* they've already gathered from the web. As one industry observer quipped, by the time a customer meets a human advisor, "Dr. Google" (or increasingly "Dr. ChatGPT") has often answered the basic questions. This dynamic fundamentally changes the role of financial professionals – they are no longer the sole source of knowledge, but rather validators and strategists building on a baseline the customer already picked up digitally.

It's also worth noting the role of online communities and peer reviews in this digital-first paradigm. Consumers frequently consult forums, social media, and review sites to see what others are saying about insurance products or companies. In fact, 89 % of customers scour the internet for customer reviews and discussions before committing to a service.[4] A person considering an annuity might visit personal finance subreddits to get unvarnished opinions, or a small business owner shopping for commercial insurance might read user reviews about an insurer's claims service. These digital word-of-mouth channels have become influential "first contacts" in their own right, sometimes even more trusted than official marketing materials. The implication is that insurers must be mindful of their digital reputations and presence in these spaces, not just their own websites.

Why do customers prefer the digital route first? One reason is transparency and control. Online, they can compare options side by side, take time to read

4 *Intuit Creditkarma*, The Rise of Fin-AI: Why Americans Are Trusting Generative AI With Their Wallets – Intuit Credit Karma (accessed 18.11.2025).

details, and proceed at their own pace without pressure. They can gather *unbiased* information (or at least information that feels unbiased) from third-party sources. This self-directed research builds a sense of confidence. By the time they talk to an insurance salesperson – if they talk to one at all – they feel more in control of the interaction, having done their homework.

Digital-first contact also aligns with consumers' busy lifestyles. Rather than schedule a meeting during business hours, many people would rather explore answers on a Sunday afternoon or late at night when they have free time. If a question pops into a customer's head ("How much would it cost to insure my new car?"), they no longer need to wait until Monday to call an office – they can get a quick answer via an online quote tool or FAQ page right away. In essence, the digital world operates on the customer's timetable, not the company's.

Interestingly, while the journey often begins online, it may still *end* with human interaction – but on the customer's terms. Research shows that while a strong majority research and even quote insurance online, many still prefer to finalize complex purchases with an agent, especially for products that are complex or costly. For instance, one study noted that 74 % of consumers research insurance online, but only 25 % actually purchase their policy fully online.[5] *Candreira/Hofer/Touska/Kumar* come to a very similar result, highlighting "A major driver of complexity is the fact that most insurers have merely digitized their existing paper forms, resulting in an online sales journey that is an extension of legacy products and requires customers to answer too many questions. Digitized paper forms often ask customers to provide excessive information up front, leading to significant drop-offs in the sales funnel."[6]

The rest eventually call or meet with a representative to close the deal, often because they desire confirmation or reassurance for such an important decision. In this way, digital and human channels are becoming complementary. The initial discovery and education are handled digitally (efficiently and at scale), whereas the final advice or trust-building step can involve a human touch. Companies that orchestrate these handoffs well – for example, by ensuring that when a customer does call, the agent already knows what the customer looked at online – are earning high marks for experience. Indeed, customer satisfaction is highest when customers can use digital tools first and only involve a person if needed, rather than being forced to go through traditional channels for basic tasks.

5 *Anderson,* 40 Insurance Marketing Statistics You Need to Know in 2026 (2025): www.invoca.com/blog/insurance-marketing-statistics (accessed 18.11.2025).

6 *Candreira/Hofer/Touska/Kumar*, Transforming Digital Sales in Insurance | BCG (2024) (accessed 18.11.2025).

For insurers, the message is clear: your digital front door is now the main door through which customers enter. Websites, mobile apps, and digital assistants need to be as welcoming and informative as a knowledgeable agent at the front desk. If customers can't easily find what they need online, they won't pick up the phone – they'll likely just try a competitor's site instead. As *J. D. Power* noted, digital channels must be able to answer all common questions and provide critical information, because satisfaction "plummets" when users are forced to switch to a call center after failing to find what they need online.[7] In a digital-first era, the onus is on insurers to keep that first contact digital *and* delightful, then provide both digital end-to-end self-service and seamless human advisor handovers.

III. 24/7 availability and instant service expectations

Alongside going digital-first, consumers have developed a heightened expectation that services be available around the clock and deliver results instantly. In the on-demand economy, patience has become a rare commodity. Whether it's streaming entertainment or e-commerce deliveries within hours, people are used to getting what they want, when they want it. Insurance and financial services are no exception: customers increasingly insist on 24/7 access and rapid resolution. This is a direct result of digitalization – automated systems don't need to sleep, and savvy consumers know it.

Consider availability: a generation ago, a customer with a question about their policy or a need to file a claim might resign themselves to waiting until business hours. Not today. A recent 2025 survey by *Genpact* found that 59 % of consumers expect 24/7 live customer support from their insurer, especially during critical moments.[8] This expectation is partly addressed to insurers having human support (hence "live" support), but realistically it is being met through AI-driven chat/voicebots and digital self-service. AI-powered virtual advisors are the only way to meet 24/7 demand at scale.

Speed is the twin pillar of this expectation. It's not enough that an insurer is *available* at 8 p. m. on a weekday – the customer also wants their question answered or their issue resolved almost instantly. In claims, for example, there

7 *J. D. Power*, Insurance Digital Experience Study (24.5.2024): www.jdpower.com/business/press-releases/2024-us-insurance-digital-experience-study (accessed 18.11.2025).

8 *Genpact*, Genpact Study Shows Insurance Customers Embrace AI When Value and Benefits Are Clearly Demonstrated (29.4. 2025): https://media.genpact.com/2025-04-29-Genpact-Study-Shows-Insurance-Customers-Embrace-AI-When-Value-and-Benefits-Are-Clearly-Demonstrated (accessed 18.11.2025).

is growing enthusiasm for what some call the "instant claim." The same *Genpact* study showed that 46 % of customers support greater AI adoption if it *speeds up* the claims process.[9] Faster claims payouts and approvals are highly valued; consumers are basically saying, "I'll embrace the tech if it means I get my money or answers faster." And the industry is listening. Leading insurers have been investing in straight-through processing and AI assessments to cut claim cycle times from days to hours, or even minutes—with a clear path towards instant-claims at scale.

One example comes from *Allianz Direct*, which set a benchmark with its flagship "60-second claims" service. By leveraging AI for loss assessment and automating verification, *Allianz Direct* allows customers to settle a simple auto insurance claim in under one minute. This is no theoretical lab project; it's a live service that has been rolled out.[10] Once more insurers improve their claims cycles, minutes instead of weeks becomes the new standard against which all insurers will be measured. Once customers know that near-instant service is possible, a process that drags on for days or even weeks feels archaic and unacceptable—leading to an increased number of complaints for lengthy claims processes.

The push for instant gratification extends to other areas as well. Prospective customers expect quotes on the fly—if it takes two days to "get back to you with a rate," you've likely lost that sale to a competitor's instant quote tool. Policy documents and proof of insurance are expected to be available immediately via email or app in the retail sector—but instant quotation is increasingly being offered in commercial insurance as well.

It's important to note that 24/7 service and instant response are tightly linked to AI and automation. You simply cannot have humans instantly process thousands of requests at any hour—it's not feasible or cost-effective. But AI can. For example, AI chatbots and voicebots can handle routine customer inquiries (from "Where can I download my policy?" to "What does this coverage term mean?") with lightning speed, any time, through the customer's channel of choice, be it text, voice or even a photorealistic avatar which looks like the

9 *Genpact*, Genpact Study Shows Insurance Customers Embrace AI When Value and Benefits Are Clearly Demonstrated (29.4.2025): https://media.genpact.com/2025-04-29-Genpact-Study-Shows-Insurance-Customers-Embrace-AI-When-Value-and-Benefits-Are-Clearly-Demonstrated (accessed 18.11.2025).

10 *McKinsey & Company*, Case Study: Allianz Direct: Insurance's digital transformation (2024): www.mckinsey.com/capabilities/tech-and-ai/how-we-help-clients/rewired-in-action/allianz-direct-advancing-as-europes-leading-digital-insurer (accessed 18.11.2025); *Boshnakova,* Connected Platforms will make insurance of the future ultra-personalised | Allianz (2025) (accessed 18.11.2025).

customer's advisor or the insurer's brand ambassador. On the claims front, AI models can analyze photos of car damage in seconds, estimate repair costs, and initiate payment – tasks that would take a human adjuster days with scheduling and paperwork. The result is not just faster service, but often a *better* customer experience. Customers feel a sense of relief and delight when something that they dreaded (like a claim) is resolved almost as soon as it happened. The overarching goal is near-instant gratification without sacrificing empathy and trust. The best companies set bold speed goals (like "60-second claims") while also offering easy access to human support whenever the customer needs the comfort of speaking to a person – establishing one consistent hybrid omnichannel experience.

In summary, the modern insurance customer expects service on-demand and in real time. They want insurers to be "always on," just like their streaming services or online shopping sites. And when life throws a curveball – a car accident, a burst pipe, an urgent question – they expect solutions in minutes, not days. This expectation has been enabled by digital technology and is increasingly fulfilled by AI. It is no longer futuristic to talk about 24/7, instantaneous insurance services; it's here now in pockets and will soon be the norm. Insurers that deliver on this expectation win not only in customer satisfaction but also in loyalty. After all, if your company saves me time and hassle when it matters most, why would I ever switch?

IV. The rise of AI assistants in consumer finance

If digital channels are the new front door for customers, AI assistants are fast becoming the guide inside the digital house. In the past two years, there has been an explosion in consumers using AI-powered tools – from chatbots to voice assistants to sophisticated generative AI platforms – also to help with their financial decisions. What began with simple FAQ chatbots on insurer websites has now evolved into something far more transformative: consumers delegating research, comparison, and even decision-making to AI assistants. This rise of AI in the customer's personal toolkit is a game-changer for insurance distribution and advice.

A striking recent statistic underscores this trend. According to a 2025 survey by *Intuit's Credit Karma*, asking for financial advice is now the *second most common use-case* for generative AI platforms like ChatGPT, right after health queries.[11] The same survey revealed that 66 % of Americans have used AI to

11 *Intuit Creditkarma*, The Rise of Fin-AI: Why Americans Are Trusting Generative AI With Their Wallets – Intuit Credit Karma (accessed 18.11.2025).

seek out financial advice, and among Millennials and Gen Z that figure jumps to an astounding 82 %.[12] In other words, a majority of young consumers – and a solid majority of all age groups combined – have turned to an AI chatbot to get help on money matters. This could be anything from "Can I afford a new car?" to "What's the best credit card for travel rewards?" to "How much life insurance do I need?" The sheer volume of usage represents a paradigm shift: AI is becoming a mainstream financial advisor (or at least a financial research assistant) for everyday consumers.

But why are people flocking to AI assistants for help with finances? Part of the appeal is convenience and immediacy (as we discussed – answers on the spot, 24/7). But there's more: AI tools like ChatGPT provide a conversational, non-judgmental environment to explore what can be sensitive topics. The Credit Karma survey found that three in four users felt AI lets them ask financial questions they'd be too embarrassed to ask a human.[13] Money is personal, and many feel shy admitting ignorance or mistakes to a live advisor. An AI, however, does not judge – it patiently explains even basic concepts and can be queried repeatedly until the user understands. As *Thomas Nitzsche* from the non-profit credit counseling agency *Money Management International* put it, generative AI is like "an enhanced and more interactive Google search" for finances.[14] It can not only retrieve information but also engage in a dialogue, asking follow-up questions to clarify your needs and providing tailored suggestions. Or in the case of *Xaver*, as shown in the case study[15], also fully sell insurance products, open investment accounts and execute full processes. This dynamic, iterative guidance and execution feels to users like their 24/7 available, personal financial advisor.

To be sure, AI assistants are not perfect – they lack the fiduciary responsibility and nuanced understanding of a human advisor. Even with those caveats, the trajectory is unmistakable: AI assistants are playing an expanding role in how consumers make financial decisions. We can break this rise into two related trends, one building on the other:

12 *Intuit Creditkarma*, The Rise of Fin-AI: Why Americans Are Trusting Generative AI With Their Wallets – Intuit Credit Karma (accessed 18.11.2025).

13 *Intuit Creditkarma*, The Rise of Fin-AI: Why Americans Are Trusting Generative AI With Their Wallets – Intuit Credit Karma (accessed 18.11.2025).

14 *Sidorowicz*, More people turning to AI chatbots for financial advice. Can you trust it? CBS News Philadelphia More people turning to AI chatbots for financial advice. Can you trust it? – CBS Philadelphia (accessed 18.11.2025).

15 See *Bachem*, *Xaver* – An AI-native Fintech (in this volume) 69 ff.

A. AI assistants as research partners and second opinions

First, consumers are using AI assistants as tools for initial research, verification and increasingly also comparison. Think of this as the AI acting like a super-informed friend for the customer. For example, a person might receive an insurance quote from their agent, then head straight to ChatGPT or a similar AI and ask, "Is this a good deal? What other options should I consider?" The AI can instantly summarize the key features of the quoted policy, highlight pros and cons, and even generate a quick comparison with alternative products available in the market. Traditionally, a customer might have had to call around to multiple insurers or consult an independent broker to get a second opinion. Now, they can obtain a broad overview in seconds from an AI – empowering them with more information before making a decision.

We see evidence of this behavior in how people describe their use of AI. Many say they treat ChatGPT as a research assistant. It's common to hear anecdotes like, "I asked the chatbot to explain the difference between term and whole life insurance and which one might suit me, and it gave a pretty detailed answer with definitions, benefits, and considerations." Some users are even more specific: they'll feed the AI details – e.g., "I'm 30 years old, married, with one child, making $100k a year; what kind of life insurance coverage might I need and are there coverages for our child I should consider?" – and get personalized-seeming guidance in return. It's not that the AI knows the user intimately, but it can apply general financial planning principles to the scenario, much like a junior advisor might. The fact that already nearly 20 % of retail investors worldwide use AI tools to help make or adjust investment decisions is telling.[16] These investors use AI to crunch the numbers or gather insights, effectively augmenting their own decision process. In the insurance context, we can expect similar adoption – for instance, using AI to scan and summarize the fine print of two competing policies, or to simulate different coverage scenarios ("what if I raised my deductible to $1,000 – how much could I save?").

AI as a research partner also shines in its ability to handle complex comparisons instantly. Humans often struggle to compare apples-to-apples across financial products with myriad variables. An AI, however, can be tasked with, "Compare comprehensive car insurance from Company A and Company B for a 2018 Toyota, and highlight differences in coverage and price." This level of on-demand analysis was cumbersome for consumers before; now it's becoming accessible. Importantly, AI can incorporate *consumer reviews and forums* in

16 *Katanich*, Personal finance and AI: Should you trust ChatGPT's investment advice? Euronews (30.10.2025): www.euronews.com/business/2025/10/30/personal-finance-and-ai-should-you-trust-chatgpts-investment-advice (accessed 18.11.2025).

its synthesized answers, giving a blend of factual comparison and anecdotal feedback ("Company A has slightly cheaper premiums, but Company B customers report better claims service"). Such a holistic view in one place is immensely valuable to a savvy shopper and is increasing expected in today's world of transparent mass customer reviews.

Perhaps the most mundane but impactful use of AI assistants is simply to answer those nagging financial questions instantly, without having to call or email anyone. "I just had an accident, how do I file a claim with my insurer?" "Is X covered under by policy?" Instead of navigating an insurer's site or waiting on hold, customers can ask an AI in natural language and usually get a useful answer. As generative models are increasingly integrated into search engines and voice assistants, this will only grow. We are quickly moving to a world where, rather than scrolling through FAQ pages, a customer can just ask their phone or smart speaker a coverage question and get a direct response.

All of this positions the AI assistant as an empowering force for consumers. It lowers the knowledge barrier, making it easier for everyday people to access information that used to be locked up in dense brochures or inside an expert's head. It also introduces more objectivity into the process: The AI isn't on commission, it doesn't upsell (at least not yet, unless programmed to), and it can present multiple options without bias. This means customers can approach financial decisions feeling more informed and confident. From the insurer's perspective, however, this trend can be double-edged: a more informed customer will ask tougher questions and be less likely to accept a subpar offer. Also sales agents from insurers and brokers have to be prepared for customers pre-advised by their AI assistant. On the positive side, if the insurer truly has a strong value proposition, the AI might highlight that and steer the customer toward them. But if not, the AI could just as easily lead the customer elsewhere. In essence, AI assistants are becoming the new information gatekeepers – much like how internet aggregators became powerful in insurance distribution over the last two decades. Insurers will need to ensure that their offerings are favorable in the eyes (or algorithms) of these digital assistants.

B. Full AI-driven advice and transactions

The second, more forward-leaning trend is the emergence of AI assistants taking on end-to-end advisory and purchasing roles. Here, the AI is not just providing a second opinion or research help while the human remains the primary decision-maker. Instead, the AI starts to *lead* the process, either guiding the user through complex decisions or even executing decisions autonomously on the user's behalf. This is where we move from today's early adoption into the realm of transformative potential for the industry.

Many experts predict that this is the direction we're headed. *Cognizant*[17] foresees that by 2030, personal AI assistants (ChatGPT, Gemini, Apple Intelligence, etc.) will through their MCP connectors to insurers and third-party enablers, be able handle every aspect of insurance buying – from comparing policies, to negotiating terms, to actually binding coverage to delivering the documents – without the customer directly interacting with the insurer. In such a scenario, you as a consumer might simply tell your AI assistant, "Find me the best home insurance policy for my new house and get me covered," and the AI agent will go do it. It will fetch quotes, vet the coverage, decide on the optimal choice based on your preferences (which it knows), purchase the policy, and set everything up. This isn't science fiction; it's a logical extension of capabilities already being developed. In fact, by the end of this decade, *Cognizant* expects that most insurance transactions will involve AI assistants acting on behalf of human policyholders.[18] These "digital agent" intermediaries will become common. Your AI will talk to my insurance company's AI to sort out the best offering – essentially an AI-to-AI negotiation.

We've already seen a glimpse of this future in experimental form, when in 2025 *Xaver* demonstrated the first fully autonomous, compliant advice session, customer profiling, product recommendation and sale of a life insurance policy via a public generative AI interface, specifically, through ChatGPT and *Claude*. In this illustrative case, a user literally gave an instruction in natural language to their AI: "Please analyze my financial situation and recommend a suitable life insurance policy to fill it." From that single command, the AI (ChatGPT connected to *Xaver's* AI financial advice and sales platform) went on to conduct a full needs analysis, determine the coverage gap, recommend an appropriate life insurance product, obtain a real-time quote, and bind the policy – all on autopilot. This case study, while cutting-edge, shows what's technically possible: an end-to-end advisory and sales process executed by AI build with compliance-by-design. It's a radical departure from the traditional agent-driven sale and even from the earlier era of robo-advisors, because here the AI was not a tool used by the consumer, it effectively *was* the consumer in the eyes of the insurer's system (acting as the customer's agent).

The implications of such AI-led commerce are profound. For consumers, it promises unparalleled convenience – the ultimate anytime available, personal financial concierge. Imagine never having to comparison-shop for insurance

17 No more human customers (2025): www.cognizant.com/en_us/about/documents/cognizant-how-ai-could-transform-insurance-by-2030.pdf (accessed 19.11.2025).

18 *Cognizant*, No more human customers (2025): www.cognizant.com/en_us/about/documents/cognizant-how-ai-could-transform-insurance-by-2030.pdf (accessed 19.11.2025).

again because your AI monitors the market and switches you to the best deal automatically. Indeed, AI assistants could routinely negotiate with insurers, switch providers for you when better options emerge, and manage your policies over time, all while you sleep.[19] They won't forget to renew your policy on time. They won't ignore a suboptimal rate out of laziness. They'll diligently optimize your coverage and cost because that's what they're programmed to do for your benefit. From a consumer standpoint, having such a tireless advisor could mean better coverage at lower prices with far less hassle.

However, this also introduces a new intermediary in the classic insurer-customer relationship: the AI as customer. Insurers will effectively be selling to algorithms as much as to people. A personal AI will comb through product details in milliseconds – far faster than a human ever could – and will spot any gap or disadvantage. If an insurer's product is too restrictive or overpriced, the AI will likely pass it over, no matter how clever the advertising might be. This will force insurers to compete on true value and API, MCP, and A2A-enabled accessibility, rather than marketing alone. To put it bluntly, insurers whose systems cannot seamlessly interface with these AI assistants risk becoming invisible to an entire generation of consumers. Successful insurers, on the other hand, are in a first step already working on making their products "machine-readable" and easy for AI to plug into. The second step is to make today's digital sales journeys "AI agent ready" (and have for all products – also more complex products – digital sales capabilities). As a third step, developing robust APIs/MCP connectors and data standards so an AI agent can get quotes, submit applications, and sell products. We are still in the early innings of this transformation.

Regulators are watching closely. In the EU, fully autonomous financial advice is tightly regulated, and none of the publicly available LLMs is authorised to act as a regulated financial adviser. *OpenAI* itself describes ChatGPT as "a general-purpose conversational assistant" and notes that, for "sensitive or consequential topics like financial decisions, the assistant is trained to offer information without giving definitive advice".[20] This is precisely the gap regulated AI Fintechs like *Xaver* address: they enable financial institutions to deliver compliant financial advice and sales journeys at scale, including the integration into personal AI assistants which, on their own, cannot provide regulated financial advice.

19 *Cognizant*, No more human customers (2025): www.cognizant.com/en_us/about/documents/cognizant-how-ai-could-transform-insurance-by-2030.pdf (accessed 19.11.2025).

20 *Katanich*, Personal finance and AI: Should you trust ChatGPT's investment advice? Personal finance and AI: Should you trust ChatGPT's investment advice? | Euronews vom 30.10.2025 (accessed 18.11.2025).

And customers and their comfort levels using full AI processes increase. Surveys show consumer openness creeping upward: in the UK, the share of customers comfortable with AI making insurance decisions for them (without human input) rose from 21 % to 34 % in just one year.[21] Each year, as AI systems prove themselves and guardrails (like independent audits of algorithms) are established, more people will take the leap.

In conclusion, the AI assistant is set to become an indispensable part of the consumer's financial life. Today, it's an advisor in your pocket—ready to answer questions and offer a second opinion at any hour. Tomorrow, it will be your fully empowered personal financial advisor. For consumers, this promises greater convenience and potentially better outcomes. For insurers, it presents both an opportunity and a challenge: an opportunity to tap into an "AI channel" that will bring in business at lightning speed, and a challenge to remain relevant when loyalty shifts from traditional brand relationships to whichever insurer's product an algorithm deems best. In this AI-driven future, the winners will be (a) those companies that can either position themselves with a holistic omnichannel financial advisor with customers and (b) those able to integrate with personal AI agents and prove their value in an algorithmic comparison—essentially, those that can appeal to the customer's AI as much as to the customer themselves. One thing is for sure, the age of the AI-empowered consumer is dawning, and it will redefine the rules of engagement in insurance and beyond, requiring insurers to adapt and transform.

References and resources

Anderson, 40 Insurance Marketing Statistics You Need to Know in 2026 (2025): www.invoca.com/blog/insurance-marketing-statistics (accessed 18.11.2025)

Bitkom, Versichert per Klick: 83 Prozent schließen Versicherungen online ab, Presseinformation Bitkom e.V. (12.11.2025): www.bitkom.org/Presse/Presseinformation/83-Prozent-schliessen-Versicherungen-online (accessed 18.11.2025)

Boshnakova, Connected Platforms will make insurance of the future ultra-personalised | Allianz (2025) (accessed 18.11.2025)

Candreira/Hofer/Touska/Kumar, Transforming Digital Sales in Insurance | BCG (2024) (accessed 18.11.2025)

Cognizant, No more human customers (2025): www.cognizant.com/en_us/about/documents/cognizant-how-ai-could-transform-insurance-by-2030.pdf (accessed 19.11.2025)

21 *Guidewire,* Customer Suspicion of Insurers Using AI Softens (14.5.2025): www.guidewire.com/about/press-center/press-releases/20250514/customer-suspicion-of-insurers-using-ai-softens (accessed 18.11.2025).

Genpact, Genpact Study Shows Insurance Customers Embrace AI When Value and Benefits Are Clearly Demonstrated (29.4.2025): https://media.genpact.com/2025-04-29-Genpact-Study-Shows-Insurance-Customers-Embrace-AI-When-Value-and-Benefits-Are-Clearly-Demonstrated

Guidewire, Customer Suspicion of Insurers Using AI Softens (14.5.2025): www.guidewire.com/about/press-center/press-releases/20250514/customer-suspicion-of-insurers-using-ai-softens (accessed 18.11.2025)

Intuit Creditkarma, The Rise of Fin-AI: Why Americans Are Trusting Generative AI With Their Wallets – Intuit Credit Karma (accessed 18.11.2025)

J. D. Power, Insurance Digital Experience Study (24.5.2024): www.jdpower.com/business/press-releases/2024-us-insurance-digital-experience-study (accessed 18.11.2025)

Katanich, Personal finance and AI: Should you trust ChatGPT's investment advice? Euronews (30.10.2025): www.euronews.com/business/2025/10/30/personal-finance-and-ai-should-you-trust-chatgpts-investment-advice (accessed 18.11.2025)

McKinsey & Company, Case Study: Allianz Direct: Insurance's digital transformation (2024): www.mckinsey.com/capabilities/tech-and-ai/how-we-help-clients/rewired-in-action/allianz-direct-advancing-as-europes-leading-digital-insurer (accessed 18.11.2025)

Sidorowicz, More people turning to AI chatbots for financial advice. Can you trust it? CBS News Philadelphia More people turning to AI chatbots for financial advice. Can you trust it? – CBS Philadelphia (accessed 18.11.2025)

Walker, Personalization Is Now the Core of Insurance Customer Strategy (2025): https://insurance-edge.net/2025/10/15/personalization-is-now-the-core-of-insurance-customer-strategy/ (accessed 18.11.2025)

Where AI meets insurance: A look into the crystal ball (Transforming the insurance industry)

Christina Lucas
Global Market Leader, Insurance for Google Cloud

Abstract: This chapter examines the technologies and strategies redefining one of the world's oldest industries, presenting a unique opportunity for the next generation to build a more resilient future. It explores the AI-driven transformation of the insurance industry, detailing its shift from a reactive 'repair and replace' model to a proactive 'predict and prevent' ecosystem. Driven by forces like climate change and cyber threats, AI is creating hyper-personalized 'living' policies and real-time risk mitigation. Discover how AI augments human expertise, transforming traditional roles into strategic, data-driven careers.

Keywords: Artificial Intelligence (AI), Insurance, Digital Transformation, Predict and Prevent, Risk Mitigation, Hyper-personalization, Insurtech, Insurance Careers, Protection Gap, Climate Risk, Parametric Insurance

Contents

https://doi.org/10.33196/9783704698520-113

I. The drivers of change

A. Introduction: From next best to big leap

As we reimagine the future of insurance, let's first look at an analogy from the past. Twenty years ago, you watched whatever programming was available on the local network. Today, you stream personalized content, on-demand, anywhere. The companies that just tried to build a better lineup of pre-defined shows have almost vanished; the companies that built a data-driven utility (like *Netflix* or *Spotify*) have defined our reality today. The insurance industry is on a similar trajectory: for several decades the insurance industry has also been stuck in its "standard programming" mode, only implementing incremental changes based on an established playbook, but as described in previous chapters of this book, the industry is ready to leap into transformational change.

The big transformational leap is this: the insurance industry is experiencing a complete paradigm shift from a reactive **"repair and replace"** model to an energized, proactive **"predict and prevent"** ecosystem. The future of insurance isn't just how to issue a policy document faster; it's a critical rethinking of the value proposition of what that policy represents — an easily accessible and obtainable agreement defined by near real time, multi-modal, multi-channel first and third party data. This new way of viewing a policy is how the industry finally fulfills its original promise: to build collective societal resilience.

This needed paradigm shift, however, immediately clashes into the industry's current reality. As noted in this book's introduction[1], insurance was an IT pioneer in the 1980s, one of the first industries to go all-in on mainframes. However, being the tech leader of the past has become its greatest liability. Today, as data-driven industries like banking and finance leap forward, multiple studies confirm that insurance consistently ranks in the bottom third of AI maturity.

This conflict creates what *Challapally et al* call the **"GenAI Divide."** At the beginning of 2025, **95 % of organizations reported zero returns** from their AI initiatives.[2] They are all trapped in "pilot purgatory" — high adoption, zero transformation. This isn't a failure of the tech. It is a failure of strategy, culture, and foundations. Despite these stats, the race is on and the next 10 years will be defined by the widening gap between the early adopters and those who choose to "wait and see". For those who embrace this change, the opportunity

1 *Münkel*, Artificial intelligence (AI) in the insurance industry – An introduction (in this volume) 1 ff.

2 *Challapally et al.*, The GenAI Divide, 3 (2025): https://mlq.ai/media/quarterly_decks/v0.1_State_of_AI_in_Business_2025_Report.pdf (accessed 24.11.2025).

is epic: to finally close the global protection gap and architect a more resilient world for everyone.

B. The five catalysts: Existential threats as innovation accelerators

An industry entrenched in legacy systems does not change because it's convenient; it changes due to dire necessity. True transformation requires external, existential force. Today, insurance faces five such forces. These challenges are the primary accelerators that will finally energize the industry, forcing it to abandon analog-era inertia and embrace a digital-first, AI-native future.

1. Climate change

From: Reactively processing claims *after* a catastrophe.

To: Proactively mitigating risk via AI-powered climate modeling and real-time geospatial data. This creates a massive new market for scalable parametric products.

Market Imperative: As previous authors have noted, Q1 2025 was the costliest first quarter for catastrophes since 2011.[3] Insurtechs like "*Descartes*" are already using AI to analyze multispectral imagery and run complex physics-based models to simulate wildfire risk, while *Moody's* acquisition of *CAPE Analytics* for its geospatial AI shows this "predict and prevent" capability is a high-value strategic asset.[4]

2. Cyber threats

From: Insuring the financial loss *of* a data breach.

To: Becoming a real-time cyber resilience partner, offering AI-powered platforms that monitor, predict, and neutralize threats 24/7.

The Dual Risk: As *Woodward et al.* highlight, this is a double-edged sword. Insurers must insure against escalating cyber threats, but they must also manage the cyber risks *of AI itself*. AI systems create novel vulnerabilities like data poisoning and model theft.[5] The future insurer must be an expert in both, creating resilience for its customers and its own intelligent systems.

3 *Gallagher Re*, Global InsurTech Report: Q2, 23 (2025): www.ajg.com/gallagherre/news-and-insights/global-insurtech-report-q2-2025/ (accessed 24.11.2025).

4 *Gallagher Re*, Global InsurTech Report: Q2, 39 (2025): www.ajg.com/gallagherre/news-and-insights/global-insurtech-report-q2-2025/ (accessed 24.11.2025).

5 *Woodward et al*, Tech-tonic shifts, 9 (2024): www.swissre.com/institute/research/topics-and-risk-dialogues/digital-business-model-and-cyber-risk/ai-and-the-industry-risk-landscape.html (accessed 24.11.2025).

3. Emerging markets and population growth (the protection gap)

From: Traditional, complex products that are inaccessible to millions of people.

To: Easily accessible, mobile-first insurance. Using AI to create and price micro-insurance and on-demand products at scale, distributed through platforms people already use.

The Resilience Opportunity: The protection gap is a global crisis; in 2022, **only 45 % of global economic losses from natural disasters were covered,** leaving communities financially shattered.[6] AI-driven efficiency provides one of the few viable economic model to create and distribute affordable micro-products, finally bringing billions of people and small businesses into the system of financial resilience.

4. Sustainability (ESG)

From: A peripheral corporate metric or marketing slogan.

To: A core, quantifiable underwriting principle. Using AI to analyze vast, alternative datasets (satellite imagery, supply chain data, public sentiment) to create a true ESG risk score, enabling new products that incentivize sustainable corporate behavior.

The AI Energy Conflict: This catalyst creates an immediate operational paradox. Research highlights that **72 % of insurers struggle to balance the immense energy demands of training AI models with their ESG commitments.**[7] The leading insurers of the future will be forced to become pioneers in energy-efficient AI, championing smaller, domain-specific models and green computing infrastructure.

5. Parametrics

From: A niche, complex product for specific, large-scale catastrophe risks.

To: A mainstream, AI-enabled solution for a wide range of risks. AI is the key that unlocks this market at scale. It is crucial for refining triggers, minimizing basis risk (the gap between the index and the actual loss), and integrating first and third party data sources – like drone footage, ground sensors, and real-time weather feeds – to validate events instantly, making parametric insurance faster, more transparent, and scalable for everyone.[8]

6 *Owen/Mullins/Sheehan*, Generative AI Adoption, 2 (February 23, 2025): http://dx.doi.org/10.2139/ssrn.5227619.

7 *KPMG*, Intelligent Insurance, 10 (2025): https://assets.kpmg.com/content/dam/kpmgsites/xx/pdf/2025/03/intelligent-insurance-web-report.pdf.coredownload.inline.pdf (accessed 24.11.2025).

8 *Tarr A./Tarr J./Thompson/Wilkinson* (eds), The Global Insurance Market, 9 (2024): DOI:10.4324/9781003319054.

II. The AI-native insurance ecosystem

The path to the "predict and prevent" future is full of opportunity that requires a complete reimagining of the insurer's business model. What's exciting is that many components of this new framework are already being built and deployed by market leaders such as *Baloise* today.

A. The foundational shift: From on-prem to cloud-native

The single greatest barrier to the AI-native future is the technological foundation of the past. As noted by *Münkel*,[9] the industry's history as an IT pioneer in the 1980s has become its greatest liability. Many insurers are running core systems from the 80s and 90s—a motley of poorly documented, monolithic code that is expensive and difficult to maintain.

This creates the dreaded "Iceberg Effect": a handful of modern, customer-facing apps floating atop a massive, outdated back-office mainframes, disconnected data silos, and even paper files still stored in cabinets. This legacy debt is the primary reason for the "GenAI Divide." It's why *KPMG* finds that **59 % of insurers still rely on on-premises AI solutions**, 72 % cite data as their primary challenge to scaling AI, and only 13 % have a real-time data warehouse.[10]

A cloud-first architecture is not merely a change in IT hosting; it is the fundamental enabling operating model for the AI-native state. It provides the elastic scalability, the data fluidity to finally break those silos, and the direct access to cutting-edge AI services that are necessary to compete. This makes the case for a flexible, API-first architecture absolute. You don't build a new, bigger mainframe; you build an intelligent, distributed plug and play system of services that can evolve as fast as the technology does. Many organizations are turning to cloud providers, with nearly 90 % of generative AI unicorns[11] and over 60 % of funded GenAI startups being cloud customers. For example, Definity partnered with a leading cloud provider to migrate critical insurance data into a unified data warehouse, laying the groundwork for AI innovation across its business.

---

9 *Münkel*, Artificial intelligence in the insurance industry—An introduction (in this volume) 1 ff.

10 *KPMG*, Intelligent Insurance, 8, 10 (2025): https://assets.kpmg.com/content/dam/kpmgsites/xx/pdf/2025/03/intelligent-insurance-web-report.pdf.coredownload.inline.pdf (accessed 24.11.2025).

11 AI unicorns are private companies in the artificial intelligence sector with a valuation of $1 billion or more.

B. The insurtech catalyst: Forcing the pace of change

Incumbent carriers, burdened by legacy systems and quarterly earnings pressure face the steepest challenge to adopt a high-risk (but high reward) paradigm-shifting approach to adopting AI. As in other industries, the innovative nature of start-ups, specifically InsurTechs have stepped up to fill the industry's needs for unique point-to-point solutions that fulfill specific business needs. These firms, unburdened by technical debt, are frequently acting as the distributed, hyper-agile R&D to help jump start the transformative innovation for the industry.

With over **$60 billion invested since 2012** and approximately 25 % of recent funding directed at AI-native technologies, Insurtechs are the pioneers rapidly testing the new products (parametric wildfire models) and distribution channels (embedded APIs) that the legacy companies cannot.[12]

Bringing it all together, the future winners in the insurance AI race are not builders; they are companies that adapt the strategy of a master integrator. The "AI Readiness Index" from *CB Insights* confirms this: market leaders like Cigna and Travelers are accelerating their transformation not just through internal builds, but through aggressive acquisition, strategic investment, and deep partnership with the Insurtechs that have already proven the path forward.[13]

C. The end of silos: The inevitable rise of platforms and ecosystems

This leads us back to the core tenets of this paradigm shift: from closed, mainframe systems to open, API-driven platforms. The future insurer does not simply sell a policy; it is helping the insured implement a strategy that delivers value to the policyholder through products that target both risk mitigation and loss prevention, different from the legacy view of a simply a legal contractual agreement that pays out in the event of a loss.

For example, think of the latest fleet of electric vehicles. Instead of re-issuing a policy every 6 months based on the prior 6 months of driving history, the car's (and driver's) data feeds a dynamic UBI (Usage-Based Insurance) ecosystem that:

- **Prices risk** with real-time accuracy (pricing precision).
- **Actively coaches** safer driving behavior through in-car alerts (loss prevention).

12 *Gallagher Re*, Global InsurTech Report: Q2, 5, 6 (2025): www.ajg.com/gallagherre/news-and-insights/global-insurtech-report-q2-2025/ (accessed 24.11.2025).

13 *CB Insights*, AI Readiness Index, 4 (2024): www.cbinsights.com/research/ai-readiness-index-insurance/(accessed 24.11.2025).

- **Predicts maintenance** needs before a component fails (risk mitigation).
- **Fully automates** First Notice of Loss (FNOL) by detecting a crash, dispatching emergency services, and initiating the claim simultaneously (claims servicing).

D. The reimagined workforce: Human expertise, augmented by AI

We do recognize that there are two components to transformation: technology and the people who support/use (or are impacted by) it. Increasingly in the news we see stories that show a fear of how AI will drive mass job displacement across industries, including insurance. The reality is one of mass talent *augmentation*, elevating human expertise above repetitive, manual tasks to complex, judgment-based work. As *Bockelmann* noted in his chapter, successful AI implementation is never just a technology problem; it is overwhelmingly a human one. The **"70 % Rule"**—that success is **10 % model, 20 % technology, and 70 % change management**—is the critical lesson for any leader.[14] The failure of the 95 % of companies stuck in the "GenAI Divide" is a failure of this 70 %; they are focusing only on the technology while ignoring the human transformation required to unlock its value. The reality is that in a 400 year old industry that has experienced little role change over the centuries, AI unlocks many new interesting career paths for the next generation that combines technical acumen with empathetic EQ. Examples of these paradigm shifts in roles include the following:

The underwriter as a portfolio strategist

Today: Manually assesses individual risks by reviewing siloed documentation.

Future: Manages a portfolio of AI underwriting models. Their expertise is used to refine algorithms, set risk appetite, design parameters for new products, and handle the complex risks that AI cannot parse.

Benefit: This democratizes expertise, leveling the productivity gap by boosting the performance of junior staff while still providing continuous learning for more experienced professionals.

The claims adjuster as an empathetic crisis manager

Today: Spends the majority of their time on damage assessment, paperwork, fraud checks, and validating coverage.

14 *Bockelmann*, AI in a European Insurance Group (in this volume) 33 ff.

Future: AI could handle the vast majority of personal lines claims without human touch. Computer vision[15] can analyze damage from photos and video; GenAI can summarize the event; and automated processing can issue an instant payment greatly reducing the time to settle a claim while increasing customer satisfaction (faster payment, happier customer). For example, *Five Sigma's Clive*, an AI Insurance Claims Adjuster, leverages advanced AI and natural language processing to analyze claims data, automate processing, and provide recommendations to human adjusters.

Benefit: This frees the human adjuster to become a true crisis manager, handling the most complex, severe claims where empathy is paramount. They will be focused on the how of the customer's experience, not the what of the paperwork, using AI-driven tools for triage, intelligent data extraction, and automated routing.

The risk manager as a corporate futurist

Today: Assesses historical risk data and industry benchmarks for corporate clients.

Future: Uses AI-powered "digital twins" of a client's operations—like a simulation in a video game—to model future scenarios.

Benefit: They will model the cascading impact of climate change on a global supply chain or test the resilience of a network against a AI-generated cyber threat, moving their function from risk assessment to active, predictive risk elimination.

The broker/agent as a holistic digital advisor

Today: Focuses on product sales, comparisons, and lead qualification.

Future: The agent's routine tasks will be fully automated by Agentic AI. Think of this as live coaching for a broker that involves a multi-agent system, retrieving data, and generating quotes. A large UK automotive insurer, for instance, used generative AI to provide real-time suggestions and auto-fill forms for call center agents, improving efficiency and customer satisfaction.

Benefit: This elevates the human broker into a true holistic advisor, providing the strategic risk judgment and empathetic relationship management that AI cannot.

E. The hyper-personalized product: From static policies to living

In this new ecosystem, the static annual policy becomes an artifact. AI is the engine for "living protection": policies that are parametric, on-demand, and deeply embedded.

Use Case: Travel insurance that, without a claim form, queries flight data, detects a 4-hour delay, confirms policy conditions are met, and instantly deposits payment into the traveler's digital wallet before their plane even boards.

15 Computer vision is a subfield of artificial intelligence that equips machines with the ability to process, analyze and interpret visual inputs such as images and videos.

Use Case: Income protection for a gig economy worker that dynamically adjusts coverage and price based on data from their work platform, scaling protection up during busy months and down during quiet periods. This creates a safety net for a growing segment of the global workforce that was previously uninsurable.[16]

Role of Generative AI: GenAI will instantly create and explain policy documents in simple, personalized language for every single customer, ending the era of opaque, one-size-fits-all contracts.

The best of all of this is that it is not just a theoretical concept in a streaming movie, insurers who are already leveraging hyper-personalization are realizing significant improvements in their risk prediction accuracy that enables them to provide targeted value to policyholders while also maintaining a profitable book of business. For example, as *Bockelmann* discussed in a previous chapter, *Baloise's* "Baloise FX" tool, which uses a GenAI assistant trained on **70,000 past financial plans** to help human advisors build better, data-driven, optimized plans for new clients, is a concrete example of this powerful new generation of human-AI collaboration.[17] *Max Life Insurance*, for example, built a chatbot to help customers with questions and connect them with relevant products.

III. Charting the course: Trust, technology, and society

Change is multi-dimensional and this transformation is no different. It represents not just a technological paradigm shift, but one that has social, ethical, and political implications. Navigating the path forward means solving the fundamental barriers of trust and regulation, turning them from anchors into accelerators.

A. The new consumer benefit: From "necessary" purchase to valued service

For decades, insurance has been the ultimate "purchase of last resort" – a product customers are forced to buy and hope to never use. The ultimate benefit of this AI-driven transformation is the fundamental re-architecting of this relationship, creating new avenues for resilience.

16 *Tarr A./Tarr J./Thompson/Wilkinson* (eds), The Global Insurance Market 7 (2024): DOI:10.4324/9781003319054.

17 *Bockelmann*, AI in a European Insurance Group (in this volume) 33 ff.

The "invisible" claim

A smart home IoT sensor detects a water leak. An automated, agentic AI process files the claim, dispatches a pre-approved plumber from its partner ecosystem, and handles payment without the homeowner needing to make a single call. This seamless fulfillment is what consumers already expect. The *Deloitte* study confirms that consumers have the strongest preference for digital channels in servicing functions (managing contracts, filing claims), which is precisely where insurers currently have the largest digitalization gaps.[18] AI directly closes this experience gap.

Embedded Protection: Insurance is seamlessly included at the point of purchase or activity.[19]

The Result: The consumer's perception of insurance shifts from a necessary evil to a valuable, invisible background service that actively reduces risk, simplifies life, and prevents loss. This model allows insurers to finally reach previously uninsurable communities and build resilience for all.

B. The trust equation: Navigating the privacy paradox

The future of insurance is also built on a massive, constant flow of personal data, which creates another important challenge: trust. The data is clear that this is a primary barrier. Research shows **57 % of insurance professionals** already mistrust the reliability and accuracy of GenAI,[20] and nearly half of industry leaders share those reservations.[21] Furthermore, as preceding chapters noted, insurers demonstrate a far higher caution around data governance than even banks (**56 % vs. 39 %**), reflecting a deep-seated institutional awareness of this challenge.[22]

This history of caution, however, is an asset. The task isn't to *create* trust from scratch, but to *prove* their existing trust models can be mapped onto these powerful new tools. This requires a new social contract built on transparency, user control, and privacy-preserving technologies like federated learning. The value exchange must be explicit and undeniable: consumers will willingly share

18 *Deloitte*, Digital Insurance Maturity, 16 (2025): www.deloitte.com/ce/en/related-content/digital-insurance-maturity-2025.html (accessed 24.11.2025).

19 *Tarr A./Tarr J./Thompson/Wilkinson* (eds), The Global Insurance Market, 8 (2024): DOI:10.4324/9781003319054.

20 *Owen/Mullins/Sheehan*, Generative AI Adoption, 30 (February 23, 2025): http://dx.doi.org/10.2139/ssrn.5227619.

21 *KPMG*, Intelligent Insurance, 9 (2025): https://assets.kpmg.com/content/dam/kpmgsites/xx/pdf/2025/03/intelligent-insurance-web-report.pdf.coredownload.inline.pdf (accessed 24.11.2025).

22 *Münkel*, Use of AI in various industries (in this volume) 27 ff.

their data because they receive undeniable value in return—lower risk, tangible prevention services, and significantly reduced costs.[23]

C. The regulatory handshake: Partnership in innovation

The greatest barrier to this future is not technology, but regulatory ambiguity. As highlighted by *Owen/Mullins/Sheehan*, the lack of clear guidelines is the **#1 barrier (cited by 62 % of professionals)** to GenAI implementation.[24] The industry is trapped, fearing that innovation will be met with punitive regulation.

This highlights the **"blessing and a curse"** of the European regulatory framework: comprehensive consumer protection has also created intense bureaucracy that slows innovation and, ironically, protects slow incumbents from the very competition that would benefit customers.

> **From:** Regulators as slow-moving gatekeepers applying analog-era rules to digital-first models.
>
> **To:** Regulators as innovation partners. This requires a consensus shift—already championed by *The Geneva Association* and *EIOPA*—away from broad, horizontal mandates (like the EU AI Act) toward **principles-based, sector-specific regulation.**[25] Regulators must co-create "regulatory sandboxes" to safely test new AI-driven products and focus on algorithmic accountability and fairness of *outcomes*, not just inputs.
>
> **Government's Role as an Enabler:** This future should involve public-private partnerships where governments provide access to large-scale, anonymized datasets (e.g., public health, weather, transit data) to help train more accurate risk models for the public good, directly helping to close national-level protection gaps.

D. Call to action: A roadmap for transformation

This transformation will not be defined by a single big leap; the competitive landscape will be decided by a phased roadmap, aligning practitioner strategy with the transformation model from *KPMG*.[26] This maturity journey is

23 *Noordhoek,* (The Geneva Association), Regulation of Artificial Intelligence in Insurance: Balancing consumer protection and innovation 24 (2023): www.genevaassociation.org/publication/public-policy-regulation/regulation-artificial-intelligence-insurance-balancing (accessed 24.11.2025).

24 *Owen/Mullins/Sheehan*, Generative AI Adoption, 28 (February 23, 2025): http://dx.doi.org/10.2139/ssrn.5227619.

25 *Noordhoek,* (The Geneva Association), Regulation of Artificial Intelligence, 34 (2023): www.genevaassociation.org/publication/public-policy-regulation/regulation-artificial-intelligence-insurance-balancing (accessed 24.11.2025).

26 *KPMG,* Intelligent insurance, 14 (2025): https://assets.kpmg.com/content/dam/kpmgsites/xx/pdf/2025/03/intelligent-insurance-web-report.pdf.coredownload.inline.pdf (accessed 24.11.2025).

not strictly linear—different parts of the organization will move at different speeds—but follows a clear strategic logic.

Phase 1 (The foundation/"enable")

The immediate focus is mastering the data infrastructure and, most importantly, the people. This means migrating core systems to the cloud, creating unified data lakes, and attacking data silos. Critically, this phase is about building AI literacy across the entire workforce, leveraging **"Embedded AI"** in standard software and deploying **"Self-Service GenAI"** tools (like an internal chatbot) to democratize AI skills and achieve quick, low-risk wins. Success is measured in efficiency gains and employee adoption.

Phase 2 (The ecosystem/"embed")

The focus shifts from isolated AI projects to rewiring entire domains and building external platforms. This phase requires forging the deep, data-sharing partnerships with auto manufacturers, healthcare providers, and smart home tech companies that define a true ecosystem. Insurers will scale parametric and embedded products and empower **"Low-Code Enablement"** for business users, while targeting investment in strategic **"High-Code Applications"** for core processes like claims and underwriting that can be performed by more tech savvy IT developers, following *McKinsey's* "domain-based" transformation model.[27] Success is measured in new product velocity and the ROI of rewritten core processes.

Phase 3 (The AI-native insurer/"evolve")

This is the end state, where the insurer achieves the vision of insurance as a fully embedded, background utility. The majority of revenue is tied to prevention and risk mitigation services. The organization's operating model is fully **"High-Code,"** run by sophisticated, agentic AI systems that orchestrate entire business functions. Human expertise is focused entirely on managing the AI ecosystem, designing future-forward risk products, and providing high-empathy crisis management.[28]

When all of these elements are pulled together, it not only represents a transformation in the way the insurance company works, but also in the way that the consumer experiences an insurable event that is seamlessly integrated into their life, and not as an additional burden endured after a loss. A use case that is not too far off in the future is a classic homeowners policy that can transform from a simple cover to proactive wildfire risk mitigation plan leveraging *Google*

27 *Milinkovich et al.* (McKinsey & Company), The future of AI, 17 (2025): www.mckinsey.com/industries/financial-services/our-insights/the-future-of-ai-in-the-insurance-industry (accessed 24.11.2025).

28 *KPMG*, Intelligent insurance, 26 (2025): https://assets.kpmg.com/content/dam/kpmgsites/xx/pdf/2025/03/intelligent-insurance-web-report.pdf.coredownload.inline.pdf (accessed 24.11.2025).

Earth Engine and *Waymo*. Imagine a homeowner in a wildfire-prone area. Instead of simply insuring against loss, their policy actively works to prevent it.

Risk Assessment & Monitoring: *Google Earth Engine* continuously analyzes satellite imagery, weather patterns, and vegetation data to create a real-time, hyper-local wildfire risk score for the homeowner's property. This data is fed into an AI model (running on *Gemini* Platform) that predicts the likelihood and severity of a wildfire event.

Proactive Mitigation: If the risk score crosses a predefined threshold, the system automatically triggers a series of preventative actions:

- **Automated Alert:** The homeowner receives an immediate alert *via Google Assistant* or their preferred smart home device, advising on specific actions like clearing brush or preparing an evacuation plan.
- **Waymo-Enabled Response:** In extreme risk scenarios, *Waymo's* autonomous vehicles, equipped with specialized fire suppression equipment or even *Wing's* drones for aerial assessment, could be dispatched to high-risk areas to create firebreaks or apply preventative treatments, all coordinated through *Google Maps* and real-time traffic data.
- **IoT Integration:** Smart home sensors (e.g., Nest Protect) detect early signs of fire, automatically shutting off gas lines, activating sprinkler systems, and alerting emergency services via *Google's* communication platforms.

Dynamic Policy Adjustment: The homeowner's insurance premium dynamically adjusts based on their proactive mitigation efforts and the real-time risk assessment, incentivizing safer behavior and rewarding risk reduction.

Seamless Claims Processing: In the unfortunate event of a fire, AI-powered image recognition (*Gemini*) analyzes drone footage and satellite imagery to assess damage instantly, and claims are processed and paid out automatically via *Google Pay*, minimizing human intervention and accelerating recovery.

This integrated example of end-to-end insurance coverage represents that paradigm shift from a reactive "repair and replace" model to a proactive "predict and prevent" ecosystem, leveraging *Google* and *Alphabet's* advanced technologies to create a truly resilient and safer environment for policyholders.

IV. Conclusion: Build, empower, or be disintermediated

The preceding chapters show how the insurance industry, an IT pioneer now defined by its legacy, is a laggard poised not just for disruption, but for impactful transformation. The data proves a deep structural divide is already here and accelerating. The 224 % 10-year TSR for *ACORD*'s "Digital Competitors" versus 64 % for "Digital Laggards,"[29] combined with *McKinsey's* finding that

29 *ACORD*, Insurance Digital Maturity Study, 6.

AI leaders generate 6.1 times the shareholder return,[30] confirms this is not just the next step; it's a giant leap in a winner-take-all realignment of the industry.

More broadly this transformational shift is how the insurance industry finally fulfills its foundational societal promise. The core idea of insurance—a risk community providing collective aid—has always been hampered by analog friction. AI can now provide the toolset to dramatically close the global protection gap, enabling the creation of affordable, accessible insurance and parametric products that can bring millions of underserved people and businesses into the formal system of financial resilience. The path to this empowered future is defined not by technology, but by leadership who can foster an environment that incorporates the change management, the new skills, and the cultural courage required to effectively drive technological change.

For any young person starting their career today and looking to make a tangible impact, the insurance industry is, perhaps for the first time in a generation, the most exciting place to be. Forget the outdated stereotypes. The industry is no longer just looking for people to sell policies or to answer phones to register a claim; it is desperately seeking a new generation of collaborators, advocates, and strategists. It needs people who can incorporate both problem-solving and empathy to create risk solutions that help real people address real risks. The challenge is immense to reimagine one of the world's oldest industries to not just indemnify a loss but to prevent it from even happening; and in the event of the loss, to pay what is fairly owned on precisely what exactly was indeed lost. This is not just an opportunity to build a career; it is an opportunity to build a safer, more equitable, and more resilient world for everyone.

References and resources

ACORD, Insurance Digital Maturity Study (2025)

Aragani, Venu Madhav, "Revolutionizing Insurance Through AI and Data Analytics: Innovating Policy Underwriting and Claims Management for the Digital Era, FMDB Transactions on Sustainable Computer Letters 2, no. 3, 176–85 (2024): doi.org/10.69888/ftscl.2024.000243

CB Insights, AI Readiness Index. Which insurance giants have the most AI innovation? Our AI Readiness Index shows Cigna is leading the pack (2024): www.cbinsights.com/research/ai-readiness-index-insurance/ (accessed 24.11.2025)

30 *Milinkovich et al.* (McKinsey & Company), The future of AI, 4 (2025): www.mckinsey.com/industries/financial-services/our-insights/the-future-of-ai-in-the-insurance-industry (accessed 24.11.2025).

Challapally et al., The GenAI Divide: State of AI in Business 2025, MIT NANDA (2025): https://mlq.ai/media/quarterly_decks/v0.1_State_of_AI_in_Business_2025_Report.pdf (accessed 24.11.2025)

Deloitte, Digital Insurance Maturity: Assessment of insurance digitalisation in the EMEA region (2025): www.deloitte.com/ce/en/related-content/digital-insurance-maturity-2025.html (accessed 24.11.2025)

Gallagher Re, Global InsurTech Report: Q2 – Property (2025): www.ajg.com/gallagherre/news-and-insights/global-insurtech-report-q2-2025/ (accessed 24.11.2025)

Milinkovich et al. (McKinsey & Company), The future of AI in the insurance industry (2025): www.mckinsey.com/industries/financial-services/our-insights/the-future-of-ai-in-the-insurance-industry (accessed 24.11.2025)

KPMG, Intelligent insurance: A blueprint for creating value through AI-driven transformation (2025): https://assets.kpmg.com/content/dam/kpmgsites/xx/pdf/2025/03/intelligent-insurance-web-report.pdf.coredownload.inline.pdf (accessed 24.11.2025)

Noordhoek, (The Geneva Association), Regulation of Artificial Intelligence in Insurance: Balancing consumer protection and innovation (2023): www.genevaassociation.org/publication/public-policy-regulation/regulation-artificial-intelligence-insurance-balancing (accessed 24.11.2025)

Owen/Mullins/Sheehan, Generative AI Adoption and Barriers: The Case of the Insurance Industry (February 23, 2025): http://dx.doi.org/10.2139/ssrn.5227619

Pingili, The Role of AI in Personalizing Insurance Policies, International Journal of Scientific Research in Computer Science, Engineering and Information Technology (2024): DOI:10.32628/CSEIT24106194

Woodward et al, Tech-tonic shifts: How AI could change industry risk landscapes (2024): www.swissre.com/institute/research/topics-and-risk-dialogues/digital-business-model-and-cyber-risk/ai-and-the-industry-risk-landscape.html (accessed 24.11.2025)

Tarr A./Tarr J./Thompson/Wilkinson (eds), The Global Insurance Market and Change: Emerging Technologies, Risks and Legal Challenges (2024): DOI:10.4324/9781003319054

List of authors

Max Bachem

is Co-founder and CEO of the fintech “Xaver”. Prior to that, he was CEO of the insurtech Luko Insurance AG (formerly Coya AG). At AXA Konzern AG, Max Bachem was Head of Group Development, responsible for strategy, investments and strategic partnerships for AXA in Germany. He began his career in strategy consulting at Oliver Wyman in Zurich and Hongkong. He holds a master’s degree in strategy & international management from the University of St. Gallen, a bachelor’s degree in general management & business law from the European Business School in Oestrich-Winkel, and a degree in Artificial Intelligence from MIT.

Dr. Alexander Bockelmann

is Chief Technology Officer and member of the Management Board of the Baloise Group since 2019. He started his IT career as a strategy consultant at the Boston Consulting Group with a focus on IT in Financial Services and held various IT management positions at Allianz SE in Germany and the USA for many years. At the end of 2013, he joined UNIQA Insurance Group AG in Austria as Group CIO, where he was responsible for IT in Austria and all IT issues and IT services for the UNIQA Group as Chief Digital Officer and Group Chief Information Officer. He studied environmental sciences at the Universities of Bayreuth (Germany) and East Anglia (UK) and obtained his doctorate in geosciences from the Eberhard Karls University of Tübingen.

Christina Lucas

serves as Global Market Leader, Insurance for Google Cloud, leading strategy and innovation at the intersection of insurance and technology. Previously, she served as Global Head of Industry Advisory at Guidewire and President of Envista Forensics. An AIG alumna who held senior leadership roles across Europe, Asia, and Latin America, Christina worked in consultancy at Deloitte and Booz Allen prior to joining the industry. She holds a B. A. in Economics from Georgetown University and a master’s degree in information technology from American InterContinental University. Christina Lucas actively serves on various corporate and non-profit boards within the insurance industry.

Thomas Münkel

is an insurance manager, board member and angel investor in start-ups. He has many years of experience in the insurance industry, including as Chief Administrative Officer and Chief Governance Officer at Allianz SE and as Chief Operating Officer at UNIQA Insurance Group. He is familiar with the insurtech sector as co-founder and CEO of Coya AG (later Luko Insurance AG) and as an investor and board member in other fintech companies. Thomas Münkel holds a degree in psychology from the University of Heidelberg. He teaches at Johannes Kepler University in Linz on the topics of digitalisation and artificial intelligence in the insurance industry.

Dr. Christoph Nabholz

is CEO of RiskInsight Consulting GmbH, a consulting firm focusing on foresight, sustainability and innovation. He has more than 20 years of leadership experience at Swiss Re, where he served as Chief Research & Sustainability Officer and Managing Director of the Swiss Re Institute. He championed the introduction of GenAI and machine learning in underwriting and oversaw Swiss Re's publications on digital trust and silent AI risks. Before joining Swiss Re, he was a postdoctoral fellow in genomics at Harvard University. He holds a PhD in molecular genetics from the University of Freiburg and a degree in biochemistry from the University of Basel.

Igor Raičević

is the Head of Group IT at the GrECo Group, the leading insurance broker in Austria and CEE. He led the company's entire IT organization since 2016. He specializes in IT strategy, digital transformation, and technology management within the insurance sector. As graduate of the Chief Technology Officer Programme at Cambridge Judge Business School, Igor Raičević brings expertise in IT leadership and strategic technology management, backed by over twenty years of experience in the insurance industry.

Dr. Danilo Raponi

is the Group Head of Innovation at Generali and Managing Director of the company's Innovation Fund, where he oversees a number of product and business innovations with a focus on AI and GenAI. He is Chairperson of the Board of Directors of the House of Insurtech Switzerland, and is responsible for Generali Ventures. Danilo Raponi is a member of the Supervisory Committee of Mundi Ventures, a Partner at 9"inch Capital, and an angel investor in several AI and tech startups. He is in the Advisory Board of MIT Technology Review Italy and has lectured at the University of Zurich and at the Goethe University of Frankfurt. Danilo Raponi holds a MSc summa cum laude from LUISS University in Rome, an MBA from the Bocconi School of Management and a PhD from the University of Cambridge.

Brian Walsh

is the CEO and co-founder of Resolve, a specialist enterprise software company serving the insurance, banking, and asset management industries. Under his leadership, Resolve has been recognised by Deloitte as one of the fastest-growing technology companies in

EMEA and named among the Top 100 Global InsurTechs. Drawing on his background in actuarial science and software engineering, Brian Walsh has led the development of IntegraLynx, Resolve's flagship data integration and automation platform for financial services. Brian Walsh holds a degree in actuarial mathematics and a master's degree in software engineering

Simon Woodward

is a freelance writer and insurance specialist. He worked in the reinsurance industry for over 20 years and moved from Converium to the Swiss Re Centre for Global Dialogue, where he focused on digitalisation. Simon Woodward then worked as an editor, writer and researcher at the Swiss Re Institute, where he authored publications on artificial intelligence and digital trust. Before joining Swiss Re, Simon worked in the field of sovereign and political risk. He holds degrees from St Antony's College, Oxford, and Birmingham University.

Dr. Michael Zimmer

is Chief Data and AI Officer of the W&W Group and Head of Data, Processes and AI. In this role, he drives the data- and AI-driven digitalisation of W&W as an integrated financial group. Before joining W&W, he was Chief Data Officer of the Zurich Group Germany and worked in consulting for 15 years. Michael Zimmer is a publisher, speaker, author and fellow of TDWI (= association "Transforming Data with Intelligence").